Contemporary Christian Music

Contemporary Christian Music

Where It Came from, What It Is, Where It's Going

Paul Baker

Crossway Books • *Westchester, Illinois*
A Division of Good News Publishers

Cover concept by Jeff Barnes.

First printing, 1985.

Printed in the United States of America

Library of Congress Catalog Card Number 84-72002

ISBN 0-89107-343-4

Portions of the history of contemporary Christian music as included in this book have appeared in slightly modified versions in the following publications: Rock in Jesus, Right On!, Harmony, *and* Contemporary Christian Music.

All secular record chart numbers included in this history are as tabulated in Joel Whitburn's Top Pop Records 1955-1982 *book, compiled from* Billboard's *pop charts. This book is published independently. Write to: Record Research, P. O. Box 200, Menomonee Falls, Wisconsin 53051.*

This book is dedicated to the girl at the New Year's Eve concert in Denver whom I didn't hug, and to Charles McPheeters, who would have.

Contents

Prelude—1979

Here's everything you ever wanted to know about Jesus music, and didn't know to ask! Paul has done an amazing and thorough job of researching this whole latter-day phenomenon, getting right back to its early wellsprings in traditional Christian music and tracing each tributary as it flows into the cascading river of living water that Jesus music is becoming.

I find the chronicle very exciting, having been involved in it from one of its earliest stages. I've watched this new crest developing, and have earnestly paddled to try and stay in the sweep of it. I remember being stopped in my tracks the first time I heard Paul Stookey's song, "Hymn." It was sung by a virtually unknown trio of boys at a Youth for Christ beach rally in Florida in the late sixties.

I got goose bumps. It hit me like a brick or one of those beach hot dogs. "Of course—it's possible! Why not talk to young people about Jesus in their own language, and with the sound of their own music? Why not be completely honest about a human being's search for something real in a world that so often accepts substitutes and dehydrated religion?"

Soon after, I began to hear other songs and know other Christian artists who were doing just that: Larry Norman and Randy Matthews and Paul Johnson and Jimmy Owens, and on and on. I recorded my own first Jesus music album, and even established a new label, Lamb and Lion Records, to serve as a fresh channel for this modern music.

Like so many, continuing right up until now, I was so frustrated that this wonderful new music couldn't find distribution or air space on the radio. Here was a totally new avenue of Christian expression, one that would communicate immediately with millions of young people in a way they could understand—and nobody knew what to do with it! It was too "religious" for pop stations, and too "pop" for religious stations.

Obviously, new channels would have to open up, and I decided to be one of them. It seems to have been a long and frustrating struggle, but now the doors are opening. More and more Christian stations have accepted Jesus music in its varied forms and are spotlighting the whole galaxy of dedicated and talented new artists. Now even the secular and rock stations are beginning to perk up their ears and listen to the sound of young people singing about Jesus in a musical form that is every bit as commercial and entertaining and arresting as any of the secular artists.

The tide is irresistible now, and chinks in the dam are appearing everywhere.

In the 96th Psalm, and a number of other places, David cries,

> Sing to the Lord a new song:
> Sing to the Lord, all the earth.
> Sing to the Lord, praise His name.
> Proclaim His salvation day after day.
> Declare His glory among the nations,
> His marvelous deeds among all peoples.

On the day of Pentecost, the Bible tells us, "every man heard in his own language."

People used to ask me, "What is this Jesus movement, anyway?" I replied, "It's Jesus moving, that's what it is." No human people originated or organized the Jesus movement; Jesus did it, through yielded young hearts.

Now they're asking, "What is Jesus music anyway?" I reply, "It's Jesus singing, in the hearts of young people by His Spirit!" Again, no person conceived or organized Jesus music; it's just happening in the hearts and talents of young people, and building to an undeniable crescendo of testimony and praise.

I'm grateful to Paul Baker for bringing the whole dynamic history of Jesus music into sharp focus and giving credit where credit is certainly due. Praise the Lord!

Pat Boone
Beverly Hills, California

Foreword—1979

There was a time I felt quite alone with my music. I had gone forward in church to accept Christ when I was five. I strained to reach the high notes when we sang the hymns, and I struggled to understand the lyrics which were filled with things like "bulwarks never failing." If the hymns seemed archaic to me, well, that made sense. God was very ancient too. These hymns were probably written back when He first made the world.

When I was young I heard Elvis Presley sing "Hound Dog" on the radio, and I began to wonder why there couldn't be church music that sounded a little more modern. And so I began to write songs in the fourth grade. A few years later I sang "Moses" and some other early songs at the church picnic, but I felt embarrassed and just a little angry when no one really understood what I was trying to do.

My father, bless his heart, did not allow me to listen to the radio anymore and tried to "encourage" me to give up music entirely. I was obedient on the first count, but couldn't bear to stop writing songs. And so for many years I felt alone in my enthusiasm for Jesus-rock music.

Periodically I performed in public and upon leaving school I signed with Capitol Records, but it was a long time before I met anyone who "understood" me.

Then in 1967 my sister told me about this boy who had seen me perform in concert with my band, People, and wanted to meet me. I didn't think much about it until one day I came home to find my sister sitting on the couch and heard someone singing in the other room. I walked into the next room and saw this skinny little high-school kid singing "Bluebird" at the top of his lungs. I joined in on the harmony.

That's how I met Randy Stonehill. Although it was a few years before he would become a Christian, he identified with Jesus rock from the time he first heard it. And so, quite suddenly there seemed to be two of us.

In 1969, after the release of my third album for Capitol *(Upon This Rock)*, it seemed that people were ready for a modern approach to Christian music. Within two years there were a dozen or so groups or solo performers just in California who were recognizably "contemporary."

So you can imagine my joy when not too much later I found out there were many more scattered all over America. A disc jockey named Paul Baker had a Jesus-rock radio show, and a writer named Brooke Chamberlain had written a few articles about contemporary Christian music, and I met a guy named Frank Edmondson who seemed to know all about Jesus music. He not only "understood" it, but was explaining it to everyone who came near. Now further imagine my surprise when I found out that not only were Paul Baker and Brooke Chamberlain the same person, but that both of them were also Frank Edmondson.

Frank explained that he had been in radio for a long time and had experimented with different jock "handles," as most disc jockeys do, and that gradually it became convenient to let Paul continue to do the radio show and let Brooke move into writing while he, Frank, remained himself.

When I got to know him better I found out that not only did he have three different names, but he seemed to have the energy of three different people.

He not only had a three-hour radio show, every night at one point, but he had started a magazine called *Rock in Jesus.* He wrote it, edited it, printed it, assembled it, stapled it, addressed it, stamped it, and mailed it. He also paid for it. After all, what publisher could be convinced that Jesus rock was a viable and spiritual art form? Most people seemed convinced that rock and roll was of the devil and that God would never use it.

So Frank stood alone and did it all by himself. He was a tall skinny kid who had great enthusiasm for his belief in Christ and gentle empathy for those who did not believe.

To those who disagreed with his understanding of Christian music he could discuss church history and church music and back the conversation up with that nice smile of his. Not only did he have a nice attitude but he had nice looks too, which helped. I mean, it wouldn't be easy to convince a grown-up that Jesus rock was a legitimate direction in Christian music if you looked like a leftist—drugged—burned out—Communist—faggott—weirdo.

But for all his rapport with the grown-ups and the establishment, to me Frank didn't look exactly "straight." He had longish hair and looked like the street people. But because his looks and personality also passed inspection with adults, Frank sat on the borderline and communicated to both sides and helped bring them a little closer together.

By the time Explo '72 occurred in Dallas, Texas, Frank had a wealth of "research" material crammed into his tiny apartment. His clothes remained in drawers or hung over chairs because his closet was filled with records. He had albums and singles stacked everyplace. He thumbed through them and showed me songs I never heard on any radio show except his. He had songs written by Christians (and others by non-Christians which had only a passing reference to Christ or God), but he had them all! And he knew which was which. He sensed that a very large "Jesus-music" culture was going to develop, and he was more than prepared for it. It looked to me as though he were the sole historian of a new era in church music.

Frank not only chronicled the Jesus-music history in his magazine, but he helped to make it. As early as 1971 he was already stretching the dimensions of religious broadcasting by experimenting with its possibilities in format. Besides playing obscure gems from his private record collection, he once set up a room for an audience right in the radio station and had me do a live concert on the air. It was the first time many of my songs had been on the air because I had not previously released them on record. I did "The Tune" that night on his show and though it had never been heard before (or since) on any radio program anywhere, it suddenly became the most requested song in my concerts. I was amazed at how far-reaching Frank's radio show was in its influence on the grapevine.

There were a few other Christian disc jockeys like Scott Ross who played contemporary Christian music, but none of them were as avant-garde as Frank. None had access to his mammoth collection of records, so none had such a staggering playlist of different selections. And none were quite daring enough to risk alienating a religious sponsor or associate with an experimental format; so Frank made important cultural inroads into what Christian radio could become.

I guess I've known Frank for almost nine years now. He kept his radio show going for all those years and later worked for Word Records, pioneering radio coordination and format and helping disc jockeys understand how to improve their technique in a field that Frank more or less pioneered—Jesus-rock radio. And later he was asked to head up the FCCM, the Fellowship of Contemporary Christian Ministries.

Right from the first time I met Frank and heard Paul Baker on the radio and read Brooke's articles in *Rock in Jesus,* I thought Frank should write a book. He finally has.

LARRY NORMAN

Introduction 1979-1985

1979

I was one of the rock generation. I can still remember "borrowing" my father's turquoise transistor radio (the first such radio I had seen) when he brought it home one day. I don't know if he ever had a chance to use it again after that day either, because everywhere I went thereafter I had it with me, next to my ear.

The music on that radio was usually rock and roll: "Peggy Sue" by Buddy Holly; "Bird Dog" by the Everly Brothers. Why I was attracted to the rock station I can't really say. I had my choice of country, religious, mood music, and rhythm and blues. But as an adolescent, even though I didn't like *all* of the rock and roll, I guess I was drawn to the energy and excitement which rock music carried inherently.

Bill Haley rocked with his Comets, Elvis Presley rolled out a song about his "Teddy Bear," Jerry Lee Lewis sang about "A Whole Lotta Shakin' Goin On." Rock music (even the mellowest of rock ballads) became the headache of older Americans. Rock was crude to the older folks, but definitely "cool" to the young people.

The furor over rock and roll music started in the fifties and never really abated until the late sixties and the early seventies, when adults simply got tired of fighting it. By then the "beautiful music" of the adults ironically was very often music written and originally performed by rock musicians such as Elvis and the Beatles. When drums and rock rhythm were added to orchestra recordings, the adults somehow didn't seem to mind it as much as they had originally.

I also grew up "in the church." My parents took the whole family to church each week, and I know my personal faith is now as strong as it is because of the Bible study, the worship, and the fellowship I enjoyed there.

Unlike many peers, to whom such music was at the least "foreign," I enjoyed the music of the church. By the time I had reached my high school years, though, I began to yearn for *contemporary* music which conveyed my faith in Jesus. I wanted music I could share with my unchurched friends—music which wasn't strange to them.

I first experienced such music in the form of Christian folk songs, sung on Thursday nights at a "Christian hootenanny" across town from where I lived. While the guitar players and washtub bass "experts" accompanied, we sang songs which I'd sung many times at church fellowships and socials— "Do Lord," "When the Saints Go Marchin' In," "Give Me Oil in My Lamp"—but for some reason they took on a vitality I had never experienced in them before. Somehow with the guitars and basses I didn't feel as embarrassed asking my out-of-church schoolmates to join us on Thursdays.

My next encounter with contemporary Christian music came a few years later when I attended the World Baptist Youth Congress in Berne, Switzerland. A smartly uniformed youth choir performed a new musical entitled *Good News* before the six thousand delegates. *Good News* utilized folk music mostly, but even went so far as to put in a few semirock licks which would then and for months to follow drop the jaw of many a staid church member.

Next, it was through a subscription offer in *Campus Life* magazine and membership in Word, Incorporated's Young America Record Club that I began amassing a collection of every contemporary and quasicontemporary Christian music album there was. The names of the performers seem quite tame now: Cliff Barrows and the Gang, The Melody Four Quartet, The Teen Tones. But at the time they were a big step in the direction of new music for Christian young people like myself.

In 1970 a singer named John Fischer came through my hometown of Tampa, Florida, while touring with evangelist Leighton Ford. I was excited about the music he had performed, so I introduced myself and we spent an afternoon together discussing what he kept calling "Jesus music." I liked the expression, and I immediately caught on to using it, just as hundreds of other young people around the country were already doing.

I kept hearing the words "Jesus music" more and more frequently. When a group known as the Pilgrim 20 from Wichita, Kansas, sang it in a Tampa church recreation hall they called it

"Jesus rock." When a group known as the Spurrlows came through town for a performance, it was "sacred music with a new flair." But it was all *Jesus music* to me.

Those are recollections of my first impressions of a music style which would greatly influence my life. While I was delving deeper and deeper to find more of this exciting, fresh music, thousands of young people across the country were writing it, discovering it, singing it, and sharing it.

During the years covered in this book, I had the good fortune to live in Florida, Kansas, California, Texas, Colorado, and Europe. Living in these geographically diverse areas provided grand opportunities for me to observe what was happening in Jesus music and to be an active part of it all. Thus this history of Jesus music and the Jesus movement is a history as I saw it and often participated in it. That is why I occasionally lapse into the first person in the pages that follow.

In 1968, when I first began collecting my Jesus-music records and dreaming of what contemporary Christian music could be and could accomplish, I had no idea it would grow as fast as it has. The growth has been literally stupendous. Now that it *has* grown, it's time we learned from the zealousness of the young people in the early days. Even more important, we need to see where, in certain instances, our priorities have been turned topsy-turvy. I hope we can learn from looking back, taking stock, and then moving forward with a renewed vigor and perspective.

Rock music about Jesus hasn't really found favor with adults any more easily than did secular rock. But regardless of one's stance in the question of Jesus-rock music—pro or con—the fact remains that rock music has had the ears of the nation's youth since its inception. Likewise, Jesus music has emanated from people for whom rock music has been a natural language. It has communicated, often where no other language has.

By the time of the writing of this book, there were so many people involved in contemporary Christian music, there was virtually no possible way to chronicle or credit everyone who had a part. Quite honestly, that was the most frustrating part of writing the book. There is a natural tendency for us to venerate the well-known performer and pass over or simply forget the lesser-known musicians who have done the Lord's work just as diligently, but in less visible ways or perhaps on a local basis. In fact, in some cases they were the hardest workers.

For every well-known musician, there is a lesser-known roadie who assists in setting up concerts. Likewise, there is also a person to invite that musician to perform the concert, radio broadcasters to publicize and advertise the concert, people to get the musician to and from the airport, record company personnel to release and record his albums if he records, personnel to promote and publish his music, and so forth, not to mention supportive brothers and sisters praying for him, and the audiences who listen to him and buy his albums if any are available.

Thus, at times I have spent more time describing the work of people "in the wings" than the people "in the spotlight," for this is mainly a history of the *work* done by people glorifying God through Jesus music, not necessarily the people doing it. Most of the musicians would agree that their names are not so important as the lives changed by their music.

I wish to thank a few of the "anonymous" and better-known people who have helped me through the years in various ways: Dallas Albritton, and Mosie Lister for introducing us; Victor Salem; Henry Webb; Daylon Rushing; Herb Hunt; Dan Vap and the others who helped me with *Rock in Jesus* magazine; Billy Ray Hearn; Larry Norman; Gary Elrod; Mark Puckett; John Grable; John Styll; Erwin Hearne; Bob Freeman; Gary Dick; Freddy Piro; Bob Cotterell; Jack Bailey; Robbie Marshall; and of course, my parents, Frank and Doris Edmondson. Their encouragement, help, and exhortation were invaluable and still are greatly appreciated. Also, I deeply appreciate the many people who have so generously supported my radio show, "A Joyful Noise," since it began in 1970.

I owe unending thanks to the scores of people who, in private interviews or casual conversations, helped me so much to recall the important people, places, dates and events which make up the history of Jesus music.

My appreciation also goes out to Lou and Peggy Hancherick of *Harmony* magazine for their inclusion in the magazine of my articles on the history of Jesus music. Many thanks also to Dan Hickling, publisher of the *Foreversong Journal*.

Also, a big thank you to the many people at Word, Incorporated, from the warehouse to the front offices, who made my three and one-half years there so memorable and enjoyable. The biggest thank you of all goes to my wife Debbie, who "inherited" the book, which was in the process of being written when we were wed. Her suggestions were invaluable, her patience was unbelievable, her tolerance was insurpassable, and her assistance, especially those final nights of getting the book finished by working all hours of the night, were the ultimate in selfless giving.

1984

A history is an amazing phenomenon. In preparing one, such as this book, by the time the writing is completed, the text itself is history! Within the span of just the few weeks between the time of submission of the manuscript to the publisher and the time it is sent to the printer, there have already been countless new developments and events which need to be chronicled.

That's what had happened by the time the preceding paragraphs were written. And now, history literally repeats itself as I write these few additional paragraphs exactly six years later.

Since the typewriter coughed its last gasp at the end of the book's last chapter, singer Amy Grant has performed to sellout crowds at Radio City Music Hall, and she has been featured in *Life* magazine. Petra has completed the most extensive Christian rock concert tour in history, performing before 429,000 people in 166 concerts on two continents. Word Records has announced that both Grant and Petra will be having their next albums released on Christian labels and the secular A & M label, in a major secular distribution pact. *Bullfrogs and Butterflies* by Candle has been awarded a gold record, making them the first group in gospel music to win two such honors. Meanwhile, Candle and all of the Agape Force gang mentioned in one chapter of this book have relocated from Lindale, Texas, to Tacoma, Washington.

Compact discs, the latest audio revolution, have been introduced by Benson, Sparrow, and Word Records. Christian rock releases are coming out at an unprecedented clip, on Myrrh, Refuge, Exit, A & S, Heartland, Patmos, Enigma, and at least a score of other labels. By the time the Music Comparison Chart in the back of this book was completed, the labels had come up with at least two dozen more artists who had been waiting in the wings. And, sure enough, rock was beginning to show up on Christian radio with much more regularity than had been predicted.

And the beat goes on . . . .

History is to be enjoyed and learned from. I hope that the reading of this one will provoke thought, prompt reassessment and renewal, enlighten the novice, rejuvenate the discouraged, and most of all, glorify God.

There must be a few names added to the list of my thank yous from a few years ago, people who have provided inspiration, help, and just good, old-fashioned friendship: Jan Dennis at Crossway Books, who was always open to new concepts and shared indispensable discussion; Bob Larson, who confronted and challenged me in some tight times; Thom Schultz and everyone at *Group* magazine and the National Youth Congresses, for making me a part; Tom Green, for his sagacious advice ("Don't quit for your convictions; get fired for them!"); Will McFarlane and the Muscle Shoals folks, for sharing their contagious enthusiasm; John and Candi Staton Sussewell, for their open doors, for their exuberance, and for being there at the right time; Paul Wilkinson, Leen LaRiviere, Marc Brunet, Steve Vaughn, Jose de Segovia, and Luis Alfredo Dias, for the armchair trip around the world; Danny Taylor, for the trip through the past and the present; Earl Paige at *Billboard,* for his precious counsel; Bob Payne; Bill Scarborough; Chuck Clements; and those always-anonymous "and others." My thanks also to the people at the record companies who made themselves available, and as always, my wife, Debbie.

Most of all, thanks to my Lord, who has placed me in such a fascinating variety of vantage points from which to view contemporary Christian music. As always, the Lord has been my light and my salvation.

PAUL BAKER
Birmingham, Alabama

Part I
1955–1978

1 / *Eve of Destruction*

> The babies born just after World War II came booming into the Sixties and nearly caused a national nervous breakdown. . . . That decade ranks as one of the most convulsive periods of social ferment and change in American history.[1]

How we ever made it through that decade is a mystery. The sixties were filled with major sociological problems, and one of the most perplexing was the generation gap. America's youth were exasperated with the materialistic living of their elders, the very lifestyle for which the parents had toiled and struggled so much to give to their children.

In his book *The Jesus Generation* Billy Graham said, "We came through the Depression and World War II. Hardship and death made us determined that our children would never have to go through another depression or another war. In pursuit of that goal, we chose the wrong means. Instead of turning to spiritual values, we turned to materialism."[2] Graham added that two of the things which drove so many of the youth into radical fervor and revolutionary fever were "the soulless materialism and the deification of technology in America."[3]

The youth reacted by throwing everything back into their parents' faces. They protested wars ("we're on the eve of destruction," one song announced), greediness, hypocrisy, pollution, bigotry, technology, and the Establishment in general. The noisy radicals, the "stoned" hippies, and the quiet flower children became the revolution.

For the radicals, the solution was to destroy. "Burn, baby, burn" was the call to arms. For the less aggressive hippies, the best way to handle everything that was going down was to "get stoned" and escape into the world of drugs. For the flower children, the desired world was one of peace, brotherhood, love, and understanding—a sort of "back to the basics" attitude. Their ideals were admirable, but the youth lacked the knowledge of how to realistically live them out.

Many of the youth of each type found themselves searching the teachings of scores of foreign and domestic, ancient and brand-new philosophies, religions, and sects. The youth were trying desperately to find answers which technology could not provide, and solutions which American Christianity had failed to convey to them.

In his study of the generation gap, evangelist Billy Graham listed what he felt were the causes of the rift:

> The natural rebellion of the human heart; the emptiness evident everywhere; the constant erosion and dehumiliation of personality by a machine-oriented age; the lack of purpose and meaning; the tragic failure of our educational system which seems more and more to alienate the young and consequently anger their parents; the overriding social problems that have no foreseeable solutions; the failure of government to understand that the basic gut-level problems facing the nation are not materialistic and social but moral and spiritual.[4]

When it came to spiritual values, the young people were more disillusioned than ever. The motto "In God We Trust" seemed to them not a creed but a mockery. The youth were convinced that there must be a better way to do things.

In their zeal to find meaning for their existence, however, the youth hastily concluded that it was "thumbs down" to all of Christianity. They failed to carry their investigations past the obvious mistakes and blunders of some of their Christian parents and the "American" style of Christianity. They failed to realize the source of the faith: Jesus Christ.

Some church leaders saw the increasing friction and tried to alert the established church to the growing chasm between the youth and the establishment. Almost prophetically, author Dennis Benson warned in 1969: "How long will it be before the silent Sunday morning army of youth realize what poor fare it has been fed and will turn away from the church?"[5]

Benson wasn't through. He warned further:

Youth's orientation asks of the church "How does it smell, feel, sound, or appear?" No longer acceptable are answers such as, "It must taste like communion wafers and grape juice; or it must smell like damp carpeting and moldy basements; or it must feel to the touch like glass beads; or it must sound like songs pitched too high for men to sing and phrased in language too quaint for this age; or it must appear only at a given time during the week in the dress of the ladies and gentlemen."[6]

Not only were the youth growing tired of the hypocrisy in what they saw as Christianity, they were also discouraged by the lack of interest the established church was taking in spiritual matters. In 1971 Norman Vincent Peale admitted:

For years we watched a spiritual vacuum growing in our young people. All the signs were there: dissatisfaction with a materialistic and affluent society; impatience with old forms of worship; a groping for fulfillment—first in rock music, then in various kinds of mysticism, finally in drugs. The churches turned off emotionalism and put all their chips on intellectualizing Christianity. Result: They priced themselves out of the youth market. We saw all this happening. But did we reach out eagerly and offer the seekers a solution they could accept in terms they could understand? I'm afraid many didn't.[7]

There were, fortunately, some youth who did not pass up the possibility that perhaps the trouble with America and American Christianity existed not in the faith's early foundations, but rather in the more recent waverings from "gospel truth." These youth had the maturity to "hang in" with the Christian faith. Rather than break with the church entirely, they began their own movement outside of the church to relate teachings and lifestyles which they felt more closely paralleled the early church. They sought to "get back to the Bible."

Thus, an "underground church" began again, as it had in catacombs and private dwellings centuries before. It had no organization; it consisted of individuals, sometimes thousands of miles apart, who had the same goals: communicating Christ to millions of stranded and confused young people caught in the middle of a generation gap, and instilling joy and excitement about true Christian living to the millions of churched young people who had grown tired of church life.

In his book *The Underground Church* Edward Plowman, a noted historian on the Jesus movement, observed:

> They are not flag-waving destructionists bent on overthrow; basically they seek spiritual renewal and satisfaction for themselves. They hope the wider Church will join their quest. I have found little bitterness among them and almost no inclination to mount a holy war of liberation against the formal church.[8]

The beginning of the Jesus movement in modern America has been traced back to 1967, when the Christian World Liberation Front opened the first Christian coffeehouse in the Haight-Ashbury district of San Francisco. Haight-Ashbury was a gathering-ground for every imaginable type of dissident youth. A freckled street minister, "Holy Hubert" Lindsey, preached on the street corners of Berkeley, telling dissidents and derelicts alike about Jesus Christ.

As Lindsey recounts it: "In 1965, there were fifteen thousand rioting students at Berkeley. In 1966, they didn't have a riot at Berkeley. In 1967 we had a revival! We turned that revolution into revival!"

By early 1968 another street preacher, Arthur Blessitt, was spending his Tuesday nights preaching to club-goers at Gazzarri's Hollywood-A-Go-Go on Sunset Strip. "I kept going into Gazzarri's trying to witness to him and all the nightclub people," explains Blessitt. "Finally one night he agreed to let me do a gospel rally. After that, it became a regular weekly thing, 10 to 12 each Tuesday."

Calvary Chapel, a small Orange County church, was beginning to experience growing pains. The congregation was growing so rapidly that a large circus tent had to be raised to house the growing throngs of California youth and adults. Pastor Chuck Smith led his congregation with a special sensitivity for the young people.

Before 1969 had passed, the increased activity of the Christian youth underground also included the publication of newspapers (called "Jesus papers") and their free distribution on street corners and on college and high school campuses. At Berkeley, *Right On!*, the pioneer Jesus paper, debuted as a Christian response to the radical underground *Berkeley Barb*. Twenty thousand copies were distributed. In Seattle *Agape* hit the streets. *The Hollywood Free Paper*, later to have the largest circulation of any of the papers, was started by former entertainer Duane Pederson in October 1969. In Spokane, *Truth* began publication.

These papers made no secret that they were Jesus papers. They mainly consisted of testimonies, Bible studies, and comics relating gospel-oriented tales. *Right On!*, published from a more intellectual perspective, was devoted to attacking propaganda from radical non-Christian groups.

All of the action wasn't in California, though. In the small berg of Freeville, New York, an ex-rock disc jockey from New York City, Scott Ross, was celebrating his discovery of Christ by broadcasting a radio show on five New York stations from Buffalo to Albany. Ross also founded "Love Inn," an old barn which had been converted in more ways than one. The renovated barn became one of the earlier Christian communities of the Jesus movement.

In West Palm Beach, Florida, the movement was gathering momentum under the auspices of the First Baptist Church. First Baptist had seen the early warning signs of restless youth. Fenton Moorhead, a professor at Palm Beach Atlantic College and specially appointed "Minister to the Generation Gap," was stirring up the enthusiasm of Florida teens. Despite opposition from some church members and West Palm Beach citizens, the youth of the church as well as college students from all over the country were challenged to reach the estimated forty thousand hippies, radicals, flower children, and others who were to attend the 1969 West Palm Beach Rock Festival. The extravaganza featured Janis Joplin, the Jefferson Airplane, the Rolling Stones, and may other top rock performers. Arthur Blessitt led a special training session, and then the Christians descended on the festival. The result was an admirable witnessing effort. An estimated three thousand youth responded by becoming followers of Jesus Christ.

There were plenty of other places where the Spirit was stirring, leading into a climactic decade of spiritual renewal: Dallas, Wichita, Palo Alto, even Waikiki.

Like the waves of Waikiki, the expanse of the Jesus movement swelled. Sometimes through the efforts of earlier pioneers and sometimes through their own searching, the youth of the generation gap began studying the character of Jesus more closely than they had in decades. They found that Jesus Christ had taught the very things for which the youth of the twentieth century were striving.

For these youth, the words of Christ spoken two thousand years ago could have been spoken just as well in the 1970s. Two thousand years ago Jesus said of love: "This is my commandment, that ye love one another, as I have loved you."[9] Of peace, Christ preached on the Mount of Olives: "Blessed are the peacemakers: for they shall be called the children of God."[10] On brotherhood, Jesus' advice was: "Whosoever is angry with his brother without a cause shall be in danger of the judgment."[11]

More and more youth were rediscovering the classic words of Jesus of Nazareth. Norman Vincent Peale described it this way:

> So what happened? A miracle, in a way. Without much leadership from anywhere, some of these young seekers groped and blundered and fought their way to an encounter with a Person so majestic, so appealing, so loving, so life-giving that the aching void in their lives was filled with a tremendous explosion of joy.[12]

Joy was the most noticeable attribute of the Jesus people. Even *Time* magazine was impressed: "What startles the outsider is the extraordinary sense of joy that they are able to communicate."[13] Those outsiders, on the whole, welcomed the exuberance of the Jesus people.

By 1971, the movement was going full steam and had drawn the attention of *Time, Life, Look,* CBS-TV, and NBC-TV. Even *Rolling Stone,* the bible of the antiestablishment youth underworld, reported:

> This new-style fundamentalist revival has spread rapidly across the country. "Every day with Jesus is sweeter than the day before," say these mostly young, long-haired children of America: Middleclass teenagers from the suburbs, ex-drug addicts and acid cultists, blacks from big-city ghettos, and babyfaced veterans of Vietnam. All of them born-again Christians.[14]

That was reported in June 1971, several years before a man named Jimmy Carter would cause worldwide awareness of the term "born again."

Time magazine appeared to have a running commentary of God in American life on its covers. The April 8, 1966 issue of *Time* had sported a cover asking, "Is God Dead?" On the cover of the last issue of 1969, the question had been "Is God Coming Back to Life?" Then, in the same week as the 1971 *Rolling Stone* article on the Jesus movement, *Time* featured a modernistic cover painting of Jesus and ran a feature article on the "Jesus revolution." Said *Time:*

Jesus is alive and well in the radical spiritual fervor of a growing number of young Americans who have proclaimed an extraordinary religious revolution in his name. Their message: the Bible is true, miracles happen, God really did so love the world that he gave it his only begotten son.[15]

Time had answered its own questioning covers.

Miracles come with just about any large spiritual revival, and one of the miracles of the Jesus revolution was the penetration of its message into so many different types of lifestyles. The movement permeated all portions of the youth culture: Satanists, dropouts, rock musicians, flower children, cultists, athletes, students, and even the not-so-rebellious, but often apathetic "straight" youth. Jesus' teachings were as full of salvation for one type of person as for another.

The common language of youth in the sixties and seventies assured rapid transmission of "new" ideas. It wasn't so much in the cute cliches of that era—"feelin' groovy," "right on," "far out," and "heavy"—though these exclamations were very much a part of the Jesus movement. It was in the methods of communication. Among the youth, word of Christ was not spread to any great degree over the airwaves or in books, as was so common with many other ideologies or current "fads." The method was ancient—from one person to another. It was an amazing example of the power of "word of mouth" and street witnessing. The message was taken to the streets.

As often as it was spoken, the message was sung. Just as the work of the Spirit knew no boundaries, neither did music. There may have been differences as to what style of music was preferred, but hardly a person did not relate in some way to music. And the people of the Jesus movement used music to its fullest advantage.

2/ He's Everything to Me

During the early sixties, folk songs were one of the most popular forms of music. While Chubby Checker was twisting and Bobby Rydell was singing "Wild One," folk-music "hootenannies" were becoming the Friday-night fare on college campuses. Some songsters traveled to the remotest parts of the Appalachians in search of more folk songs that could be recorded, introduced to the public, and in many cases exploited. But while the raw folk music was touching a limited audience with songs of unrequited love and bluetail flies, needles and pins were being woven into the fabric of the more public folk songs of Joan Baez, Bob Dylan, Ian and Sylvia, and Peter, Paul & Mary. Theirs were the folk songs of protest lamenting the woes of the younger generation as the gap began widening.

Though folk music was just about the simplest and most innocent form of music in America, the protest songs caused nearly all folk music to fall out of favor with the adults. In their eyes, all of it was lumped into one unacceptable category. Folk music was for beatniks and hippies, not respectable people.

Most churches of America continued with the hymns and many allowed their own style of folk music, though it was not recognized as such. The fellowship choruses such as "Do Lord," "Say 'Amen,' " "Give Me Oil in My Lamp," and "I've Got the Joy, Joy, Joy, Joy Down in My Heart" were the most contemporary of all Christian songs. They were used in Sunday-night fellowships and at camp, but hardly ever in the churches' sanctuaries. In the actual Sunday services the music was most often a selection of hymns ranging anywhere from ten to three hundred years old. Usually, the "special" music in each week's services was either of a country gospel or operatic nature, depending on the size, geographical area, and denomination of the church. Folk music was new and virtually untried.

One of the earliest denominations to utilize modern folk-style music was the Catholic church. The more liberal Catholics were working on the infusion of folk music into the church liturgies. As early as 1964, Ray Repp produced a "folk mass," something completely new to the church scene. Repp's *Mass for Young Americans* was a forerunner of numerous folk masses which would be performed around the nation in a sweep of the Catholic churches. Christian folk records began to come out of the Catholic church also. FEL and Avante Garde were two companies which built up entire lines of Christian folk-music recordings.

Youth for Christ (YFC), a Christian teen organization, also had its own spokesman for contemporary Christian music during the early 1960s. He was Thurlow Spurr, who had originally formed a group known as the Spurrlows to minister at a local YFC rally in Winston-Salem, North Carolina:

> Earlier I had heard Fred Waring and the Pennsylvanians in concert, and I was completely knocked out by the beautiful sound of the orchestra and singers. I knew then that I wanted to do something like that except I wanted to do it for the Lord.[1]

It wasn't too much later that Thurlow put the Spurrlows on the road full-time. The work of keeping the group touring led Thurlow to leave YFC in 1960.

The Spurrlows created smooth harmonies and modern arrangements to favorite hymns, traditional songs, and occasionally new music. As the years progressed, the style of the music they performed paralleled more and more of the current popular styles in secular music; the group developed an increasingly contemporary sound. By the late sixties, they were mixing in rock numbers at a regular pace.

Much of the support for the Spurrlows in the early sixties came from the Chrysler Corporation, which sponsored the group as they toured high schools all over America, promoting drivers' education and safety. They did their Chrysler work in school assemblies by day, and perfomed both secular and Christian contemporary music in local churches and auditoriums by night. More than a million people heard the Spurrlows each year.

Cam Floria, who worked with Youth for Christ in Portland, Oregon, developed a group very similar to the Spurrlows. Cam's group, the Continentals, developed their own tour patterns, and by the early 1970s they were literally spanning the globe with contemporary Christian music.

The Continentals and the Spurrlows were in reality made up of numerous teams, all using the parent names, each touring different geographic regions in America and abroad. Groups such as the Continentals did much more than just convince adults to listen to pop music styles. They provided training for the singers—not just in performing, but in living in group situations and in relating their faith to others. As one leader described it, the objective was not to be selective in finding the most spiritual and the most professional singers and put them on tour. Ron Bowles, who directed several of the Continental tours, added, "The idea was to enlist those young people who were interested in growing first in their faith, then in their musical proficiency. The singers and musicians in those groups, however, were still above average because of the intense training they went through prior to their tours."

Ron explained why he felt the group experiences were invaluable. "People," he said, "were originally against the idea of contemporary Christian music because they had never heard it performed well. So, they were thinking the *music* was bad rather than the *performers*.

"One of the ways in which the Continentals were an asset was the way they brought quality performance of contemporary Christian music into the church. People were able to see it inside the church and see that it *did* have an effect."

Many of the members of the Spurrlows and the Continentals later went on to form their own local groups. Very often, their concerts were the first taste churches had of anything related to the music of the 1960s and 1970s.

Both Thurlow Spurr and Cam Floria were aided in their endeavors by Ralph Carmichael, who would eventually record both groups on labels which he worked with or owned. Carmichael's crusade to contemporize Christian music had begun as early as 1947.

"Way back then," Carmichael explains, "there was a rhythmic sound that people were listening to on their radios. Just a gentle bass and then a backbeat on the guitar was all there was to it.

"We had music that could be played on keyboards that fit into those tempo slots, but the minute you put the bass and guitar and drums with it, and got it to where it was the sound the populace was listening to, then the church folk took exception to it. They would listen to it so long as it wasn't church music, but then they would come to church on Sunday and it had to be just the keyboards again.

"I couldn't figure that out," Carmichael continues, "because I knew that I liked the sound. I loved the strings. I loved the pulse, the rhythms. I didn't understand why we were always having to sing in half notes and quarter notes and whole notes. You could never use the strings, the brass, the woodwinds."

Carmichael began to search for ways to make those sounds and use them in the Christian field. "How can you sing about the joy of the Lord," he pondered, "when you can only use the organ or the piano? You couldn't sing about the joy of the Lord using instruments like in the Old Testament—the drums, the cymbals, the sackbut, the stringed instrument, or the loud-sounding brass! It didn't make sense to me! Did God change His mind somewhere between the Old Testament and the New Testament?"

When Carmichael was about eighteen, his ideas started to develop and his experimentation with sounds began. When he was twenty-one, he organized a band and traveled on holidays.

"We would get thrown out of churches," he recalls. "We had it all there—four trumpets, four trombones, five saxes, rhythm, and sixteen male singers. Things *really* started to happen when we went on television.

"We began to be accepted using strings and a moderate beat, too. There were several years when everything was comfortable because we had fought that battle and they were listening to the strings. I had made an album entitled *102 Strings,* and we were doing big things with big choirs."

Just when Carmichael had "won the battle," secular music began changing, making a turn toward rock. "Some musicians made that transition," Carmichael adds. "By that time I had started to do some secular things. I was experimenting and learning my lessons, always hoping that what I learned in the secular field I could bring over and use in the Christian field.

"I didn't like rock. My daughter used to buy rock records and I would break them. I remember the day I went out to my car and I found *her* station on! We developed this 'her' station/'my' station syndrome. She would play the rock and I wouldn't play it. I would play only *my* station. I wouldn't even let her buy rock records with her allowance.

"Then one day Roger Williams called and asked, 'Can you write rock?' Well, of course *that* was getting into my *pocketbook,* so I said yes, and hung up the phone asking myself, 'Why did I say *that?*'

"Roger Williams isn't a rock musician, but things were happening in the commercial field with the influence of rock, so we did a record with a moderate rock beat. It was even eighth notes, if that made it rock.

"The song was 'Born Free,' and it was a hit! So my daughter

came home from school one day and she had bought *Born Free,* as did about two or three million other people. She flipped the album down and said, 'Is that the same Ralph Carmichael that doesn't like rock?' She had caught me!"

Carmichael continued to experiment. Soon Billy Graham began production of a film entitled *The Restless Ones,* an evangelistic thrust into the youth scene via film. Carmichael was asked to compose the score. Although by today's standard the music would seem tame, it caused waves among the conservative churchgoers because of its contemporary nature.

"I saw the film and it was so relevant," Carmichael recalls. "The message hit right where people lived. I thought to myself, 'Dear Lord, I hope I can do something more than just the hearts and flowers and the strings and oboe and that kind of thing. Let me do something that really says something to the kids.' So we went in and did a score with a fender bass and drum added to everything else. 'In the stars His handiwork I see . . . He's everything to me.' "[2]

The fact that *The Restless Ones* had been produced by the Billy Graham Association tended to ease the worries of the dubious. The film was quite a success at church and youth-group showings around the world. The music from the film, especially "He's Everything to Me," is still sung in churches today, many of those churches the same congregations which earlier would not allow it.

Not long after Carmichael had finished the soundtrack of *The Restless Ones* in 1965, Bob Oldenburg, Billy Ray Hearn, Cecil McGee, and a few other cohorts composed the first of at least a score of Christian folk musicals which soon would inundate the churches and religious bookstores of the nation. The first musical was *Good News.*

"What really sparked the idea," recalls Hearn, "was the big movement at that time toward the big road shows like 'Up with People.' We saw a lot of our church kids leaving the church to join up with groups like that.

"So a bunch of us got together during Recreation Week at the Baptist Assembly in Glorieta, New Mexico, and asked ourselves why we couldn't develop our own 'Up with People' music. We decided to write some music like that by the next annual Recreation Week.

"Meanwhile, we got together a bunch of kids who were there at Glorieta, and some guitars. We started working on some known spirituals and folk songs, and doing some hymns in a folk style. There were about eighty kids, about twenty guitars and a bass, but no drums. *That* was still a little far out."

The youth performed for the Recreation Conference audience

in 1966. In 1967 the men completed *Good News,* which was performed for the first time at Glorieta, and shortly after that at the Ridgecrest Baptist Assembly in North Carolina. In 1968, the musical was performed by one thousand three hundred young people and a fifty-piece orchestra at the Southern Baptist Convention in Houston. From there, *Good News* fever took over.

Kurt Kaiser, a composer who worked at Word Records in Waco, Texas, flew to Houston to see the musical. Kaiser and Hearn then phoned Ralph Carmichael and discussed the possibility of composing more *Good News*-type musicals. All three men saw that music such as that in *Good News* was what the churches *and* the young people needed.

"We discovered that there was a great gulf developing between the youth and the traditional church," Carmichael remembers. "There were very few youth choirs. The church didn't like the kids' music, and the church didn't like the way the kids were dressing. They didn't like their hair styles, and the gulf was growing wider and wider. The churches were making the kids more and more uncomfortable. There were a lot of influences, but the result was that we decided to try something for the kids."

Carmichael and Kaiser then began writing *Tell It Like It Is.* Billy Ray Hearn moved to Waco and joined the Word staff to promote the musical, and in 1970 *Tell It Like It Is* was released as a record and music folio.

"The gospel was very plain, but the music was those even eighth notes," Carmichael adds. "Different choir directors started to see the potential, and youth choirs started growing. One lady who wrote to me said she had two or three kids who would meet with her on Saturday afternoons. She played *Tell I Like It Is* for them, the kids had become involved in it, and six months later there were forty kids in the youth choir. This happened over and over. I think we ultimately sold something over a half million of that $2.98 music folio, *Tell It Like It Is.*"

Carmichael and Kaiser then progressed to other musicals—*Natural High* and *I'm Here, God's Here, Now We Can Start.* The two composers gradually pulled away from the "folk" category of the earlier ones and began writing them in a contemporary, quasirock style. Not all of the later musicals, however, met with the success of *Good News* and *Tell It Like It Is,* probably for two main reasons. First, the impact of musicals was lessened by a sudden flooding of the market by more and more of the same. Second, many of the follow-up musicals were hastily prepared and too closely resembled their more successful and better predecessors.

Other notable musicals, however, were Otis Skillings' *Life* and *Love*, and Jimmy Owens' *Show Me*, which was performed in the spring of 1971 at Disneyland, as well as in hundreds of churches. Later Jimmy and his wife Carol would team up to write *Come Together*, *If My People*, and *The Witness*.

Composer Owens met with considerable opposition in the late sixties, as did the other writers who wanted to introduce contemporary music styles into the church. By 1972 he had found the going somewhat smoother but still difficult.

Said Owens in an interview at that time, "For the first time since right after the Civil War we are able to use contemporary music in the church. All through history there have been periods when the church would for a time speak the language of the people with its music, and then the music would become crystallized. The world would continue to grow while the church would hold sacred the styles that had evolved to a certain point. The attitude was like 'If it was good enough for our grandfathers, it's good enough for us. No one can change it. If you change it, you get kicked out.'

"The first guy who tried part-singing in church," Owens continued, "was excommunicated and his soul consigned to hell because they only sang in unison then. I could give example after example all through church history of that type of thing, which stems from not being open to the Spirit.

"The Salvation Army Band is a good example. The Army was founded by General Booth, and at the time the brass band was the hottest popular music of the day. Every little town had one, and every little town said, 'our brass band is better than your brass band.' You could put a brass band on a street corner and draw a crowd immediately.

"That's what the Salvation Army did because that was the pop style of the day. But, as one Salvation Army major said to me a few years ago, 'All progress ceased at General Booth's funeral,' " Owens added. "Everything crystallized, and anyone who dared change it was changing 'holy tradition' that had come down through General Booth. So the brass band continued on until it was no longer acceptable to the general public. There are still people who love brass bands, but the brass band has become a sort of mockery of the Salvation Army.

"Within the last ten years," Owens concluded, "there have come up leaders within the Salvation Army who have seen that we have to be bold and we have to change things. If Booth were still alive, progress would have continued; it wouldn't have stopped at the brass band. General Booth was a visionary who would have been using rock music by now."[3]

While thirteen hundred Salvation Army units still existed around the country playing the traditional instrumental hymns in 1973, a few rock groups sponsored by the Army began showing up in the Midwest and Canada. In England, Joy Strings, a Salvation Army contemporary music group, had released a record album as early as 1965.

According to a February 1973 article in *Right On!*, the few Army rock groups had caused some disgruntlement with the more traditionalistic, old-guard members, "who wonder at the merits of using rock music in the salvation of souls." The rock groups were composed of guitarists, an organist, a drummer, five singers, and a large brass section (keeping up the family tradition), sending forth the music in the vein of then-popular rock groups Blood, Sweat and Tears, Lighthouse, and Chicago. The article quoted the Army's supervisor of the rock band as saying, "It's not the type of music, but the saving of souls that's important." One Army major stated, "We've found that direct person-to-person relationships are most effective, and the way to get to the kids is through their music."

Another Army officer working in the New York area recalled General Booth's statement that he "would use the devil's own tune if it would turn one soul out of darkness."[4]

3/ Jesus Is Just Alright

"He's Got the Whole World in His Hands." "When the Saints Go Marching In." "There'll Be Peace in the Valley." "There's a Gold Mine in the Sky." "He." "Angels in the Sky." "The Bible Tells Me So."

It may sound like a grand old sermon, but actually it is a list of songs which were popular in the mid- and late 1950s—and not just popular in churches and at camp meetings, either. The songs, recorded by artists such as Pat Boone, Fats Domino, Elvis Presley, and the Crew Cuts (Does anyone remember the Crew Cuts?), made their way to the top of the secular hit charts.

Popular music of the 1950s was a potpourri of musical styles, ranging from "Sixteen Tons" by Tennessee Ernie Ford and "Around the World" by Mantovani to "Heartbreak Hotel" by Elvis Presley and "Rock Around the Clock" by Bill Haley and his Comets. The variety of pop styles allowed some inspirational or gospel songs to become hits right along with the other pop songs.

In the early 1960s, however, the musical tastes of America began to change. The "war babies," conceived in the years of World War II, had become high-school teenagers and would soon be in college. The comfortable "Fabulous Fifties" faded, and there began the growing unrest of civil rights inequities, and later a Viet Nam war.

The generation gap widened. Religious sentiments in pop songs faded. From 1961 until 1964, except for Christmas music each December, there were no major pop hits of a religious nature.

In 1964, the nation's music entered a new phase. The music industry was jarred so radically by the Beatles that in some ways it was as if popular music had just started. The mood was brightened by British rock, and in the midst of the renewed enthusiasm and hope pop hits of a religious nature began showing up again. Peter, Paul & Mary made the Top 40 charts with "Go Tell It on the Mountain." The Bachelors sang "I Believe." "You'll Never Walk Alone" was a hit twice in two years, 1964 and 1965.

Also in 1964, the nation was treated to a motion picture starring Sidney Poitier, entitled *Lilies of the Field.* The movie carried a religious theme and featured "Amen," a gospel song written by Jerry Goldsmith. "Amen" quickly caught on as a hit for a soul-music group known as the Impressions, and reached #7 on the national charts. The Impressions had recorded "Amen" with a march beat rather than a gospel beat; the brass choir in the recording gave the effect of a Salvation Army band, which was many people's idea of what "religion" was supposed to sound like.

In fact, the images of "religious" people and religion in general were an interesting concept. Most people outside of Christianity had been convinced through motion pictures that in order for someone to be "religious," one had to be a mild-mannered, meek priest wearing a clerical collar, or a nun dressed in her habit, feeding and caring for orphan children. Even less sympathetic views of preachers were the ranting, raving images presented in *Hawaii* and *Elmer Gantry.* To the Hollywood directors and producers, an average, everyday, level-headed, commonly dressed businessman could in no way represent Christianity or religion.

Thus, the people began believing the images they saw—one extreme or the other, pious or delirious, seldom normal. God was given the image in music of being "the Man upstairs." Seldom was He portrayed as Something or Someone touchable and real. He was nearly always kept aloof. Thus, the religious feelings in pop songs had to be subdued, couched in nebulous terms. Religion was kept cute and harmless, never convicting.

Though the songs weren't always evangelistic, religious music managed to break into the top 20 several times during 1965. The Impressions, hot on the heels of their success with "Amen," recorded "People Get Ready," which reached #14.

Elvis Presley sang "Crying in the Chapel" in 1965 too, and the song smashed all the way to #3. But the top religious hit for the year was the Byrds' recording of "Turn! Turn! Turn!," composer Pete Seeger's paraphrase of Ecclesiastes 3, with certain alterations given to make it a "peace song." "Turn! Turn! Turn!" became the #1 song in America on October 23, 1965.

Then, in the late sixties, another trend in religious pop songs began. Just as the Jesus movement was drawing people into recognizing Jesus as a personal Savior, the name of Jesus began appearing in pop songs for the first time. Heretofore, song lyrics had referred to God only as "He" or "Him" or "the Lord."

In 1968 Simon and Garfunkel recorded the soundtrack music to a movie entitled *The Graduate*. The most popular song from the film became "Mrs. Robinson," in which this line appeared: "Here's to you, Mrs. Robinson; Jesus loves you more than you will know."[1] The song was a tongue-in-cheek poke at religion and was by no means religious, but it was apparently the first time in the rock era that the name Jesus actually appeared in a popular song. It was ironic that it should take a sarcastic song to open the floodgates of Jesus music!

The ironies didn't end with "Mrs. Robinson" though. In the late sixties, a group of black California high-school students, known collectively as the Northern California State Youth Choir, recorded a hymn which was more than two hundred years old.

The recording of the hymn was sent to a few radio stations in California, and soon people were calling and asking to hear "that choir record." A large record company caught wind of what was happening with the song and pressed a new copy of the single for national distribution. To remove some of the religiosity from the group's name (so more pop stations might play their music), the name was changed to the Edwin Hawkins Singers.

"Oh Happy Day" was the hymn. Legend of how the record became a hit says that the song was played as a joke by a rock disc jockey in San Francisco. The joke backfired, and the phones started ringing with requests for it. The superhymn began its stupendous climb all the way to a #4 chart status in June 1969 and sold over a million copies. The message "Oh happy day, when Jesus washed my sins away" was being heard by millions in a popular song.

A two-century-old hymn sung by a black choir had become a top hit in a rock world. Even more ironically, the name of the record company which distributed the first "Jesus hit" was Buddah Records. The popularity of "Oh Happy Day" heralded the start of a long succession of hit songs mentioning Jesus.

Just as a hymn was an unlikely candidate to find its way into the top record charts of the late 1960s, so was a country gospel recording. While "Oh Happy Day" was still selling in stores all over the world, an unknown singer named Lawrence Reynolds recorded a song entitled "Jesus Is a Soul Man." Warner Brothers Records released the single, and it emerged on the national hit charts in September 1969 and managed to rise to #28 in *Billboard*. Not only was it country music, it was country *gospel* music—unlikely company for the Beatles and the Rolling Stones.

Norman Greenbaum, another newcomer to the charts, was the next artist to use Jesus' name in pop music. "Spirit in the Sky," which first seemed to be a genuine Jesus-rock song, was later exposed to be a tongue-in-cheek flay at the Jesus people who were actively witnessing all over the West Coast. Greenbaum told *Hit Parader* magazine, "I wanted to write a thing called a religious song. Jesus Christ is popular and in actuality I used the most popular religious character in my song . . . I'm not a Christian and I don't go to church."[2] Regardless, thousands of young people adopted the hit as a Christian "theme song" during that year. "Spirit in the Sky" became the nation's #3 song in February 1970.

There were several reasons why songs about Jesus began showing up more and more frequently in 1969 and the early seventies. The Jesus movement was gaining momentum, and the Jesus theme was a little more acceptable than it had been in years past. Secondly, the youth of the generation gap were opening up to *any* possible religion. They were considering each faith's claims and experimenting with each, searching for spiritual fulfillment. To these youth, Jesus represented just another religious possibility. Though many of them had turned down the Jesus of their parents, they felt they had discovered a *new* Jesus, with long hair, a beard—so many of the characteristics adopted by the prodigal youth of the late sixties and early seventies. To them, Jesus was a revolutionary.

A third reason for the increasing number of "Jesus" hits was the simple fact that fresh new lyrics were needed as more and more pop songs were vying for hit status. The lyrics seemed to appeal to the masses; so more and more record companies followed the lead established by "Oh Happy Day."

Though not generally recognized by the public as a "Jesus song," the late-1962 #2 hit of singer Tommy James, "Crystal Blue Persuasion," was written as a result of James' realization of Christ as Savior.

The Youngbloods' recording of "Get Together," which had already been a hit in 1967, returned to the charts in 1969 and reached #5. "Get Together" is one of three "Jesus hit" recordings to become hits in two different years. The other two were Billy Preston's "That's the Way God Planned It" (1969 and 1972), and the questionable "Superstar" (1970 and 1971).

One of the classic albums of Jesus-rock music was released in 1970 by Cotillion Records. The album, which unfortunately never reached the hit charts, was *Mylon,* and featured Mylon LeFevre and his band performing a dozen Jesus-rock songs. Mylon had been a part of the Gospel Singing LeFevres, a family southern-gospel group. He was singing at the early age of five, when, he recalls, he would "stand on the end of a piano bench and face the microphone." He continued to sing with the other LeFevres until he was twenty-five, when his long sideburns and his love for rock music caused a rift.

Mylon had already written songs for Elvis Presley, Merle Haggard, Johnny Cash, Don Gibson, Porter Wagoner, and Mahalia Jackson. Some of the songs became award-winning gospel favorites. But Mylon wanted to rock. He explained to everyone, upon his resignation from southern-gospel music, that he wanted to "reach young people with what I believe in—that Jesus gave His life for my sins—but I'm not gonna shove religion at them."

Mylon's debut rock album contained nearly all Jesus music. His subsequent recordings drifted from the Christian theme, but the first remains an important event in the history of contemporary Christian music.

Ray Stevens, whose "Ahab the Arab" and "Gitarzan" had record buyers assuming that the singer never took things seriously, recorded a song in April 1970 which turned many heads and sold a million copies. "Everything Is Beautiful" easily reached #1. Although the composition itself was not actually Jesus music, the lyrics told of love for one's fellowman. What put it into the Jesus music category was the children's chorus of "Jesus Loves the Little Children" at the beginning of the recording.

Later that year the popular Columbia recording group the Byrds released "Jesus Is Just Alright." Though the song was caught up by many Christians, the recording never scored as a big hit. More successful was Pacific Gas & Electric, another popular rock group. Their record, "Are You Ready?," was a powerhouse single that even to this day is not recognized by some as Jesus rock, although the entire content of the lyrics is spiritual and scriptural. The song managed to secure the #14 spot in the nation in the summer of 1970.

The year 1970 was also a banner year for non-Jesus music "inspirational" hits. They were songs which were more or less worldly carbon copies of the trendy Jesus-music songs.

Simon & Garfunkel's "Bridge Over Troubled Water" was wrapped in an ethereal aura and became a hymn for the pop world. The music was right, the lyrics and recording were stirring; thus, to many people, it was religious. But it was *not* Jesus music. Indeed, its lyrics were suspected of having extensive references to drugs.

James Taylor, Johnny Rivers, and R. B. Greaves all reached the Hot 100 in 1970 with Taylor's composition "Fire and Rain." Here, once again, was a borderline case as to whether or not the song was really Jesus music. The song alluded to a definite call for help from Jesus, but Taylor tended to use the word euphonically rather than with conviction. The Taylor version of "Fire and Rain" hit #3 on the charts.

The Jackson Five produced a stir with "I'll Be There," a song assuring that when everyone else had deserted, "I'll be there to protect you." No one seemed to mind that the singer providing all the reassurance, Michael Jackson, was an adolescent.

Motown Records, who released the Jackson Five song, also had a #7 hit in 1970 with the Supremes' "Stoned Love." The song passed by many people without their realization that the lyrics in part spoke of God's great love, citing the sun in the sky as a "symbol" of that love.

Much more obvious were the lyrics of "Amazing Grace," an astonishing hit indeed for Judy Collins in 1970. The hymn was written by converted slavetrader John Newton in the second half of the eighteenth century. Collins' #15 recording of "Amazing Grace" was not an updated version, but rather a traditional, congregational singing of the hymn.

In 1971, there was hardly a week when at least one "Jesus song" was not on rock radio stations coast to coast. B. J. Thomas sang "Mighty Clouds of Joy." Kenny Rogers and the First Edition even nudged the Hot 100 with another handclapper, "Take My Hand." Rogers, in a personal interview, said he had been influenced by his Baptist upbringing in writing the song. (Several years later he would make a hit country recording of the hymn "Love Lifted Me.") Johnny Rivers sang "Think His Name." Sha Na Na even contributed a parody of all the Jesus hits: "Are you on the Top 40 of your Lordy, Lordy, Lordy?" Ray Stevens revived a 1938 song, "Turn Your Radio On," all about gospel radio.

One of the most memorable of the 1971 "Jesus songs" was the #2 hit for a Canadian group, Ocean. The song, "Put Your Hand in the Hand," was picked up and recorded by scores of other artists, but Ocean's version stood alone on the charts.

Noel Paul Stookey, on his own as a solo performer following the breakup of Peter, Paul & Mary, made a hit out of a song he had written for Peter Yarrow's wedding. Noel felt so impressed that the Lord had given him the words for "Wedding Song (There Is Love)," he published it under the "Public Domain Fund," and most of the proceeds from royalties for the #24 hit were sent to "The Children's Foundation."

"I assigned the writing and the publishing to them," Stookey said, "because I didn't really feel it belonged to me. I had put up the request before Jesus to write the song for Peter's wedding. It took two or three days for me to get out of the way, but eventually Jesus created the tune. I just wrote it down when it came."

Songs such as "Wedding Song (There Is Love)" and "Amazing Grace" were true Christian songs in the midst of many trendy Jesus songs. At times the dividing line was hard to draw, but in general the Jesus songs of the late sixties and early seventies were no more than pop songs about a current topic. By 1971, it was nearly impossible to *avoid* hearing mention of Jesus in pop music. For some people it was a pleasant state of the art. Other people had almost had their fill. But the most publicized exploitation of Jesus in the rock-music world was just around the corner.

4/ Jesus Christ, S.R.O. (Standing Room Only)

Just as a choir was responsible for bringing Jesus music to America's hit charts, a schoolboys' choir was indirectly responsible for what turned into one of the high points in Jesus music's history.

In London, Alan Doggett, head of the music department of Colet Court School, needed a musical piece for his schoolboy choir to sing at their end-of-term concert. Doggett appointed two young British men to compose the appropriate piece.

The result was a fifteen-minute "operetta" entitled *Joseph and the Amazing Technicolor Dreamcoat,* first performed March 1, 1968, at the school by the schoolboy choir. *Joseph and the Amazing Technicolor Dreamcoat* was just what the title implied: a contemporary musical story of Joseph. By incorporating the varying styles of rock and roll, the Joseph story took on new life, and the presentation was a success.

The musical was performed again during the several months following its debut, and by late 1968 it had been lengthened to thirty minutes and recorded. The initial album of *Joseph* was released in England in January 1969 and, in the words of *Joseph's* composers, it "received several good reviews but did not set the commercial pop world alight." Copies of the libretto started finding their way into churches and schools in America, but not much more attention was given to it.

By mid-1969, the composers of *Joseph and the Amazing Technicolor Dreamcoat,* Andrew Lloyd Webber and Tim Rice, decided to "have a go at writing something else" since they had been fairly successful with *Joseph.*

Both Webber and Rice had been raised in the Anglican church, but neither found themselves believing in the deity of Jesus Christ. Rice was to later express to *Time* magazine, "It happens that we don't see Christ as God, but as simply the right man at the right time in the right place."[1] This perspective is most likely what prompted Webber and Rice in 1969 to begin their second work together, one which would view Christ through the eyes of Judas Iscariot, perceiving Christ as a man rather than the Son of God.

The two composers started full steam in that direction. To drum up backing for the musical's completion, the duo composed Judas' theme song, which was also the theme of the opera-to-be: *Jesus Christ Superstar.*

> Jesus Christ, Jesus Christ
> Who are you? What have you sacrificed?
> Jesus Christ Superstar
> Do you think you're what they say you are?*

The production of the single record "Superstar" was accomplished in September 1969, only two months or so after the song had been written; Murray Head was the singer chosen to record it. Released in late 1969, the recording only reached #74 during the seven weeks it was on the American charts.

"Superstar" broke no popularity records at first outing. Its brazen questioning of Christ was too radical for many people. On the surface the record didn't appear to stir much interest in the American public. But John K. Maitland, the newly appointed head of Decca Records, was impressed by the preliminary work on the full opera he had heard and gave the monumental musical a full go-ahead.

And monumental it was. The project called for eighteen months of work, four hundred hours of studio time, a cast of eleven lead singers, two choirs, six major rock musicians selected from the finest British groups, and a Moog synthesizer. As if that wasn't enough, also employed were the strings of the City of London and an eighty-five-piece orchestra directed by none other than Alan Doggett, who had first commissioned Webber and Rice to write *Joseph and the Amazing Technicolor Dreamcoat.* The man chosen to portray Jesus was Ian Gillan, star of the popular rock group Deep Purple.

Jesus Christ Superstar was tagged a "rock opera," a term which had been first used in billing a highly successful work, *Tommy,* only

---

a few months earlier. The *Superstar* material was written between October 1969 and March 1970, when the recording of the work began. By July the sessions were completed and the historical release date was October 27, 1970.

The eighty-seven-minute, two-record rock opera immediately drew publicity from all corners. *The New Yorker* quoted a "major religious leader," Pastor Ralph E. Peterson, as saying "I liked it. It reached me. But the composers are hung up on old-fashioned piety."[2] The writer quoting the pastor said, "Theology-wise, updated, reworked, some nice points, wanders from the book."[3]

Time stated: "What Rice and Webber have created is a modern-day passion play that may enrage the devout but ought to intrigue and perhaps inspire the agnostic young."[4] *Newsweek* called the rock opera "Nothing short of brilliant—and reverent. . . ."[5] "A rock opera about the Passion of Christ is a double-barreled provocation. It trespasses on a sublime musical terrain and threatens to profane Western civilization's most sacred religious belief."[6]

From the Christian press came views confirming the prophecies of *Time* and *Newsweek*. Cheryl A. Forbes, in *Christianity Today,* observed that "the wordless finale . . . leaves Christ in the grave. No faith and no victory emerge from this weary music, but the relentless quest remains, haunting and hollow."[7] But Forbes also conceded, "*Superstar* tells what young people are saying."[8]

The *Jesus Christ Superstar* album was sure to be controversial. The shock of hearing a song about Jesus, much more one *questioning* Jesus, was traumatic for many Christians. For others, the recording was a breakthrough—the first time the person of Jesus Christ was put in a "believable" light. Said one observer:

> A common reaction to Superstar is: It was the first time I ever thought of Jesus as a real person. The Phantom-like portrayals of an other worldly Christ on decades of funeral home calendars and Sunday School walls apparently makes the focus on Jesus as a real person a remarkable revelation to this generation.[9]

For some young people, *Superstar* was a crack in the dike of staunch antipopular-music feeling within the established church. Not long after the debut of the album, *Superstar* songs were being used in church services all over the country. One theater group, The American Rock Opera Company, managed to perform twenty-two unauthorized performances around the nation before the copyright holders put a halt to the "bootlegging."

By early 1971 talk was beginning about a Broadway presentation of the successful rock opera. Successful, in this case, would be an understatement. According to *Business Week,* "in eight weeks, a touring toupe of about 25 singers and 30 musicians took in more than $2,000,000 in box-office receipts,"[10] while by October of 1971 the album had sold 3.5 million copies, for a total gross of $40,000,000. As a Tom Paxton song said, "Jesus, You're S.R.O. on Broadway."

The machines of big business had never before seen so much profit off the Man from Galilee. *Time* described it as "the Gold Rush to Golgotha."[11] The title of the rock opera turned out to be prophetic, too. *Newsweek* said that

> the opera makes it natural to see Jesus as a superstar, the new Messiah, who's at "the top of the poll," with Mary Magdalene as chief groupie, Judas as conniving manager, the Apostles his turned-on band, the priests the blind guardians of rigid law and order, Pilate a kind of smooth university president, and Herod, governor of the state.[12]

Opening night at the Mark Hellinger Theatre was the epitome of superstardom for Webber and Rice's Jesus, with advance sales at $1.2 million, one of the largest in Broadway history. People from all sorts of backgrounds attended the theatre to see this man called Jesus to which the marquee in the east had led them. The majority of the public attending loved the show, and the critics generally hated it. The production of Tom O'Horgan (who had also staged the first American rock musical, *Hair*), had turned a fairly acceptable rock opera into a series of "bizarre effects and for-the-shock-of-it images."[13] *Time* stated, "O'Horgan's aim is mainly to shock the sensibilities; often alas, that is all he manages to do."[14]

And then there were the protestors—placard-carrying pickets marching outside the theater, rebelling at the Superstar hat being placed on their King of kings. The American Jewish Committee issued a seven-page study condemning the anti-Semitic feeling of the play.

Billy Graham wrote in his 1971 book, *The Jesus Generation:*

> I don't particularly like the rock opera *Jesus Christ Superstar* because it treats Christ irreverently and perhaps sacrilegiously. But its fatal flaw is that it doesn't go far enough—it leaves Christ in the grave. And without the Resurrection there is no Christianity, no forgiveness, no faith, no hope—nothing but a hoax.[15]

However, a rock music publication later quoted Graham as softening his stand against *Superstar:*

> It doesn't mean that they accept Him, but they are taking a new look, because the young can identify with Him. He taught love, peace and forgiveness. He had a beard and long hair. He is seen as a revolutionary in whom they can believe and with whom they can share an experience.[16]

Another writer responded to *Superstar* with this observation:

> Pastors who are looking for the record *Jesus Christ Superstar* to make more Christians are going to be greatly disillusioned. A warning is also in order for those who seek after the novel. But, for a look into the souls of men who have confronted the person of Jesus and have not known what to do with Him, *Jesus Christ Superstar* will provide a window. One student remarked that it was too bad that a Christian had not written the contemporary religious sensation. That's right, it is too bad, but then we would not know how the unbeliever feels. Of course, don't get offended by the attitude of confusion of the disciples, the scheming of Judas, the political maneuvering of the priests, etc. This is just the way we all would have acted, if God had placed us in that history instead of the present. I get the impression that the composers would have preferred that Jesus would have never existed. They can't and don't want to believe in Him, but they can't get rid of Him.[17]

Jesus Christ Superstar had its pros and cons, but one thing was for sure: the rock opera, the play, and the movie (which was released in the summer of 1973) opened several avenues for Jesus music. In the first place, it came into popularity at the same time the Jesus movement was reaching its fullest strength. Whether *Superstar* helped the Jesus movement receive more news coverage, or the national awareness of the Jesus movement helped draw more crowds to *Superstar* is still open to conjecture. Most likely, each helped the other.

Another avenue opened by *Jesus Christ Superstar* was the financial backing behind it. It would have been a hard task indeed for any Christian body or corporation to utilize the publicity and finances in getting a show off the ground with the same strength and success as MCA managed in promoting *Superstar*. Even though the play nullified the divinity of Christ, it did, as Billy Graham had stated, draw many people to the point of considering Jesus for the first time.

Thirdly, *Jesus Christ Superstar* encouraged struggling contemporary Christian musicians to work harder than ever at producing quality, up-to-date Jesus music. These musicians saw that the public *did* respond to music about Jesus much more than they would have imagined, and who was to say it couldn't happen again, this time from the Christian camp?

Perhaps the hardest pill to swallow for Jesus musicians was the fact that someone in the secular world took the honors for creating mass awareness of Jesus, limited though the perspective was. Encouragement and a challenge, however, came from Cheryl A. Forbes in *Christianity Today* right after the *Superstar* album was first released. "Perhaps," she wrote, "some Christian composer will take the cue and produce a rock opera about Christ that ends not with hollow questions but with triumphant answers."[18]

5/ Little Country Church

With the popularity of Jesus as the subject of secular songs increasing in the early 1970s, it would seem that early Jesus musicians would have had excellent opportunities to have hit records, too. Such was not the case, however. Most of the songs which were hits were attempts by secular record companies to cash in on a fad. Very few stations even auditioned the music on the religious labels. Secular radio programmers said the music was too religious, while the religious programmers said it was too worldly. The records of Jesus-music performers were either trashed or given away.

Though the issue against Jesus-rock music was a moral one for many concerned adults, it was far from that for the youth. It was an excruciating dilemma. Antirock evangelists were stirring up adults against Jesus rock, while many of the youth were trying to explain to their parents that rock music did *not* cause them to fall into evil habits as the evangelists warned.

Larry Norman wrote the rallying song for the Jesus-music fans, "Why Should the Devil Have All the Good Music?":

> I want the people to know
> That he saved my soul
> But I still like to listen to the radio
> They say "rock and roll is wrong
>   we'll give you one more chance"
> I say I feel so good I got to get up
>   and dance
>
> I know what's right I know what's
>   wrong, I don't confuse it
> All I'm really trying to say is

Why should the devil have
all the good music
I feel good every day
Cause Jesus is the rock and he
rolled my blues away.[1]

In the Southern Baptist churches a point well-made by a
preacher would receive a hearty "Amen!" from someone in the
audience. In the world of the 1970s, the musicians became the
ministers, and their points well-made in song earned an abundance
of "Right on!" exclamations and plenty of approving applause from
thousands of teens.

But the applause often wasn't so much for the performer as it
was an outward manifestation of their free expression. Someone was
finally saying it as they believed it. When the applause began, Larry
would point his index finger upward as if to say "Give God the glory,
not me." The teenagers quickly caught on, and the one-way sign
became the flag of the Jesus movement.

One way, one way to heaven
Hold up high your hand.
Follow, free and forgiven,
Children of the Lamb.[2]

With his long, straight blond hair, his incisive lyrics and his
gutsy rock tunes, Larry shocked just about every adult who came into
his path. Enigma though he was, he carried the Good News of Jesus
via a medium which was readily understood by the young people.

Larry had been playing musical instruments since he was three.
His first guitar had been slipped under the bed to hide it from his
father. Being a musician was not exactly the most respectable or
profitable job in the eyes of his dad, but to Larry it was just about
everything.

By the time he was a teenager, Larry was singing in his San
Jose, California, neighborhood with other musical friends. His band,
People, managed a fair degree of success in the Bay Area, and
Capitol Records signed them. Their first recording, "Organ Grind-
er," was not a rousing success, but their second was. "I Love You
(But the Words Won't Come)" sailed to the #14 position on the
national hit charts in April 1968.

Larry was already a Christian when the hit came. He was
already a bold young man, too, wanting to alert people to the truth in

unorthodox ways. So he and the band titled their first album *We Need a Whole Lot More of Jesus and a Lot Less Rock and Roll*. But when Larry wanted a picture of Jesus on the cover, Capitol put the proverbial foot down. It was much too risky and not commerical enough. The LP, with the modified, unimaginative title of *I Love You*, and a photo of People on the cover, was released.

On the very same day, Larry broke with the band. He went on to do his own creative "thing," doggedly determined not to let "commercial" strictures stifle his creativity and his desire to sing about Jesus.

Only a year or so later Capitol Records invited Larry back to do a solo album. The result was *Upon This Rock*, one of the first American Jesus-rock albums. Though the album never made a hit, it did affect the lives of numerous young people who heard what Larry said in his songs. A good example of those people affected was Kurt Dillinger, then a young Michigan resident.

"I had rebelled severely against my church and its doctrinal teaching," Dillinger recalls. "I had turned to peer pressure, drugs, and similar things in order to be popular. At that time there was a big Christian movement throughout the United States. Many friends of mine tried to show me that living in Christ was the only way for me to live.

"Music had influenced me greatly as to the direction my life was going, and my idea of *Christian* music was pretty well warped. I thought that to be a Christian you had to fit into the mold that was already set for musicians at that time.

"The people who were leading me to Christ had Larry Norman's album *Upon This Rock*. They had opportunities to share that album with me. I automatically related to Larry Norman, because he seemed to rebel against most Christian music, and was sort of the pilot for Christian rock. Larry seemed to be really speaking a solid message, something that wasn't redundant or being overdone all the time. It was new and refreshing. I don't really think it was the lyrics that got to me as much as the way Norman was free to explain things in his words. They weren't the typical hymn-type songs. I had always thought that music of the Christian world was the hymns or the quartets or some of the music which made me feel like I was going to a funeral every week. Larry's music was lively instead."

> I ain't knocking the hymns
> Just give me a song that has a beat
> I ain't knocking the hymns

> Just give me a song that moves my feet
> I don't like none of the funeral marches
> I ain't dead yet.[3]

"I believe that Larry Norman's album had direct influence on my decision for Christ," Kurt continues. "At that time, I turned about and went directly in the opposite direction that I had been going. After that, his songs encouraged me to bring music into the church, into our youth group. The group grew, and seventy people came to know Jesus. It was because of the freeing power that Christ has, and Larry letting Christ use him through his music."

Upon This Rock wasn't Larry's only Jesus-rock album in the early years. Larry produced two albums in 1969 for his own One Way record label, *Street Level* and *Bootleg*. The music on all three of the Norman albums was definitely on the fringe of understanding for adults, but the teens grabbed every word. "Sweet Sweet Song of Salvation," "Right Here in America," "One Way," "Let the Lions Come," "UFO," and "Why Don't You Look Into Jesus" became the bootlegged songs of the underground church.

The words of Christ in Luke 17:34-36 concerning the Second Coming were Larry's inspiration to write "I Wish We'd All Been Ready," which would become his most popular Christian song. Unlike most Jesus music, the song was a lamentation.

> Life was filled with guns and war
> And everyone got trampled on the floor;
> I wish we'd all been ready.
> Children died; the days grew cold
> A piece of bread could buy a bag of gold;
> I wish we'd all been ready.
> There's no time to change your mind
> The Son has come and you've been left behind.[4]

"I Wish We'd All Been Ready" became the anthem of preparation for Christ's return. Teenagers picked up the sorrowful ballad, campfire groups sang it, and soon church youth groups were singing it and trying to teach it to their parents.

> A man and wife asleep in bed
> She hears a noise and turns her head; he's gone
> I wish we'd all been ready
> There's no time to change your mind
> The Son has come and you've been left behind.[5]

A trademark of the Jesus movement was the cry "Jesus is coming soon!" Perhaps never since the Apostle Paul's warnings of Christ's imminent return had there been such an electric air of expectancy. Rev. David Wilkerson was sharing his visions and telling congregations that his "bags were packed." Hal Lindsey was shocking the world with his revelations of coming events in *The Late Great Planet Earth,* which would become reportedly the best selling book of the decade.

The eschatological fervor of the Jesus movement ran especially heavy at Calvary Chapel in Costa Mesa, California. Pastor Chuck Smith, whose Pacific Ocean mass baptisms were given national publicity, formed a new ministerial outreach called Maranatha! Music. The meaning of *maranatha* is "The Lord cometh."

Maranatha! Music released its first album in 1971. *The Everlastin' Living Jesus Music Concert* was an immediate sellout among the Jesus people of California, and numerous copies drifted eastward. Friends mailed other friends copies of the albums, and those who received the records were quick to play them for *their* friends at first chance.

The cover of the *Everlastin' Living Jesus Music Concert* album, which later became known as *Maranatha! 1,* featured the words of Psalm 150:

> Praise the Lord! Praise God in His sanctuary: praise Him in the Heavens of His power! Praise Him for His mighty acts; praise Him according to the abundance of His greatness. Praise Him with trumpet sound; praise Him with lute and harp! Praise Him with tambourine and dance; praise Him with stringed and wind instruments. Praise Him with sounding cymbals: praise Him with loud clashing cymbals. Let everything that has breath praise the Lord! Hallelujah!

Everything in the Jesus-movement years crackled with joy and exclamation; the true Spirit of the Lord was manifest in the young people. For the first time in that generation of wars, riots, and tumultuous unrest, the young people were being offered the love and peace of Jesus on recordings which could be played over and over, ministering in their own special language.

In the earliest days of Jesus music, there were scattered albums of folk or rock music which had been recorded by specific groups on their own labels. The greatest problem for these musicians was getting their own albums publicized and distributed nationally as well as locally. Otherwise, thousands of the artists' records were doomed to their garages and bedrooms.

More than anyone else, Bob Cotterell enabled these musicians to minister through their records. Bob was a Californian who in 1966 formed Creative Sound, a record production company and distributor which was responsible for disseminating most of Jesus music's earliest albums. Creative Sound's 1972 catalog listed a wide array of Christian folk music and Jesus rock: *The Everlastin' Living Jesus Music Concert* and The Children of the Day's *Come to the Waters,* Maranatha's first two recordings; *Jesus Power,* one of Jesus music's first sampler albums; *Truth of Truths,* a rock opera based on Bible stories; *The Armageddon Experience,* Campus Crusade's contemporary troubadors; *Jesus People,* a live Jesus music concert; *Soul Session at His Place,* recorded live at Arthur Blessitt's Sunset Strip club; *Street Level,* Larry Norman's first album; *Born Twice,* Randy Stonehill's debut; *Songs from the Savior* from Paul Clark; *Agape,* by the first hard-rock Christian group; and scores of other recordings. Without Bob's vision, many of the earliest Jesus-music recordings would have never left California.

One of the musical groups on the first Maranatha album was Love Song. Their music had been a bit more raucous in days past, but by the time of *The Everlastin' Living Jesus Music Concert,* it had already become some of the most popular Christian music to be written in the 1970s.

Love Song's members had met each other through their participation in various other music groups. Jay Truax recalls meeting Chuck Girard for the first time while Jay was working in Salt Lake City as part of the rock group Spirit of Creation. "When I first met him in 1967," Jay recounts, "Chuck had just come from Los Angeles. He'd had a couple of hit records before, like 'Little Honda' with the Hondells, and 'Sacred' and 'So This Is Love' with the Castells.

"He'd been singing and playing music for a long time, and I was just playing in night club situations. I had no direction to my music. I was just kinda earning money. We were both wanting a change—a fresh direction in our lives. Some sort of goal."

Jay and Chuck started off together. Not much later a friend of Jay's in Las Vegas had stopped playing music and had gone into full-time study of the Bible. Jay and Chuck responded to the friend's suggestion to "get into the Bible." They left just about everything behind, including old friends.

Jay recalls how people looking for answers and wanting to

experience God's love began "accumulating" at their house in Pasadena.

"This is where Love Song came about," added Jay. "It was basically to share God's love. We went into bars and everything. We had some songs about Jesus and about other things. We were radical, man. We'd get kicked out of bars, and no one could even relate to us at that point."

For the next three years they went through all kinds of changes. Chuck read in Luke 18:18-25 the story of the rich man who was told to sell everything he had in order to follow Jesus. Jay and Chuck followed suit, sold everything, and went to Hawaii—the place where they "would never grow old." Their studies of Eastern philosophies became more intense.

"It started out Jesus and the Bible," they recollected, "and our minds took over from there. We never really learned how to walk in the Spirit. We tried to reach up to God instead of having him reach down to us."

Chuck recalls his stay in Hawaii. "I went to the out-island of Kauai and lived in tents, or anywhere else I could find. I became a sort of 'holy man.' I sat on a rock for five or six weeks, and gradually I began to feel a sense of doing nothing for anybody."

Chuck returned to the States, and while in Las Vegas he was arrested for possession of LSD. Meanwhile, news had filtered to him about the events and people at Calvary Chapel in California. Chuck finally decided to visit the Chapel. "When I came in that night, it was in the little sanctuary, before they had the big tent. It was a very cozy and warm atmosphere, and the people were all singing praises to God. It was a real feeling of love. I was twenty-six or twenty-seven by this time, and I wasn't too much into the emotional carryings-on, but I could perceive emotions of a true nature. I was mentally *and* emotionally affected. The whole thing just hit me. I really could feel a genuineness in those people. I felt they really *did* know God. All the other people I'd talked to were always talking about a God that they had to attain, instead of the more personal concept of having him right now.

"I'd heard about Lonnie Frisbee," continues Chuck. "He was the hippie preacher there, and I was a little disappointed when Chuck Smith came out to preach that night. Chuck was an older man, but I decided to hear him out. He came out with this big grin and the whole thing was barraging me with images. What is this guy's trip? He doesn't look like the usual guy—the sober thing happening, with a robe and everything! This was more like a mellowed, relaxed atmosphere.

"He just started rapping. It was different. It wasn't like reading a portion from the Bible and then saying a bunch of words. It was like he was sharing someone he knew—Jesus Christ. He wasn't telling me about a God I'd someday find; he was telling me about his personal Friend. He laid all the gospel down."

Girard's walls crumbled. He didn't make a decision for Jesus that night, but it wasn't long before he yielded; likewise, Jay Truax, Tom Coomes, and Fred Field. The enthusiasm of these four newborn Christians was hardly containable. As Chuck recalls, almost immediately they composed several songs expressing their faith.

"We didn't have all the right doctrine, but Pastor Chuck and Lonnie liked the songs, and pending a few changes in the lyrics, they invited Love Song to perform at the Chapel. All the gunk went away, and we revamped the lyrics to make them minister."

Love Song's increase in popularity was meteoric from then on. More and more requests for their concerts came into the offices at Calvary Chapel. Their songs, "Little Country Church," "Two Hands," "Front Seat, Back Seat," "Maranatha," and others were played and replayed. They drew more and more teenagers to a personal relationship with the Christ who had seemed so unattainable to even Chuck, Jay, Tom, and Fred such a short time before.

With the help of fellow-Christian Freddy Piro, Love Song again put their music on record. This time it was a more polished group than had been on Maranatha's first album.

Love Song, the title of their first complete album, was the premiere release on the Good News label. The 1972 record smashed through all kinds of barriers which had been set up around contemporary Christian music. Love Song's soft-rock album began going places where no Jesus-music albums had ever been. In Wichita, Kansas, the album became one of the city's top sellers in the rock record stores. In the Philippines, the title cut, "Love Song," became the number one single for the nation—and most of the Filipinos didn't even know Love Song was a religious music group!

In 1973 a seemingly impossible feat was accomplished by Love Song. Four long-haired musicians whose roots were deeply imbedded in rock and roll had produced an album of Jesus music and had seen their recording become the top religious album of the year.

Love Song went on to record a second album, *Final Touch,* in 1974. The title was appropriate, for the group went on one last national tour and disbanded. The individual members went their own ways, although a few times several of them wound up partners in other music groups.

In addition to Love Song, numerous other young musicians developed at Calvary Chapel in the early seventies: Debby Kerner, Ernie Rettino, Children of the Day, The Way, Country Faith, Karen Lafferty, Good News, Mustard Seed Faith, Blessed Hope, Gentle Faith, Selah, Kenn Gulliksen, and more. The list seemed endless.

In addition to the worship services at Calvary, there were Saturday night concerts held for the young people. The first such concert took place at Milliken High School in Long Beach. Tom Stipe, who ministered at the concerts, recalls those Saturday nights:

"We started holding the concerts," he remembers, "when Calvary Chapel had grown to the size that it needed a new building. Actually, the first few were on Friday, then we moved them to Saturday. A couple of thousand people could be seated in the tent, so we wanted to have the concerts as often as possible. At that time there was the phenomenon of creativity beginning to take place that was bringing about all of the new California music groups. The Saturday night concert platform in the tent was really a greenhouse for the growth of those groups."

Rock, folk, and country Jesus music made up only a part of the songs emanating from Calvary Chapel and other such churches and fellowships nationwide. There were the praise songs and Scripture songs, too—simple choruses which either stood by themselves or were drawn from some of the Jesus songs: Karen Lafferty's "Seek Ye First"; "Heavenly Father" and "Thy Loving Kindness," from Lutheran Youth Alive; "Holy, Holy, Holy," by Tom Coomes, which he recalls writing after his "first time through the Book of Revelation."

Meanwhile, out of the Love Inn community in Freeville, New York, drifted the choruses written by Ted Sandquist—"Lion of Judah," "My Son and My Shield," and "All That I Can Do." Pat Terry, along with two Smyrna, Georgia, neighbors, formed the Pat Terry Group, and wrote "I Can't Wait," a chorus sung around many a campfire before nearly anyone knew who had written it:

> I can't wait to see Heaven
> And to walk those streets of gold
> I can't wait to check into my mansion
> And get my sleeping bag unrolled.
>
> Tell me how it's gonna be
> Read it from the Bible again
> I can't wait to see Jesus
> 'Cause Jesus is coming again.[6]

Songs also came from Candle, affiliated with the Agape Force in California. They joined the new simple Scripture choruses going around from town to town as Christians traveled. In a very real sense, the praise choruses and the Scripture choruses were the folk music of the young American Christians.

Tom Coomes, who later became part of Love Song, remembers the impression the Scripture and praise music made upon him the night of his very first visit to Calvary Chapel. "I knew each line even before it was sung. I wasn't used to simple music like this, but it blew me away! It was music which drew people into the Lord's presence! I loved it."

Here was a rock musician, on the eve of being sentenced for a drug charge, a young man who had been to church very few times in his entire life. Yet here he was, soaking up and enjoying the songs of a most simplistic nature, almost childlike. What was the magic? Both the praise songs (taken from the Jesus music of the day) and the Scripture choruses (simple, easy-to-learn lyrics, often lifted directly from the Bible) were no more than 1970s cousins of the "Singspiration" choruses of the fifties and sixties.

For the most part people such as Tom, who had never been exposed to Christian fellowship, found the aura of love in the midst of congregational praise an exhilarating, if not awesome, experience. Their lives in the dog-eat-dog world outside had told them that true *love* was practically unobtainable, and yet they saw and felt love in the songs being sung. All the "press" given to Christianity was contrary to what happened in a service like that! Where was the hellfire and brimstone? Where were the money-grabbing preachers who cared about nothing but taking up the offering? These people were downright enjoying themselves! And look at their hair! It was long! And look at all those bluejeans! This must be heaven!

Facetious though it may sound to someone who has been raised in a true Christian home, this was the revelation of the many young people who found worship in Scripture songs so beautiful, even though in the outside world their sense of dignity and professional rock-music pride would abhor such simple, "emotional" music.

But perhaps the most redeeming feature of the praise music and Scripture music was its ability to draw the two sides of the generation gap together. The adults might not like Jesus rock, but they could tolerate and even enjoy the Scripture choruses. The young people had little trouble with the age-old, "antique" Scriptures when they were put to pleasant music which was easy to learn. Because of those reasons and more, praise/Scripture music—even though not unique—was very important in the history of Jesus music. It provided common ground on which the old people and the young people could stand together as they raised their hands and voices to praise the Lord with "vertical" music. All attention was on the Lord. As one of the popular praise songs said, they were "one in the Spirit" and "one in the Lord."

6/ *Turn Your Radio On*

The Guinness Book of World Records cites the fact that there are more radio broadcasting stations in the United States than in any other country of the world. By 1977 there were more than eight thousand,[1] broadcasting an astounding variety of general and private interest programming. A study of American radio reveals programs in languages from Czechoslovak to Navajo, and music from Krishna chants to disco rock.

Even as late as 1974, of the more than eight thousand stations in the United States, only four hundred to five hundred devoted eighteen hours or more a week to religious programming.[2] However, of *that* limited number of religious stations, not one single station devoted its entire broadcast day to young people and their music.

Many young Christians had grown up with transistor earplugs as standard equipment and rock and roll as their language. They were without one single radio station in the United States which communicated exclusively to them. If they wanted programs relative to their Christian faith, they had to tune in to stations programming music and shows geared either to senior citizens or grade-school children. It was either "churchy music" or kindergarten stories. Very few programs related to teenagers. If those same Christian youth wanted lively music to which they could relate, the Top 40 stations were the only answer. Christian programming did not provide their kind of music.

Unfortunately there was no happy middle ground for those young people. They wanted to listen to their favorite kind of music, but they wanted to sustain their walk with the Lord, too. The adults—the ones who operated, advertised on, and financially supported the Christian stations—said "no way" to the forms of music they misunderstood and literally despised in many cases. What those often well-meaning adults didn't realize was that by so dogmatically renouncing rock with "no ifs, ands, or buts," they were giving young people a blatant black or white alternative: rock or religion.

The rock choice was a much easier one to make for many youths. They loved rock, their friends loved rock, and rock was on the radio in the car, at home, even at school. "Why sit through stale 'shut-in shows' and 'old-fogey' music?" was their opinion.

Meanwhile, non-Christian youth were searching for meaning in their life which they didn't find in church music. The broadcasters, just as much as most church leaders, failed to hear the warnings:

> The church is often represented in our day as hating youth and its smell, sights and sound. The world of today's culture is exploding with smells, tastes, colors and action which call men to be alive. The church comes from another age and yet is now. This must be so. The message of the Christian faith cannot depend for its essence on the cultural needs of the time. However, the relationship between the faith of the past and the life of the present cannot remain broken if there is to be a living faith.[3]

For many Christian youth, they saw and tasted a music form which was bland and old-fashioned. So they turned back to rock, and often its evil elements—the suggestive lyrics and psychedelic, drug-steeped content.

The youth were wrong to abandon God because His message wasn't couched in their form of media. But there had to be concerned ministers who would step past their own prejudices and realize the immense mission field which existed in the world of rock and roll.

Scott Ross was such a minister, though not in the traditional sense of the word. Ross had an extreme burden to see young people touched with God's love and power. In the late 1960s the young disc jockey, who worked at one of the rock stations in New York City, became a Christian. His faith and his desire to share it with a lost generation took him in 1967 to the Christian Broadcasting Network in Portsmouth, Virginia, where he attempted to mix contemporary Christian music with the more traditional records being aired.

Pat Robertson, the head of the Christian Broadcasting Network, recalls meeting Scott at a 1968 Full Gospel Business Men's meeting in Baltimore:

At the close of the meeting this longhaired, moustached young man came up to speak to me. Despite the fact that he was dressed in a wild psychedelic shirt with tight pants and boots, I liked the sparkle in his eyes and the contagious smile he flashed through his moustache. He introduced himself as Scott Ross and said he was a radio announcer who had accepted Jesus Christ and been baptized in the Holy Spirit just a short time before.

I liked him immediately and later in the summer contacted him asking him if he would like to go to work for us directing programs toward teenagers.[4]

Scott's flashiness and radical ideas caused a considerable stir at CBN. His plans for WXRI-FM, the CBN radio station in Portsmouth, included a gospel-rock show. Said Ross:

These dudes on the beach aren't going to listen to the Haven of Rest Quartette when they're groovin' on the Jefferson Airplane and the Beatles. You've gotta start where they are and bring them up to where we are.[5]

It was an uphill struggle all the way. Scott's methods were not well-received. He managed to start his own show, but it just didn't work.

"I went on with a radio program I hoped would reach my contemporaries," Scott later explained. "I tried to play rock music, but the most I could get away with were folk records. I played Peter, Paul & Mary and 'Jesus Met the Woman at the Well,' and all of their songs of that type. Then people would call up and call them 'commies,' and they'd say to get them off the air. It was really, really difficult.

"In August of 1968," Scott continued, "CBN was given five radio stations in upstate New York. I felt the burden for them. Pat Robertson and I had prayed about it, and we felt that I was supposed to go up there and help format those stations. The whole idea was to have a format of deejays on the air playing contemporary music, mixed in with as much good Jesus music as we could find. At that time, that was maybe five albums! We also felt we should speak to the issues out of scriptural perspectives, without coming off as back-to-back preachers.

"Pat thought it was a good concept. He had given me the ball, and I had run with it. They probably were the first radio stations of their type anywhere in the world. We started moving toward it in the fall of 1968, and went on the air in January of 1969."

Before the year was out, troubles began. According to Scott, "Then the Christians started making so much of a hassle that the stations began to back off, because they were afraid of offending the constituency too much and there would be no one to support the station."

Scott recalls that the adults were doing most of the complaining. "The young people were with us! After about four months on the air there, I went to speak at a particular breakfast. I expected to speak to a couple of hundred people and a few thousand people showed up! We did a concert in Syracuse around the same time, and seven thousand people showed up. We were stirring things up. It wasn't just the music. It was the Holy Spirit. The Lord was doing it. People were coming to the Lord in droves. I went on the air with my show early in the evening and sometimes we went on till four or five o'clock in the morning, as an open-ended show. People came to the Lord, phones rang and rang, and we took calls on the air. It was exciting!"

But the hassles continued. Scott and Pat Robertson got together to discuss the situation. Pat, while in South America, had experienced a vision from the Lord concerning a program which Scott could do as a syndicated show. Simultaneously Scott had also been thinking and praying along the same lines. "Pat really believed in what the Lord had called me to do," Scott remembers. "He literally laid his ministry on the line to give me the opportunity to pursue what the Lord was telling me to do when no one else would allow it."

With Pat's help, "The Scott Ross Show" became the fulfillment of their dream. By early 1970 the show was on sixteen radio stations. The list grew at a rapid pace. Young people were getting their first taste of Jesus-music radio, with a show featuring a combination of top secular hits and Jesus rock.

One of his most notable programs in the early days was one in which Scott did a report on *Jesus Christ Superstar.* "There was a show," he recalls, referring to the rock opera and Broadway play, "that was unique in itself. It was bringing the Lord right into the midst of the whole music scene. Many people obviously had theological problems with it, but we approached it from the direction that His name is above every other name under heaven and earth: Jesus Christ. Period. You put it on the marquee, and they've got to deal with it, because that's His name.

"We straightened people out as far as the theology of it was concerned, and we had Tim Rice and Andrew Lloyd Webber on the air. It was a powerful segment for 'The Scott Ross Show,' and we made it available to the stations as a religious program."

Meanwhile, Larry Black, who had worked the afternoon shift on the CBN New York network, went on the road selling "The Scott Ross Show," which within several years would be broadcast on 175 stations nationwide—the most extensive syndicated contemporary Christian show in America.

The year 1970 was the premiere year of another nationally syndicated Jesus music show, the year I began broadcasting "A Joyful Noise." The dream of broadcasting a show of Christian pop music had been born while I worked with chapel youth groups in the service overseas. I had found a few songs which alluded to God, such as "Hymn" and "Tramp on the Street" on Peter, Paul & Mary's *Late Again* album, and was excited about the possibility that there might be more songs of that type.

As soon as I returned home from the service, I began visiting record sections of department stores, scavenging for any Christian folk or rock music I could find. In April I contacted a friend who worked for a rock-and-roll station in the Tampa area, where I lived. I asked him if he would assist me in producing a sample show in which I would feature the best pop songs about God I could find.

We both found it an exciting prospect. The first step was getting the records to play. At the radio station where my friend worked, there were two giant cardboard boxes full of "trash" records—the hundreds of 45 singles which WFSO chose not to broadcast. They were generally saved to give away as contest prizes. For me, they were much more important than any contest prize I could ever win. I hoped there would be a few God-oriented records among the box-loads, because they were just what I needed.

The search went on for hours. Each title of each song was scrutinized for any reference, direct or indirect, to God. Surprisingly, they began showing up. "Good Morning, God," "Streets of Gold"—they weren't "biggies" like the smash hits they were playing in the radio studio one door down, but who cared? They were building a repertoire for my first show! "Down on My Knees," "God Grows His Own"—likely and unlikely titles from a stack of rock records.

Then I picked up two Capitol singles which were in a stack together. The first was by Pat Boone, entitled "Now I'm Saved," and the second was one by a singer named Larry Norman, entitled

"Sweet Sweet Song of Salvation." Pretty bold Christian titles for pop records on a label such as Capitol!

I ran into the production room and reviewed each likely candidate I found. By the time I got to Larry Norman, I knew I had latched onto something. Never before had I heard such a raspy, rock-and-roll, and totally unchurchy voice singing such an obviously Christian song. As heretical as my reasoning would seem to some people, I knew I had found just the right ingredients of a shocking new form of Christian radio!

I was anxious to record my first show with these records no one had wanted. I put them with the hit Jesus songs I already had— "Jesus Is a Soul Man," " Jesus Is Just Alright," "Oh Happy Day," and a few others—and recorded the first show.

In the true spirit of a rock-and-roll disc jockey I wanted to shock everyone. Not in a negative way, but in a way which would open everyone's eyes to the reality that there *could* be dynamic rock music about the Maker. I had searched the Scriptures for references which might be appropriate for beginning the show. In that study I found more than thirty references in the Bible which entreat us to "make a joyful noise unto the Lord." With rock music we had the *noise;* what was missing was the *joy!*

Psalm 95:1 was my choice for the opening: "Make a joyful noise unto the rock of our salvation." I read the verse in a straight tone, fully expecting half the rock-and-roller listeners to cry "Yuk!" and reach for the radio knob. But what came next was the shocker. With a wailing guitar and crashing drum came a rock version of "The Lord's Prayer" (one of those giveaway singles), and "A Joyful Noise" had already lived up to its title.

Through the help of Herb Hunt at rock radio station WLCY in St. Petersburg, "A Joyful Noise" hit the air on a Sunday morning only a few weeks later. The first all-Jesus-rock radio show, featuring nothing but songs about the Lord and his teachings, was a reality.

Other rock stations got word of the show. Residents of Wichita, Oklahoma City, Denver, Nashville, Richmond, and Indianapolis were soon hearing Jesus-rock music on their favorite rock stations each Sunday morning. There were so few records at the start, each week I would play many of the same ones, rotating them into a different order to make the show sound fresh. For a while "A Joyful Noise" featured the top 10 Jesus-music records each week, only because there *were* only ten Jesus-music records.

Any discussion of pioneer Jesus-music radio should include the early broadcasting ventures of people such as Scott Campbell. Scott began a show of contemporary Christian music in 1968 on KARI in Blaine, Washington. KARI was a Christian station, and Scott recalls, "I played everything I could get my hands on that was good, contemporary Christian music."

In other areas around the U.S., other innovative Christian deejays and programmers such as Scott began playing as much contemporary music as the station managers would allow. Some of them often sat through long lectures in the manager's offices for their enthusiastic updating of the standard musical fare. Others were just plain fired.

A sad irony developed. Religious station programmers, unsure of rock music, avoided nearly all of it, regardless of lyrical content. Rock station programmers, hardly concerned about the harmful effects of rock music, turned out to be some of the first broadcasters of Jesus music, via the Jesus rock of popular performers and the authentic Jesus music on syndicated shows such as "A Joyful Noise" and "The Scott Ross Show."

As was traditional, the church fell one step behind by not opening itself more to the question of whether rock could be an efficient medium of the gospel. It would be 1975 before the first all-Jesus-music radio station would hit the air.

7/ Day by Day

The movie theater we sat in was only half-filled. The film we were about to see wasn't a box office smash as the off-Broadway play had been. But my two friends and I were excited at the prospect of viewing any "religious" film which truthfully put Bible stories on the screen.

The city streets of Manhattan, bustling with shoppers and crowds, was the unlikely setting for the film. Soon a ram's horn was heard and the strains of "Prepare Ye the Way of the Lord" emerged from the crowded streets. The fantasy began. A few New York City residents from various vocations, who were to be the main characters of the film, threw away their earthly woes and possessions and joined the singer. The din of street noise faded away as the characters danced and sang their way into the land of *Godspell*.

Then, a young white man with an afro-type hairdo appeared. He wore overalls and a Superman T-shirt. His face was painted as a clown's. He was Jesus, being baptized by John in a New York fountain.

I was totally caught up in *Godspell*. Because of the allegorical style I was taken offguard, but I was excited regardless. My two friends, however, weren't quite so pleased. After only a few moments, they left the theater.

When I saw my friends the next day, I inquired about their leaving after only about ten minutes. They explained that both of them had been offended by the sacrilegious tone of the film; it made fun of Christ by putting him in a clown suit. They didn't want to see what happened next. As far as I was concerned, I was entertained and at times edified by *Godspell*. I would see the film nearly a dozen times in the next five years, something of a record for me. Each time I was refreshed. The differing views that day in the theater were indicative of the opinions being voiced everywhere.

Godspell had been conceived and directed by John Michael Tebelak; the music had been written by Stephen Schwartz. Based on the Gospel according to St. Matthew, the play was a musical review done in what one magazine described as a mixture of "slapstick, vaudeville, satire, circus and expository preaching."[1]

The difference in *Godspell's* stage presentation and that of *Jesus Christ Superstar* was extensive. *Superstar* had portrayed Christ in a flashy, superstar role; *Godspell* showed him as a gentle clown. *Life* magazine's theater critic Tom Prideaux stated that "compared to *Jesus Christ Superstar, Godspell* is a carefree beggar beside a rich Pharisee."[2] A more humorous comparison was that offered by *The Christian Century:* "*Godspell's* ho-ho Jesus and *Superstar's* woe-woe Jesus."[3]

Superstar had never allowed the resurrection of Christ, and *Godspell* left the resurrection "just offstage." The hornets' nest stirred up by *Superstar* among the more conservative Christian population was still buzzing when *Godspell* appeared on the scene. Tebelak's portrayal of Christ as a harlequin was just as offensive to the conservatives as the deluded Jesus in *Superstar.*

What the critics censured was what the supporters applauded— a characterization of Christ as a humble and gentle leader, teaching His followers to be as little children and always to look to Him for answers. He directed them with love and wisdom so simple it was profound. The play brought to life Matthew 18:4, in which Jesus said, "Except ye be converted, and become as little children, ye shall not enter into the kingdom of heaven." The clown figure of Jesus allowed the plain message of the Gospel of St. Matthew to come through loud and clear, not just in words, but also in acted-out parables.

Director Tebelak, who had conceived *Godspell* while working on his Master's thesis at Carnegie Tech's School of Drama, stated, "The church has become so down and pessimistic. It has to reclaim its joy and hope. I see *Godspell* as a celebration of life."[4]

And a celebration it was. Stephen Schwartz composed the music and wrote new lyrics for *Godspell.* Several of the songs were Anglican hymns and anthems of yore, with new musical foundations constructed by Schwartz. According to one report, "when asked how he could give such fresh tunes to old hymns, Schwartz said it was no problem at all since he had never heard the old tunes."[5]

Schwartz's songs in the play ranged the entire gamut from rock to barroom music, each song taking on the character of the scene in which it was used. The song which rose out of *Godspell* as the greatest commercial hit was "Day by Day," one of the revitalized hymns Schwartz used. "Day by Day" reached the #13 position in national pop music charts in May 1972.

In 1973, the movie version of *Godspell* came along, following record-breaking runs for the play in places such as the Ford Theater in Washington, D.C. The movie was greeted with the same span of opinions as the play had been.

Certain Christian publications, such as *Christianity Today,* gave the *Godspell* film positive reviews. However, some other critics flayed the film for presenting a too-shallow view of Jesus and an overall too-shallow play (even though the script was lifted almost directly from a two thousand-year-old literary masterpiece). One disappointed writer went so far as to describe *Godspell* as "the Gospel according to St. Cutesy-poo."[6]

Though such critics tore down the play and the film, and though many people were greatly offended by the unholiness of *Godspell,* lives were affected. To some people the actors may have portrayed "cutesy-poo" characters, but to many the play was much more significant.

Scott Ross, whose wife, Nedra, sang for several years as part of a pop group, the Ronettes, saw *Godspell* do some heavy work. "A well-known secular record producer called Nedra and me one day," he recalls, "and asked us to come to New York City and see *Godspell,* because he wanted Nedra to record a couple of songs from *Godspell* for a secular label. I'd already seen the show, but we took up the invitation and went to New York to see it with him.

"We got to the end of the show where the Lord is crucified on the chain link fence. All of a sudden, this producer, who knows nothing about the Lord to my knowledge, grabbed my hand. I turned and looked, and he had grabbed Nedra's hand on the other side. He had sunglasses on, but I saw the tears streaming down his face. I'm not overdramatizing the instance—the tears were literally streaming down his face. I could not believe it, because I knew something about this guy's life. He trembled. He shook from head to foot.

"I looked around in the audience, and I'd say half of them were Jews, people in show business. It was a new show; everybody in town was trying to see it. People all over the auditorium were crying. This friend we were with couldn't take it any longer. He jumped up and ran out the door.

"After the end, when the cast had come down the aisle saying,

'God is not dead,' we went outside and our friend was standing on the sidewalk. He said, 'We've got to go eat something.' He was still trembling. He said, 'Tell me about Jesus.'

"We sat for five hours in his apartment telling him about the Lord. He didn't ever make a commitment, nor did Nedra ever record that album, but I know that that day something happened in his life. A seed was planted in a major way."

Though *Godspell's* producer Tebelak said he did not consider his play a part of the Jesus movement, it was. There was no way of avoiding it. The same young people who had expressed their joy in Christ in and out of churches gladly embraced a chance to experience that joy in the theaters of the nation too. To them, *Godspell* was an excellent alternative form of entertainment.

8/ Pass It On

June 1972. The Texas sun seemed to be a little hotter than usual. Texans were used to their share of sunshine, but the drought conditions of the recent few months had farmers praying for badly needed rain. It wasn't to a crucial stage yet, but the drought was causing concern.

In 1972, residents of Dallas were still living down the city's reputation of being the place where a President of the United States had been gunned down nine years earlier. Dallas Cowboy fever was somewhat a diversion as the football team became world champions at the Super Bowl in Miami earlier that year.

As early as 1971, hints had been dropped that "something historic" was going to happen in the "Big D," Dallas, in June 1972. Newspapers started to divulge more about what was being planned. Billboards announced the week of June 17-22 as that historic week-to-come, the week when an estimated one hundred thousand young people would converge on Dallas to participate in Explo '72, the World Student Congress on Evangelism.

The man behind the plan for Explo '72 was Bill Bright. In 1951, Bright, then owner of Bright's California Confections, founded Campus Crusade for Christ. Campus Crusade was to the churches of America what the Jesus movement had been to street people. Much more organized than the spontaneous Jesus movement, Crusade people had worked aggressively at winning college-aged and high-school-aged students to Jesus with the help of many churches. Bright's goal was to see by 1980 global saturation of the gospel—to see all nations have the opportunity to hear the Good News. Explo '72, the World Student Congress on Evangelism, was part of that goal.

Using the techniques and publicity methods he knew as a

businessman, Bright orchestrated the gigantic congress, to be attended by representatives of all fifty states and nearly one hundred countries. Mailers announcing Explo went out to all regional Campus Crusade offices nationwide, and the word began spreading.

In early June, teenagers, college-aged youths, and older adults began the pilgrimage to Dallas. Explo '72 bumper stickers decorated cars and luggage from Washington to Maine, and much farther. All the cars headed toward Texas.

Finally the week of Explo came. Dallas had never seen such an onslaught of young people. All airplanes into the airport were filled. Motels were packed with wall-to-wall teenagers. Backyards of private residences were turned into campgrounds as Dallas-area residents extended a welcome to the Explo crowds. A tent city was built at an RV campground near Dallas, and the rows of tents and campers seemed endless.

Although there were teaching sessions going on throughout Dallas each day as part of Explo, the main gathering place for the multitudes was the Cotton Bowl. Each night as many as eighty thousand delegates poured into the giant stadium for preaching and music. The preaching came from Billy Graham and other renowned speakers, and the music came from perhaps the widest array of musicians ever to gather to worship the Lord at one time.

The Cotton Bowl meetings were far from typical. Cheers pierced the warm Texas air: "Gimme a J! Gimme an E! Gimme an S! Gimme a U! Gimme an S! What've you got? Jesus!" The people in the crowd—a lot of them, at least— had Jesus, and much more. They had an enthusiasm which made the older guests rejoice and shudder at the same time. The young might be returning to active life in the church—but did they have to be *so* enthusiastic? Even when a full-fledged thunderstorm dumped tons of water on the Cotton Bowl crowd, the cheers turned to roars of applause for each clap of thunder provided from the heavens. As one student commented, "Almost eighty thousand people here in the Cotton Bowl prayed that it wouldn't rain tonight. There were probably about two hundred thousand farmers praying that it would. We were simply out-voted."[1]

One of the climaxes of Explo '72 was the candlelight service held toward the end of the week, when an estimated eighty thousand people in the Cotton Bowl lit candles in a "Great Commission" service. As each person lit the candle of a person next to him, the entire stadium sparkled with the beautiful light. The people sang "Pass It On," written by Kurt Kaiser as a part of the 1970 musical *Tell It Like It Is.*

Kurt remembers that night well. He was watching the television coverage of Explo from a motel room in Cincinnati. "It was probably one of the most moving experiences of my life. I never would have imagined that one simple song would go so far. But I'm so very glad it was used in that way!"

Explo '72 was a major step by the churches not only to bring back their prodigal youth, but also to refire the enthusiasm of church youth. The established church leaders trusted Campus Crusade more than the less-defined Jesus movement in the streets, which they often viewed as drawing the young people *away* from the church.

But Explo '72 was historic in another way. Noteworthy were the numerous concerts of gospel music presented at the Cotton Bowl each night, at various parks and churches throughout the week, and on the Woodall Rogers Parkway the concluding day.

The day-long concert near downtown Dallas drew one hundred and eighty thousand Christian *and* non-Christian people to hear the most varied program of gospel music in America's history. The program of performers and speakers that sultry June day was overwhelming: Billy Graham, Johnny Cash, Randy Matthews, Larry Norman, Danny Lee and the Children of Truth, Katie Hanley (star of the Broadway production of *Godspell),* country singer Connie Smith, Andrae Crouch and the Disciples, Willa Dorsey, the Armageddon Experience, Reba Rambo, Barry McGuire, Vonda Kay Van Dyke (former Miss America), The Speer Family, and many others, including an appearance by Kris Kristofferson and Rita Coolidge.

Gospel music would never be the same again. The music programs at Explo '72 gave every visiting delegate a chance to pick a favorite style of gospel music and take home word of what had been heard. For several music groups and solo musicians, Explo '72 was their springboard to national prominence.

In fact, just a few months later, several of the musicians who had performed at Explo were in Madison Square Garden for a Labor Day concert. "Jesus Joy: A Solid Rock Gathering at the Garden" featured Love Song, Danny Lee and the Children of Truth, Katie Hanley, Lillian Parker, and the Maranatha Band. Speakers included Tom Skinner, Scott Ross, Fr. Jack Sutton, Moishe Rosen (Jews for Jesus), Bob Mumford, Charlie Rizzo, and Jerry Davis (editor of New York's Jesus paper, *Good News of Jesus).*

"Jesus Joy" concerts provided the same opportunity of worship for northeasterners as had the Maranatha concerts in California and Explo in Texas. In Carnegie Hall, "Jesus Joy" had sponsored a concert a few months prior to Explo featuring Andrae Crouch and

the Disciples and Danny Taylor. The crowd at Carnegie Hall over-
flowed into a Baptist Church across the street. While Danny performed in the Hall, Andrae Crouch and the Disciples performed at
the church. Then, while everything was "cooking," the performers
switched stages and did the whole concert again. What could have
turned into mayhem turned into "Jesus Joy." Both Danny and Andrae recorded the Madison Square Garden concerts for albums.
Danny's was released on Tempo Records and Andrae's on Light.

Andrae Crouch and the Disciples were rapidly becoming the
best known gospel group in America. Andrae had made giant strides
in contemporizing gospel music, and he took much flak for doing so.
Critics lambasted his rock interpretation of the gospel, but soul
gospel music was Andrae's life and the beat didn't bother him at all.
"It's the rhythm of the heart," he'd say.

Andrae began playing piano as a mere child, and was raised in a
church environment which made gospel music second nature to
him. In 1965 he brought together a few friends to form a singing
group known as the Disciples, who stayed with Andrae through
several years of work at Teen Challenge in Los Angeles.

In 1970, however, Andrae Crouch and the Disciples became a
full-time ministry. The group recorded a single, "Christian People,"
which hit the secular charts in some locales after its release on
Liberty records.

The next step was a recording contract with Light records, and
Ralph Carmichael "adopted" them to *Take the Message Everywhere*.
Andrae's music was quickly taken up by young people, especially
songs like "I've Got Confidence," "Through It All," "I Don't Know
Why (Jesus Loved Me)," "Bless His Holy Name," and "My Tribute
(To God Be the Glory)."

Andrae's enthusiasm while performing was infectious; likewise,
the Disciples'. They even accomplished the "impossible" by appearing on the "Johnny Carson 'Tonight' Show" (he introduced him as
Andrew Crouch). By that time the Disciples were made up of Bili
Thedford, Sandra Crouch (Andrae's twin sister), and Perry Morgan.
Backing up Andrae on the show was a group known as Sonlight, who
themselves had recorded an album for Light records. Sonlight included Fletch Wiley, Bill Maxwell, Harlan Rogers, and Hadley
Hockensmith.

By 1972, the songs of Andrae were beginning to be accepted by
older Christians as well as the youth. Andrae Crouch and the Disciples' appearance at Explo '72 just reassured that acceptance. The
hands clapped. The feet stomped. The people sang and praised the
Lord with one of the men most responsible for the growth of Jesus
music.

Because of the growing response of audiences to the music such as that which Andrae Crouch and the Disciples played, Word, Incorporated in Waco, Texas, was watching ever more closely for new contemporary Christian talent. At the time of Explo '72, Word was rapidly approaching prominence as the largest religious record publisher in the world.

Word, Inc. was founded by Baylor University graduate Jarrell McCracken in 1953. In the mid-1960s, Word and Ralph Carmichael's Light Records, a division of Word, had been instrumental in modernizing Christian music. Records by the Spurrlows, the Continentals, the Jimmy Owens Singers, Ralph Carmichael, and Andrae Crouch and the Disciples paved the way in the recording industry for Jesus music.

As Word focused more and more attention on the new Christian music, the Myrrh label was established, with Billy Ray Hearn coordinating the production of albums by Ray Hildebrand, Randy Matthews, Dove, and a few of Thurlow Spurr's contemporary groups, such as Dust and First Gear.

Both Ray Hildebrand and Randy Matthews had done an album on the Word label before the formation of Myrrh. In 1962 and 1963, Ray had been "Paul" of Paul and Paula, whose recording "Hey Hey Paula" had sold close to three million copies. Ray had written the song during the summer between his junior and senior year at Howard Payne College in Brownwood, Texas, where he was an all-star basketball player. When it was time for recording the song, the scheduled singer didn't show up. So Ray did the singing with "Paula," and within a few months, he was on the road all over the world for a straight year and a half.

When he returned to Texas, Ray was soured. "I was tired of chasing around the world after something that I wasn't even sure I wanted," he said. "I had recorded a hit album, but the royalties were slipping off. I couldn't see devoting my life to dirty jokes and night clubs. What for?

"That's when I started reading the Bible again. I had been raised in a Christian family, but I had never really asked the real questions about life or my faith. That's when I realized the Good Lord was trying to teach me something."

So Ray signed with Word Records for two albums. Then he was moved to the new Myrrh label and recorded a third LP. Ray's greatest contribution to Jesus music, however, was his 1967 album, *He's Everything to Me.* The songs from that album were circulated among many churches which had previously not been open to contemporary music.

Randy Matthews was a bit more radical than Ray. He was no

stranger to rock music—his father Monty had helped form Elvis Presley's first backup group, the Jordanaires. But Randy took the rock music one step further. "I reached an age where I had to rebel from my father," Randy related. "I sang acid rock until those guttural, animalistic noises nearly ruined the quality of my voice. The band did very well. But I never wrote anything until I found Christ."

After his senior year in high school, Randy joined a gospel group called the Revelations. Though the Revelations were a gospel quartet, Randy somehow always managed to inject rock into what they were singing. The Revelations toured for two years, while Randy also attended Ozark Bible College. He then moved to Ohio to attend Cincinnati Bible Seminary, where his music took a turn to street ministry. He helped organize "The Jesus House" in Cincinnati, which two hundred and fifty young people attended weekly.

During his Cincinnati days Randy recorded his first album, *Wish We'd All Been Ready,* for Word Records. The album was quite radical for its time, and it had very few contemporary counterparts on the Word labels. In fact, Randy was the first Jesus-rock solo artist at Word. As soon as Myrrh Records had been formed to capacitate the contemporary musicians, Randy was a natural for one of the premier albums.

All I Am Is What You See, Randy's first Myrrh album, was a collection of excellent Jesus-music songs, many of which became his most popular: "Johnny," "Sunny Day," "Country Faith," and "Time To Pray." Randy moved to Nashville and took up residence as one of the east's best-known Jesus-music performers.

The work wasn't glamorous by any means, though. On a live album released in 1975, *Now Do You Understand?,* Randy told his concert audience,

> It was about four years ago now that I started traveling around the country playing my music for God. Back then they called it "gospel rock and roll." There wasn't a lot of places to play "gospel rock and roll." You couldn't play in churches; they were afraid you'd rock and roll them out of the pews. You couldn't play in colleges 'cause they were afraid that you would sell "prayer picks" after the concert. So I was left to play mostly where I could, and that was on the street payin' some dues and learning some lessons.
>
> I learned a lot of important things living on the street like that—and goin' without food. I learned that materialistic things, they just all pass away. They're of no value really at all. I also learned that for those of us that love the

Lord, everything works together for the good, even though you can't see it at the time.

Another lesson that I learned was that dill pickles can be a great comfort to you. You can buy a five-gallon jar of dill pickles really cheap, man. What you do is get it and put it in the trunk of your car, and when you get hungry you open up that five-gallon jar of dill pickles, stick your hand down in the pickle juice, and you take out one, big, green, warm dill pickle. After you've eaten one of those, you don't want to eat for a couple of days anyway.[2]

Dill pickles in jars, sardines, and pork and beans right out of the can cold, with Kool-Aid to wash it down—they might have been unusual fare for most people. But for the Jesus musicians, it was part of "payin' the dues."

9/ Fat City

Touring is what kept most of the Jesus musicians going. The lack of contemporary radio, national record distribution, and church acceptance had ostracized them from the normal church "circuits" enjoyed by the larger, more "established" music groups. While many of these other musicians sat before giant church suppers and home-cooked meals, the Jesus-music troubador often ate what food was left in the trunk of his car. Concerts came few and far between; the work hardly kept the artist alive. Some solved the problem by taking on part-time jobs; others just stuck it out.

Tom Stipe, who worked with the groups out of Calvary Chapel, observed, "If you go physically seven days or so without a good night's sleep and good meals, you will get sick. Our groups would come back from almost every tour with well over half the band sick with colds, and the things that were related to the lack of proper nutrition."

Tom recalls one of the groups going to a certain area for a series of concerts, and it had not been communicated that the sponsor was to provide meals for the group. "The group literally went two days without food," he added, "because they were broke and they felt embarrassed to bring the subject up to the sponsor.

In the words of a Michael and Stormie Omartian song, "Fat City, I could be livin' in. . . . But it wouldn't mean a thing without you."

"Probably the hardest things to take in the early days of touring," Tom explains, "were misunderstandings and the problems of growth. In one group I was in, there was a situation where we'd stay in hotels; the expenses were all included and we'd just take care of ourselves on the road. But there's a whole other world which 90 percent of the Christian groups—and in the early days 99 percent—

would fall into. That was where you would go out on the road in your van, or maybe a trailer. You wouldn't be flying all your stuff in fancy flight cases. You'd be just touring. You'd drive into a town and you'd be at the mercy of your sponsor.

"Sometimes you'd walk into a situation where the people would be absolutely ready for you. But in the early days, we found that it was really hard to communicate to people the physical needs in a touring situation. When I say physical needs, I don't mean physical *luxuries,* because hardly anyone expects luxuries on the road. But sometimes you'd walk into a situation and ask . . . 'How about blankets and a pillow?' They'd say, 'Blankets and a pillow? I thought hippies slept on the floor.' Then they'd say, "I didn't know there were seven of you. I thought there was just a soloist in this group!'

"Now, I've heard of some groups who go in and insist on a feather mattress and a certain kind of pillow," Tom adds. "That's absurd. There are some people who spend their whole time complaining about everything, but that's not the element that I'm talking about. I'm just talking about those early days when people were beginning to relate to the spiritual and physical needs on both sides—the sponsor and the group. Sometimes there was a complete lack of communication.

"Some sponsors had the idea that the communication was done simply by the name of the group. In other words, 'Well hey! These guys, they have a record out, they must be famous. We'll just spread it around a little bit.'

"So you come into a town and no one shows up at the concert. The people go tell the artist, 'I thought you'd fill up this auditorium.'

"You start asking questions. You ask them, 'How many fliers did you make up?'

" 'Well, just a few because we thought you guys were famous. We thought you'd draw in the unbelievers.'

"You start quizzing a person on how much work and prayer have gone into a situation and they really kind of expected that your presence there and your name would somehow do the evangelism for them. They never communicated things like what street the auditorium was on, what time the concert was, what type of concert, and who was playing.

"Then there were the spiritual preparations; communicating to the body of Christ as a whole just what was going to be expected spiritually," Tom continues. "There used to be a lot of gaps upon coming into a town and finding there was no prayer, or there had been disunity in the church. In many cases we'd walk into situations and find that just the planning of our concert had created great divisions in churches."

The early years of touring presented trials for the wives and girlfriends of the musicians, too. In some cases, the wives toured with their husbands. But often it was a matter of enduring at home. Tom's wife, Mary Ellen, recalls those days:

"The times that I remember were as a girlfriend when Tom was on the road. I recall the heartbreak of watching the poverty they went through in those early days—memories of them coming home from the road after being gone for two weeks with no money and then living on macaroni and cheese for a week. The girlfriends kept trying somehow to supplement the guys' incomes by bringing over meals or pinning $5 bills to their door screens or whatever we could do to get them through.

"In those days, Tom would rarely call me on the phone when he was touring because of the expense. So I mostly got letters. I can remember, too, my friendship with the different girls in Love Song, and I recall watching them go through it as they struggled financially. I often wondered then if I really wanted to marry someone who was in the music ministry. But I did. And when it came my turn, it was basically a time of learning how to get through it!

"What do you do when your husband is gone for three weeks and leaves you alone?" Mary Ellen continues. "There were other girls who had my similar problem; so what we would do was stay in the same house and share food bills. That would give us fellowship spiritually, and also someone to talk to. We weren't so lonely and we could share financial resources as well.

"We'd pick out whoever had the biggest house and just all go over there, kids included. The guys didn't normally always call on the same night, so it was really neat to stay with the other girls. One of the other girls' husbands would call and we'd have word of all of them—what they were doing and what was happening on the road. That way we interspersed the phone calling, too, and it wasn't so long between calls. You could find out what your loved one was doing from the other one's husband.

"I remember times when the guys would call us and they'd tell us that they'd had a bad gig and we'd get depressed for them. We'd share the agony and get in a circle and pray. As wives, that was the main thing that we were called to do when the guys were gone. If we were at all in the Spirit, as Christian wives it was our duty to pray. So, when they'd call and there would be a bummer, we'd pray and at times we'd think, 'Is it worth it?'

"The hardest thing for me to take would be when people weren't appreciating the talents my husband had to share, or if they belittled him in some manner. For instance, a lot of people think that the preaching ministry has some kind of supremacy over the ministry in music. Tom used to get criticized especially for his music ministry—since he has both callings—to choose music above preaching. Some people would think that was really a drag. Yet, I believed in him and I believed in his music ministry. So it used to be hard for me when people would come down on him as a musician or not understand his calling. That would be the hardest thing for me to have to handle—the hardest thing to give to the Lord. But in most cases we'd come to the Lord in prayer and he'd take it from us.

"A lot of times, wives, friends of mine, and I would go to gigs and we'd have to sit in the audience and listen to remarks from straight church members coming down on our husbands for their songs or for what they were doing. Those people had a complete misunderstanding of the musicians' calling and, at a lot of places, since we were sitting next to those people, we would be the ones who would have to take up the banner and explain to them what contemporary Christian music was all about.

"It was such a pioneering spirit involved, the whole family had to be behind it. If the wife wasn't behind him in the early days of the Christian music scene, I don't know how a man ever made it. If his wife was nagging at him to get out of the music ministry along with all the other pressures involved with just being accepted, there was no way he could ever get through."

One wife who actually worked on the road with her husband was Karen Johnson. Mike and Karen performed on stage together. Though Karen said later the two of them usually had enough to eat, she remembered most "not having a place to go home to."

For the Johnsons—Mike, Karen, their dog Jessie, and later a baby son—home was a small trailer they pulled behind their car. At nights they parked it in driveways, truck stops, roadside rest areas—"anywhere we could put it," Mike recalled later.

As hard as touring was, doing concerts was often much easier and less risky for artists or groups than investing hundreds or thousands of dollars in an album which may or may not have wound up in their garages in unopened cases.

There were quite a few Jesus musicians and groups who never even got to the stage of having a record album, but were very much a part of spreading the Word through contemporary music. Since no albums were recorded, the only legacy they left was in the changed hearts of those who heard and heeded their musical message of Christ.

One of the most common faults in the music world as fans was the haste in assuming that when no record album was released by an artist, or when there was a lull in between record releases, that meant the artist was either backslidden, a has-been, or in an unfruitful ministry. Though any or all of these might have been true, musicians sometimes felt that their concert ministries were much more important than a record.

Also, there were some musicians who simply sounded much better on stage than on record, were more humorous in person than recorded, and generally ministered more effectively face-to-face with the audience. In some of these cases, a recording and the time involved to make it would have been a diversion from the Lord's intended work in their lives.

Hundreds of small, hometown bands and solo artists with no recordings helped to keep the fire smoldering during 1973 and 1974, the "underground years."

10/ It's Only Right

One Way Inn, Jesus Christ Powerhouse, The Fire Escape, and The Belly of the Whale are just a small sampling of the descriptive names given to Christian coffeehouses in the Jesus-movement years and after. Sometimes the coffeehouses were small and quaint. But usually they were no more than rented-out storefronts. The interior decoration was colorful Jesus posters or even wall murals; the floors were a patchwork of old carpet sample squares in a rainbow of colors. There were usually a coffeemaker and a Coke machine off to one side, and there was a good chance the sponsors of the coffeehouse would set up a small "Jesus People" bookstore, with contemporary Christian books and records, gospel tracts, bumper stickers, T-shirts, and miscellaneous items for sale or for handing out.

Christian coffeehouses were spin-offs of the 1950s beatnik rendezvous in New York and elsewhere. Some served particular purposes, such as the coffeehouse founded by the Christian World Liberation Front in the Haight-Ashbury district of San Francisco in 1967. It provided a place of retreat for students and other youth during tumultuous times on Berkeley's campus.

Further down the California coast in Hollywood, The Salt Company was started around 1968 by Don Williams, college pastor at Hollywood's First Presbyterian Church. The coffeehouse was especially noteworthy because it was supported by an "establishment" church; in those days such an affiliation was rare. The Salt Company was first located on the church premises, but about two years later it was moved to a more ideal location for witnessing—across from Hollywood High School. A music group, also named The Salt Company, was formed to minister at the coffeehouse and elsewhere.

Also in Hollywood, Arthur Blessitt's His Place on Sunset Strip presented an alternative to the scores of topless clubs and bars which surrounded it. "At His Place," Blessitt explains, "we had some Jesus-music performed there, but we didn't promote that. His Place was called a 'gospel night club,' but really all we had was a piano, a stage, and people bringing their instruments and playing. We had free coffee and Kool-Aid, and we were open all night. You couldn't sleep there overnight, but you could get free food, clothes, music, and preaching at midnight.

"We did not feature rock music in His Place, because there were all of these other clubs, bamm, bamm, bamm down the Strip. We had crowds filling our building, lining the streets when there wasn't even any music. They wanted to come in for something that was casual, where some guy over here was just plunking at the piano or somebody over here strumming a guitar."

One of the musicians who performed at His Place was Charles McPheeters. Charles had been through an almost unbelievable life of drugs, the occult, "and the whole general mess," he recalled later. His travels took him from California to Seattle in 1965, where he began to minister in a trio known as the Disciples Three. "Even then," Charles remembered, "our folk style drew opposition from many church people who seemed to like their traditional type music more than what we were doing."

Charles had gradually worked his way southward—through the Berkeley "Filthy Speech Movement," as he called it, into Los Angeles to work with the Southern California Teen Challenge Center, where Andrae Crouch was directing a forty-voice addicts' choir. Charles changed his trio's name to the New Creatures (there was already a music group working with Andrae known as the Disciples), and moved to work with Arthur Blessitt at His Place.

Arthur recalls an extraordinary night at the club which served to show the important role of the Christian coffeehouses and clubs. "The sign on the front of our building said His Place," Arthur explained, "and it looked like an old bar dive. Charles McPheeters and the New Creatures were playing. This guy came walking down the street and heard the music. He was bar hopping and popping pills and he saw His Place. So he walked in loaded and sat down on the floor. The guy looked up and saw Charles. He said, 'Brother!' It turns out that this guy was Charles' brother Jim, who had just come back from Viet Nam.

"Charles didn't even recognize his brother. Charles had been converted, but Jim hadn't.

"Jim had been through the same stuff Charles had been through—the drug scene and all. He had joined the Marines, gone to Viet Nam, and come back. Charles didn't even know about his return to the United States!

"Anyway, Jim came in and sat down. He listened to Charles, but he didn't even know he was a Christian. There he was just playing gospel music! So when he finished Jim came up, and boy, they hugged!

"Later we both talked to Jim and shared with him the love of Jesus. He didn't receive the Lord that night at His Place, but the next morning he went to church with Charles, prayed, and gave his heart to Christ. Jim then started working with us, moved into our halfway house on weekends, and joined my staff."

Ultimately Jim McPheeters, O. J. Peterson, and a couple of other men formed a group called Eternal Rush, who performed at Blessitt's club and traveled with him on his famous cross-country, cross-carrying walks. His Place stayed open until 1972. "Then," explains Arthur, "we became a tourist attraction. The Jesus movement thing exploded and whammo! We were just inundated with tourists."

Charles McPheeters traveled extensively after leaving His Place. He went to New York with his wife Judy and for a while lived with the people at what would later be called Love Inn. During the summer of 1969, Charles worked a stint as midday deejay on the CBN network of stations.

By 1972 Charles migrated west again, but only as far as Denver, Colorado. There he became a youth pastor at Redeemer Temple and ultimately formed a youth ministry known as The Holy Ghost Repair Service, Inc. Working with Redeemer Temple as a missionary outreach of the church, this ministry rented a couple of storefronts and opened a coffeehouse/counseling center on East Colfax Avenue. Part of the Holy Ghost Repair Service's ministry was an underground newspaper, *The End Times*.

Coffeehouses served Christian and non-Christian youth alike. While they were missions to the wandering street people, they were also gathering places for Christian young people who found them a pleasant alternative to other forms of entertainment and fellowship. If the leaders of coffeehouses handled the operation of such houses properly, the Christian youths, after visiting several times, would be thrust into a responsibility of witnessing to the down-and-out youths, the runaways, and the drug addicts who sought solace in the coffeehouses. In many cases, the houses were the only mission work to which the Christian young people were exposed. Thus, they were places of Christian growth as well as rebirth.

Hundreds of coffeehouses appeared and disappeared, the casualties often due to lack of financial or community support, lack of proper leadership, or a lack of vision. There are still some coffeehouses existent, frequently out of the mainstream of church activity, and often receiving very little attention from anyone outside the ministries themselves. Because the mission work to drug-hooked teens and runaways is not a glamorous job, the work goes on virtually underground.

Numerous of these Christian coffeehouses around the nation provided places for the young Jesus musicians to perform. Not only were they extremely important conduits for the new tunes of the day, these houses also provided excellent training grounds for the musicians: The Avalon in Akron, Ohio, The Greater Life Coffeehouse in Dallas, The Salt Company in Detroit, and hundreds of others.

Notable as a starting ground for several musicians was The Adam's Apple in Fort Wayne, Indiana. The coffeehouse, sponsored by Calvary Temple, actually began in a tent, and director John Lloyd recalls that his first concerts featured non-Christian rock bands in order to draw a large number of young people. But some of them didn't stay non-Christian for long. John's preaching and ministry reached the musicians, too, and several of them accepted Christ through the very ministry they had played for.

The "coffeehouse" eventually moved inside a building, and the crowds filled it weekly. Soon The Adam's Apple was known throughout the Midwest for its concerts. A few of the best-known Jesus-music artists of the decade began their ministries at The Adam's Apple. Among them were Petra and Nancy Henigbaum.

Nancy had sung in non-Christian coffeehouses several years before she came to Fort Wayne. "My first coffeehouse job," she recalls, "seemed like the pinnacle of success at the time. I started hanging around with older people and doing things I thought 'mature' people did: smoking, drinking, and doing dope. I thought I really knew what life was all about. But I must have made an amusing picture—a teenage girl with braces on her teeth, singing 'I'm a mean, mean woman.' I was actually quite naive and fragile."

Nancy described her lifestyle as "rejector of conventional society—in other words, freak." Her friends began to call her "Honeytree" when they found out it was the literal translation of her German name. She and her friends experimented with astrology, tarot cards, mind-expanding drugs, Eastern religions, utopian fantasies, current movements, and "everything unusual."

It was this curiosity concerning the sciences and religion that drew her to investigate Calvary Temple in Fort Wayne while she was there visiting her sister. While at the church, she met John Lloyd, whom she heard had at one time been into drugs himself. The next day Honeytree visited with John, which resulted in her acceptance of Jesus as Savior.

As a young Christian, Honeytree tried to "live the life," but finally succumbed to drugs again. "Then it seemed like the Lord picked me up by the scruff of the neck and landed me in Fort Wayne again," she remembers. "By this time John and the other Christians had started a coffeehouse called The Adam's Apple. I found myself working in the midst of those friendly Christian freaks, happier than I had ever been before. That was when I realized that Jesus had not left me at all. He was just teaching me a lesson. I learned that joy comes from working for Jesus and being around other people who are working for Jesus too. After I learned that, I never got stoned again.

"John started dragging me everywhere to sing and give my testimony. Eventually, I ended up being John's secretary, working full-time for The Adam's Apple, and doing musical programs on weekends. God had always impressed on me that if it weren't for The Adam's Apple and the church that got the whole thing started, I would still be a confused Jesus freak, getting high to feel spiritually alive, instead of doing something fruitful with my life."

Honeytree began her recording career with *Honeytree,* recorded on a custom label, later picked up by Myrrh Records in 1973. Her excellent songwriting talents brought forth such as "Clean Before My Lord," "I Don't Have to Worry," and "Heaven's Gonna Be a Blast."

As she sang in a song she composed, "It's only right I should be singing because the Holy Spirit's bringing a little more joy, a little more love into my heart each day."

Calvary Temple in Fort Wayne and The Adam's Apple are good examples of the interaction that was possible between church and street ministries, and between churches and the Jesus musicians. Of course, Calvary Chapel in Costa Mesa was another. Out of the Peninsula Bible Church in Palo Alto, California, came support for the ministries of John Fischer and Pam Mark (Hall). Both John and Pam were "products" of the Discovery Art Guild, encouraged by Peninsula Bible Church.

In Nashville, the Belmont Church of Christ sponsored the Koinonia Coffeehouse. Across the street from the church, the coffeehouse provided a platform for top Jesus-music groups and artists such as Dogwood. Belmont proved to be the worship place for many musicians, including singer/writer Gary S. Paxton, who admits he "sat outside the church, across the street, watching for several weeks to see what the people were like" before he went in. Going to church was a brand new experience for Paxton. He had several million-selling records to his credit, but a destroyed life was all he had had to show for it.

In Van Nuys, California, a part of the Greater Los Angeles area, the Foursquare "Church on the Way" was yet another center of worship and spawning ground of young Christian talent. Pat Boone and his family, Jimmy Owens and his family (including daughter Jamie), and the Wards—Matthew and Nellie, with their sister Annie and her husband Buck Herring—all worshiped at the Church on the Way at various times throughout the years of the Jesus movement.

Out of those three families alone came several albums of contemporary Christian music, including several musicals. The Boone family recorded for Word, then Lamb & Lion Records. Jimmy and Carol Owens wrote and recorded their musicals for Light Records; their daughter Jamie recorded her first album on Light in 1973, entitled *Laughter in Your Soul*. The 2nd Chapter of Acts (Annie, Nellie and Matthew) did backup vocals for many of these recordings before doing their first album, *With Footnotes*, in 1974.

Included on the 2nd Chapter's album was a short two-minute, twenty-second song entitled "Easter Song." Written by Annie, the song almost immediately caught on as the "Hallelujah Chorus" of the Jesus movement generation.

> Hear the bells ringing,
> they're singing that we can
> be born again.

Within weeks the song was learned by thousands of people, and by the time the 2nd Chapter of Acts passed through a town on tour, nearly half the audience sang along.

> Joy to the world!
> He is risen!
> Hallelujah![1]

The jubilation of "Easter Song" pierced through the hardest hearts, and people rose to their feet whenever it was performed on stage.

The 2nd Chapter of Acts, in addition to recording their own album, began touring and singing in concerts across the country. The charisma they exuded onstage quickly captured the audiences, and joy was usually the trademark of a 2nd Chapter concert. Annie, her husband Buck (who produced the group's albums and worked the sound in their concerts), Nellie, and Matthew became the ambassadors of contemporary Christian music during the "underground years" of 1973 and 1974. Their music not only ministered to thousands of impressionable youth; it also introduced Jesus music to church leaders and congregations who were still reluctant to accept the new music into the church.

The 2nd Chapter's music wasn't usually hard rock. Granted, there were certain songs which Matthew would belt out Stevie Wonder-style, but the majority of the music was the unlikely combination of light rock tunes and hymnlike harmonies. Though Annie wrote contemporary music, the classical feel of the songs permitted adults to enjoy it as much as the youth. The 2nd Chapter was one of the very few Jesus-music groups whose music was unique; it did not have a parallel in pop music.

Then there was Barry McGuire, a former pipe-fitter who probably came as close as anyone except the Beatles and Elvis Presley to changing America with a single song.

In 1960 Barry had borrowed a guitar from a friend and had taught himself some of the more popular folk songs of the day. It wasn't too long before friends invited Barry and his guitar to parties. The next step was singing nights away in bars for $20 and tips, and Barry loved it. But the moonlighting took its toll on the singing pipe-fitter. He finally laid down the tools and joined a few friends in forming the New Christy Minstrels.

For the next four years the New Christy Minstrels were one of the top singing groups in the world. Their performances of hits such as "Green Green" and "Saturday Night" were held at such prestigious places as the White House, Carnegie Hall, Coconut Grove, the Hollywood Bowl. They also sang in Hawaii and Europe. The New Christy Minstrels were the first American recording group to have a commercial release in Russia.

"We did one-nighters for four years," Barry explains. "Friends I called would ask me, 'Where are you?' and I'd answer, 'I don't know, but the area code is 316.' "

Barry was around some of the richest people in the world—senators, heiresses, entertainers—but he noticed over and over that none of them were really happy. They were more bored than anything else.

The happy minstrel became a soured cynic. He became disillusioned and started losing respect for the people around him, including his audiences. He began to peruse books on the sciences—biology, neurology, and psychology—"trying to find out why we think and how we think." Those studies carried him deeper into the mystical sciences, existential thought, and studies of the power of the mind. Barry had always heard that "the truth will set you free," and he continued to search for that truth.

In 1965, after his breakup with the New Christy Minstrels, Barry recorded "Eve of Destruction." In spite of its banishment from numerous top radio stations in the country because of its stinging, controversial lyrics, "Eve of Destruction" became the #1 song in America. It was protest at its loudest, and it became the anthem of a generation of peace movements and antiwar sit-ins.

The fact that the song was banned in so many places caused Barry to comment a few years later, "I thought that 'Eve of Destruction' was the truth. It was just a bunch of newspaper headlines set to music. It *had* to be sung. It was the first song I'd heard that laid it down just as it was.

"When the song was banned, it showed me that people don't want to know the truth. Isn't that incredible? People want to live in that make-believe dream world, or that Hollywood playboy fantasy. Happiness is a new home. Happiness is a Ferrari. Happiness is a black book full of phone numbers of pretty girls.

"And when you get down to the nitty-gritty, nobody wants to hear that the human race is about to blow itself from here to eternity."

Barry the cynic became even more disillusioned when no one would look at the truth. But the ultimate truth came to Barry on the street one day in 1970. He and a friend were walking down a Hollywood boulevard on their way to a movie. "A guy came up to me," he recalls, "and told me that Jesus was coming back.

"I just shined him on, you know. In Hollywood, we called them 'Jesus freaks!' They were everywhere out there. I thought, 'Come on, man. Don't hand me any of that Jesus jazz!'

"But then things started happening. Everywhere I went, I kept being confronted with the name of Jesus Christ. I was at a friend's house one day when I saw a copy of *Good News for Modern Man.* It was a modern translation of the New Testament, but I didn't know that until I had taken it home to read it. I was thirty-five years old, and I had never read a New Testament in my life.

"It blew me away! I discovered the truth I'd been looking for for so many years. It was Jesus!"

At a party with some old friends one night, "the ten-thousandth party that week," Barry gave up the last hold on his life without Christ.

"I just finally yielded. I asked, 'Jesus, are you really there?'

" 'Yes.'

" 'You mean all this time . . .'

" 'Yes.'

" 'You mean all these years . . .'

" 'Yes.'

"Then Christ opened up my memory and showed me all the things that my selfishness had done to other people. All the lives that I'd ruined—people that I'd turned on to drugs."

Within three weeks Barry dissolved his contracts with the secular world. He moved out of Hollywood and was soon fellowshipping and studying with a community of Christians in Sanger, California. Barry signed with Myrrh Records to continue his singing career, but this time singing of Jesus Christ as one who knew His power.

Seeds, Barry's first Jesus-music album, was released in 1973, eight years after his "Eve of Destruction." Barry began touring with the 2nd Chapter of Acts, and after his second LP, *Lighten Up,* he joined the 2nd Chapter for a live album, *To the Bride.* He then moved to Sparrow Records and continued his ministry of Jesus music.

Barry's glowing disposition, his distinctive laugh, and his overall joy became trademarks for a man who was respected throughout the Christian music industry. He told many an audience, "I love being a full moon, reflecting the light of the Son."

11 /   The Rock That Doesn't Roll

Explo '72 was, in a sense, the "coming out" of contemporary Christian music. The fuse had been lit in Dallas. However, there was a long way to go before anything resembling an explosion in Jesus music would take place.

During the next two years or so, Jesus music was written, recorded, and performed, but one would hardly know it by listening to the radio, reading magazines, or attending church services. Like a diamond being formed in an underground bed of coal, Jesus music was being purified and molded into a distinct art form under the pressure of a dubious public.

During late 1972 and on through 1974, numerous Christian composers were writing songs and making every possible move to give contemporary Christian music a sound of its own. The writers wanted their music to have the punch of popular music, but they wanted the lyrics to contain more profound substance than the songs of the world.

There were the "radical" composers and performers such as Randy Matthews, Larry Norman, Randy Stonehill, Mike Johnson, and others who desired to write and perform "street music"—rock music with Christian lyrics, a style which parents had trouble endorsing. There were also the artists such as the Archers and Dallas Holm, whose music at that time was contemporary, but carried enough overtones of the more traditional gospel to be accepted by a more general audience. Those more "conservative" musicians—still considered radical by some churches—made up a vital bridge between street music and church music.

Benson Publishing of Nashville was one of the early builders of that bridge. The Archers and Dallas Holm recorded for the Impact label, owned by Benson. While Benson's other label, HeartWarming, carried the traditional family gospel acts such as the Rambos, Impact introduced the more progressive artists.

For a brief period of time, Impact also featured recordings by "street level" artists. Larry Norman's *Upon This Rock* was picked up from Capitol Records and finally made its way into some Christian bookstores (fifth row back, in the corner, behind the greeting cards, and next to the water fountain). Graham Kendrick and Judy MacKenzie were folk performers from England whose recordings also were picked up and released by Impact Records in America in 1972. Joshua was the name of a Jesus-rock group from the Southwest who recorded one Impact album in 1974 before they disbanded. Impact also featured the music of the Imperials, whose style was basically southern gospel; however, as time went by, the Imperials progressed into a more contemporary mode.

The more conservative musicians performed in numerous churches and crusades around the country as their music found favor with church leaders, but the radical writers and performers had a much tougher go at it. Their desire to create no-holds-barred Jesus rock met with disdain and oftentimes outright animosity from church elders and the older members of their congregations. Even when those leaders were sympathetic to Jesus music, they were still cautious.

In 1979, musician Tom Coomes recalled a 1974 concert in the Blue Church of Philadelphia where caution was the rule. "I was in the group Wing and a Prayer at that time," he recounts. "When we got to the church, we found out that they had never even had drums in that church. Here it was 1974, and we thought the question of drums had long ago been answered. But not at the Blue Church.

"We were asked to meet with the Board of Elders prior to the night's concert. Three of us went in—Tom Stipe, John Mehler, and myself. Tom remembers being nervous, but I would say I was somewhat at peace about it. It wasn't like the elders were mad, or that they hated rock music. But they *did* tell us they were very *concerned* that the music we were going to play didn't appeal to the flesh rather than the spirit. They said, 'We've heard about Jesus-rock music, and we'll be watching closely.'

"Though the warning was given as a sincere expression of their concern, it had a sound of finality to it! We could have all gotten uptight about the situation, but we didn't. The Lord gave us all a peace at that moment. In fact, I really felt it was a real privilege to be playing there. Our next thought was, should we change our repertoire? We were kind of a rock 'n' roll band. We went off and really prayed. What should we do? Should we do just a worship set? Or a set of mellow music? Or what? We prayed and we really felt a peace about doing just what we usually did.

"That night about four hundred or five hundred kids crammed into the room," Coomes recalls. "They'd never had that many young people in their church before, ever. We played just what we normally played, which included some rock 'n' roll. But we played it at 1½ on our amps! John, the drummer, did his drum solo too, but he barely tapped the drums! We could see the elders standing back in the hall. By the second or third number, we could see them smiling!

"About fifty or sixty kids came to know the Lord. As a result, the elders asked us to share with all the adults at the church service that night. Once a month to this day, years afterwards, that church in Philadelphia still has a concert."

The Jesus-music writers and performers knew what they had to do, regardless of the consequences. They had to write the songs that the Lord had given them to write; they had to perform the music that would reach the churched *and* unchurched youth; and they had to upgrade the quality of a fledgling art form.

Bob Hartman was a member of Petra, one of the first all-out Jesus-rock bands to record an album. He described Petra's reasons for existence. "We're extremely rock-oriented, but we're not oppressively heavy. The name 'Petra' has a deeper meaning to us because it's a word that's used in the Bible when Jesus said, 'Upon this rock I will build my church.' That word 'rock' is 'petra' in Greek. It's upon the confession of Jesus Christ being Lord of a person's life that our group is built, because of the experience that we have had with him. He's changed our lives and given us a whole new outlook on life, and that outlook is reflected in our music."

Petra's music was rock, all right, but with its special spiritual dimensions it became, a way of life for young rock-music fans.

"People," Bob continued, "have almost been brainwashed by other rock groups and the message they have to bring. I think it's time the people heard a positive message."

A yet harder rock group was Agape, whose two albums were released in 1971 and 1972 during the crest of the Jesus movement. They played Jesus rock at its crustiest—music which cut through the thickest defenses of the non-Christian rock fans. For those to whom hard-rock music was a language, Agape and Petra spoke—clearly. As a result, many young people, whose main defense against Christianity was its "old fashioned, hokey" music, found themselves pleasantly surprised when a friend shared Jesus-rock music with them.

Agape's and Petra's music was not the most welcomed form of music on Christian radio stations, either. Only a few such stations would even consider playing their songs. One of those few stations was KDTX-FM in Dallas.

KDTX had broadcast all of the Cotton Bowl meetings of Explo '72. Station manager Mike Burk was impressed by the contemporary gospel music he heard played there, and the way the youth responded to it. Mike opened up the 10 P.M. to 2 A.M. air shift for a Jesus-music show. On a fall night in 1972, "A Joyful Noise" became a live, four-hour nightly radio show in Dallas, hosted by one Paul Baker.

The first show was opened with a song by Myrrh recording group First Gear, appropriately entitled "Ain't No Stoppin' Us Now." For the first few nights there were a few calls of complaint about the rock music, but the calls of encouragement and thanks quickly overshadowed them. Dallas had been primed by Explo, and Jesus music filled the air nightly.

"A Joyful Noise" in Dallas became much more than just a music show. Top Christian performers were interviewed, including Andrae Crouch, Noel Paul Stookey, rock artist Chi Coltrane, and many more. Since KDTX had large studios, numerous live concerts were also broadcast as part of "A Joyful Noise." Larry Norman, Paul Clark, Ken Medema, Malcolm & Alwyn, and countless other Jesus-music artists performed. Sometimes the concerts were announced far in advance, and large crowds attended. Other times, spontaneous concerts were arranged when a musician passed through, and a handful of people showed up in time. But all the concerts were heard by thousands of radio listeners in north Texas over KDTX.

Much as "The Scott Ross Show" had done in New York state, "A Joyful Noise" provided nightly fellowship for young people and adults who preferred Christian radio over secular radio. "A Joyful Noise" continued on the air live for one year in Dallas, but KDTX (later KMGC) would broadcast nightly Jesus music for a while longer.

Meanwhile, in Washington, an innovation was being tried. In May of 1973, WCTN introduced a format of secular adult rock and contemporary Christian music combined. However, Christians in the Washington area proved to be extremely conservative. The unique format lasted only a few months before WCTN had to change to a more moderate playlist, as the CBN stations in New York had been forced to do a few years earlier. The Jesus music stayed, but in smaller amounts.

Still, whenever Jesus music was broadcast there were changed lives. Sometimes it only took a few moments of exposure to lead someone to the startling realization that Jesus was the answer, as this writer testified in a letter to "A Joyful Noise":

> Friends:
>
> I was driving from Oklahoma City to Clinton, Oklahoma, one day after being on a hard drug trip for the whole weekend, when I turned on the radio to KOMA. It was 6:30 in the morning, and I was expecting to find my usual heavy rock—but as I listened closer to the words of this different kind of rock and roll, I heard a different kind of message. A message about a person called Jesus. I started to change the station as I have for the last twenty-five years. But instead, this time I listened.
>
> After hearing such a *beautiful* message from people like myself, I startd to realize that Jesus is a more real thing than reality itself.
>
> My life has changed a lot now, as I have thrown away my man-made drugs and taken on God's love instead.
>
> Well, I'm sure you know the rest of the story . . . How can I say thank you but to say that *I love you all very much*. You people are beautiful and the message you carry is so super concrete.
>
> J. W., Medicine Park, Oklahoma

In spite of the testimonies of young people who found Christ through Jesus music, the battle against it went on. Certain evangelists would incite young people to literally burn anything resembling or alluding to rock music. There even were bonfires held for the occasion.

Evangelist Bob Larson was probably the most outspoken critic of rock music in the late 1960s and 1970s. Larson, himself a musician, wrote a book as early as 1967 denouncing rock-and-roll music as "the devil's diversion." His scathing criticisms of rock music rapidly resulted in support from the adult/parent side, while many teenagers scorned Larson.

Rock & Roll: The Devil's Diversion was followed by several more books on the evils of rock and roll: *Rock & The Church* (1971), *Hippies, Hindus and Rock & Roll* (1972), and *The Day the Music Died* (1973). Larson lectured at churches and high schools, playing demonstrations of rock music, speaking against it, and encouraging young people to destroy their rock records by burning them.

Larson's fiery antirock campaign was highly publicized by both the secular and religious press. The secular press was skeptical or critical; the religious press was generally sympathetic. However, Larson was anything but sympathetic toward Christian rock. In his book *Rock & The Church,* Larson laid down this indictment: "I maintain that the use of Christian rock is a blatant compromise so obvious that only those who are spiritually blind by carnality can accept it."[1]

He added:

> The phenomenon of Christian rock has been around only since approximately 1968. There is still some question whether or not decisions in Christian rock concerts lead to genuine rebirth. Usually there is no clear-cut invitation to repentance at such affairs. If the explanation of steps of salvation is blurred, how can the way be found?
>
> Some have speculated that more often than not, conversion to Christ at Christian rock concerts and musicals is not really a born-again experience but an identification with the person of Jesus within the perspective of the "groovy Christian life."[2]

Although many of Larson's arguments against *secular* rock were well-founded, he created great resentment among *Christian* rock musicians with blanketing conclusions such as: "Once the possibility of demon involvement is suggested, there is no way Christian rock can be justified."[3]

Other evangelists joined in denouncing rock, and the gap widened. The main support for the antirock preachers came from adults and parents who disliked rock and roll in the first place, and the antirock-music books and lectures gave them what they believed to be a biblical foundation for the abhorrence of all rock music, including Jesus music.

The Jesus musicians who witnessed and had a part in the conversion of young people through their music were not as ready to criticize the more avant-garde styles of rock gospel. Even though they themselves may not have favored all of its forms, they saw the fruits of such evangelism.

Churck Girard of Love Song, with a background in rock music, commented in 1973, "I believe God may call some hard rock band, and I believe they may do all hard rock 'n' roll, screaming Jesus lyrics. That may be all they do. I believe that where they'll be used is a different place than where we'll be used.

"I think it would be very hard for me," he continued, "if I were fifty-five or sixty-two, to believe right off the bat that this is all right on. Because I think some of it isn't. But I think it's hard for some of the older people to grasp the sincerity of the long-haired Christians at first, especially in light of the counterculture movement out of which grew the tradition of long hair and hard-rock music.

"I've had a lot of old people come up and say, 'Well, if Jesus has changed you on the inside, why doesn't he change you on the outside?' They should realize that God looks on the inner man.

"I think as everything progresses and they see that there are long-haired Christians sticking with it, faithful to the Lord, and being used as ministers, they'll understand it more."

Many Jesus-rock musicians agreed with Larry Norman that Jesus is "good for the body and great for the soul. He's the rock that doesn't roll."

Cornerstone, a paper published by the Jesus People USA, printed this letter to the editors:

> Until this past year, both of us thought being a Christian was pretty bad, no good music, old hymnbooks and a Bible that was written in old English. Not very much to interest people who were into living in the present. It wasn't until after I met Jesus and was born again that we met some other Christians who shared Larry Norman, *Cornerstone* and the Holy Spirit. So Christianity wasn't dead after all! Unsaved people hardly ever hear about this side—the true life of joy of living for Jesus in today's world, not 400 years ago.
>
> D. & C. H.
> Sarasota, Florida[4]

Cornerstone was one of the "underground" Jesus papers which published the Good News in a most unique way. The paper was sponsored by the Jesus People USA in Chicago, who also formed The Resurrection Band. The band, which specialized in hard-rock, Christian-message music, began their ministry in 1971, playing in high schools, prisons, and in the streets.

The Resurrection Band, *Cornerstone,* and JPUSA's drama troupe, The Holy Ghost Players, were the most adventurous when it came to boldness in communicating the gospel. From the mod-art design of their newspaper to the screaming guitars in their band, they dealt in forms of communication which were controversial to say the least.

Contrary to the bad images of Christian rock 'n' rollers given by the antirock evangelists, these same young people were consistently more outspoken and bold in their presentation of the life-saving claims of Jesus than most Christians. The complaints against the raucousness of their music and the admonition that no one could use rock music to witness to the unsaved became mighty weak when the work of JPUSA was studied deeply, with literally thousands of people won to Christ through their ministry.

As the heated controversy continued, undaunted young composers kept at their work, creating what they were convinced the Lord wanted them to create. Because of the lack of support, there was little money in their work, and it was next to impossible to make more than a meager living as a professional contemporary Christian musician. This kept Jesus music a fairly pure art form for several years, practically devoid of the corruption which existed in many other forms of music, including some religious music.

Though Jesus music had been shunned by the majority of church leaders, young people were finding out about it, mostly by word-of-mouth. The exposure of the music on the radio still proved to be next to impossible, and the increasing number of Jesus-music records were still hard to find in stores.

The proprietors of the secular record stores, however, had every right to refuse much of the Jesus music. Since the music was still in its fledgling stage, many of the albums being released were poor in quality. The spirit of the singers was not enough to qualify the albums as professional recordings, especially when the technical and musical quality of those albums was poor.

Also, many times the youth, in their crusade for Jesus music, became overexuberant and presumptuously expected their churches to accept the new kind of music too readily and without question. Unfortunately, there were not many adults who understood contemporary music enough to give them unbiased guidance which would encourage the young people in their musical pursuits, but at the same time calm their youthful overzealousness. In that sense, the young Christians had to make a go of it on their own.

12/ All Day Dinner

During the 1800s and early 1900s American Christian fellowship relied heavily upon the church. Before the relatively recent advent of air-conditioned church sanctuaries, congregations would join together outside in the hopefully breezy air to praise the Lord with all-day singing and "dinner on the ground," as Reba Rambo sang. Church revivals would be held outdoors under the thatched roofs of outdoor worship pavilions. On Church Picnic Weekend, whole families would climb into their buggies, wagons, and automobiles and head out to the lake or assembly grounds for a day of fun and games and rib-sticking food.

By the mid-1960s, though, most Sunday church meetings were back in the sanctuaries, at a year-round 72°. The brush arbors were hardly more than memories. A new form of fellowship grew out of the Jesus movement in the 1970s, however, which got the people back together outdoors to praise the Lord, sing, learn, and generally have a great time. Though the scene was quite different from the camp meetings of the earlier generations, the spirit of fellowship was just as evident in the outdoor "Jesus festivals."

It was natural that the Jesus festivals should grow out of the Jesus movement in the seventies. Not only did the movement itself start on the streets, on the "outside"; it also grew out of a generation enamored by the giant secular Monterey Pop Festival in California and the even more gigantic Woodstock festival of 1969, where reportedly more than five hundred thousand young people attended.

Festivals such as Woodstock were mass outdoor gatherings where young people retreated to their own world—a world virtually void of any reminder of the Establishment, except for the policemen and the chagrined residents of nearby communities. The festivals were meccas for youth who were seeking new solutions in their quest for love, peace, and often total escape from the world.

Monterey and Woodstock led to other secular festivals: the Palm Beach Rock Festival in 1969; the Atlanta International Pop Festival in 1970 (attended by two hundred thousand), the Pocono Rock Festival in 1972, and numerous others.

However, at an Altamont, California, rockfest in 1969 the utopian dream of peace, love, and brotherhood began to decay. A man was murdered by Hell's Angels directly in front of the stage where the Rolling Stones were playing before the giant crowd. The band played on, but the rock festivals were somehow never again the same. Festival promoters had more and more trouble finding places to have them, and ultimately learned to move the concerts each year to avoid confronting the same constables. Gigantic crowds of people continued to attend the rock festivals, but the events often became no more than havens for drug abuse, self-indulgence, or, at best, havens of rock music.

Except for the finale concert of Explo '72 in Dallas, Jesus festivals never reached the gigantic proportions of the rock festivals. But the organizers did experience a greater degree of support from landowners and host communities. The Jesus-festival crowds proved to be cleaner, more polite, more sober, and less rowdy. The members of the Establishment were the lawmakers. Their sympathies tended to favor youth whose beliefs were somewhat within the limits of what even the elders were familiar with—the Christian faith. The new music was different than the earlier generations', but tolerable because of the familiar message.

The first major Jesus festival was the Faith Festival in Evansville, Indiana, in March 1970. More than six thousand people were present in a stadium to hear Pat Boone and his family, Christian folk singer Gene Cotton, and Jesus rock artists Danny Taylor, Larry Norman, Crimson Bridge, and "e." In 1971, the event was repeated and fifteen thousand people attended. The 1971 Faith Festival was covered by CBS television.

Later, in May, the Love Song Festival at Knott's Berry Farm drew twenty thousand people to the Southern California amusement park, marking Knott's largest nighttime attendance in its fifty-three-year history. Several Jesus-music groups out of Calvary Chapel performed that historic night in various parts of the park. They included Love Song, The Way, Blessed Hope, and Children of the Day.

The Knott's Love Song Festival began a California tradition of amusement-park Jesus festivals. Special tickets were sold for use on all the park rides, and Christian folk and rock music wafted through the park from various strategically located performing stages. The success of their first event prompted the proprietors of Knott's Berry Farm to stage the Christian music nights more often. At first they were Love Song Festivals, but then became known as Maranatha Night at Knott's, due to the use of musical groups from Calvary Chapel's Maranatha! Music Ministry. For the next three years, three festival nights were staged annually—one in the spring, one in the fall, and one on New Year's Eve.

Californians were accustomed to the fun and flash of entertainment, and the Maranatha Music Nights provided an excellent form of Christian entertainment. There were no Bible teachings or baptisms at the amusement park festivals, nor was there much congregational worship. The Southern California youth had those forms of fellowship and worship waiting for them back at their home churches, especially Calvary Chapel.

But for young people in other parts of the country, there were often no churches such as Calvary Chapel—churches which opened their doors to barefooted, blue-jeaned teens who needed acceptance. The festivals *became* church for many young people—outdoor sanctuaries with the sky as a canopy. For many people, the Jesus festivals marked the beginning of new lives in Christ.

In August 1973, a central Pennsylvania potato field became one of those sanctuaries. Mennonite Harold Zimmerman organized Jesus '73, the start of an annual tradition. Jesus '73 featured three days of festival, with guest appearances by top-name Christian musicians and speakers.

Young people and some adults of all faiths attended Jesus '73. The breaking down of denominational barriers had already become a trait of the Jesus people. Baptists worshiped with Assembly of God members; Catholics fellowshipped with Mennonites. Musicians from the Church of the Nazarene played before Presbyterians; gospel performers from the Church of God in Christ sang for Methodists. In the midst of them all, there was a large number of non-Christians who heard the gospel and responded to it.

Jesus '73 spanned three days. Through makeshift entrance gates set up in a field passed festival-goers in automobiles, trucks, vans, Winnebagos, on motorcycles, and even on horseback. There were numerous hitchhikers, too. From all over America and from overseas people came to join in the fellowship. Visitors stopped at the entrance gates, registered, and received their "welcome packets" with information on who would be singing when, where to go for first aid, and what *not* to do while visiting the festival. By the time the first music group struck up a chord on the giant stage, a tent city stood where there used to be farmland. Rows and rows of campers, tents, and cars fashioned a pattern of lines which stretched over the next hill. A blue haze filled the air as campfires flickered throughout the campsites.

After the tents had been pitched, everyone filed to the concert area to hear and see the Christian singing groups and solo artists perform and ministers speak. For the next few days, the people present at the festival would be in a world completely different than the one from which they came. Musicians performing at Jesus '73 included Andrae Crouch and the Disciples, Danny Lee and the Children of Truth, Danny Taylor, Randy Matthews, Randy Stonehill, and others—many of the same performers who had appeared at Explo '72.

Jerry Bryant, who later became host of the nationally syndicated Jesus-rock radio show "Jesus—Solid Rock," sold records at Jesus '73. "I phoned all the religious record companies I could think of," he recalls, "and told them, 'Send me everything you've got.' Of course, I meant contemporary music, and in those days there wasn't much! Just Larry Norman, Love Song, and a few others.

"So I loaded up a Winnebago we had rented for the occasion, and carted all the albums to Jesus '73. We were packed to the gills with records, so much that the camper leaned to one side. We set up our record display, with the traditional gospel on one side and the Jesus music on the other.

"People freaked out. 'Where did you get all this stuff? We've never heard of it!' By the end of the first day, all of the contemporary records were sold."

An estimated eight thousand people attended Jesus '73. The music they heard, in many cases for the first time, was contemporary Christian music. As each person returned home, the news of Jesus music spread. One year later, Jesus '74 drew twice as many people to Pennsylvania as its '73 predecessor.

Twenty-five hundred miles away, at the Orange County Fairgrounds in Costa Mesa, California, Praise '74 attracted an estimated sixteen thousand people. Praise '74 was a combination Jesus festival/fair, with daily outdoor stadium concerts, Christian art and craft exhibits, and a steady program of quality Christian films.

John Styll, whose radio show "Hour of Praise" on KGER was the pioneer Jesus-music show in Southern California, recalled in 1978 that Praise '74 helped to introduce varied California talent, rather than solely Maranatha groups as had the amusement park festivals.

"Praise '74 was sponsored by Maranatha Village," he adds, "a local Christian bookstore which grew out of the Jesus movement. The festival featured Andrae Crouch and the Disciples, Terry Talbot and the Branch Bible Band, Love Song, the Latinos, Ralph Carmichael, Cam Floria, Jerry Sinclair, and numerous other musicians." Disneyland fireworks a few miles off lit up the sky behind the stage each night while explosive Jesus music filled the stadium.

In the summer of 1975, Cam Floria and Bill Rayborn designed and sponsored the First Annual Christian Artists' Seminar in the Rockies, held at a YMCA camp in the mountain resort town of Estes Park, Colorado. There was an abundance of music and talent. The gathering featured Evie Tornquist, Andrae Crouch and the Disciples, the Archers, the Continental Singers, Jeremiah People, the Imperials, the Hawaiians, and a wide array of other performers.

The Seminar was unlike any of its Jesus-festival progenitors, however, in that it catered to the musicians and other members of organized churches and colleges and their music more heavily than to the Christian "street people" whose tastes leaned to Jesus music. Also, the Seminar was not intended to be a festival to draw in music *fans,* except for the evening concerts. Rather, the Seminar was mainly intended for people in music ministries.

In the ensuing years the Seminar, referred to around the country simply as "Estes Park," would increase greatly from the 1975 attendance of approximately eight hundred. Seminar leaders trained musicians, music ministers, and choir directors. Concerts at night featured a potpourri of artists running the gamut from classical to rock, and a "National Talent Competition" was begun, with cash prizes and recording contracts going to the victors. Probably the most important contribution the annual gathering offered was a much-needed time of fellowship between musicians. For some, it was the only true retreat for fellowship they had during the year.

1975 was also the year that Jesus festivals sprang up everywhere. There was Jesus '75 in Pennsylvania, where rain turned the festival grounds into a quagmire of mud, though it failed to dampen the festival-goers' spirits. In Michigan, Salt '75 featured "twenty-five hours of music, teaching, Bible study, and prayer." The music was performed by Simple Truth, Randy Matthews, Good News Circle, Oreon, Honeytree, the Continental Singers, and others.

At the northern end of the scenic Blue Ridge Parkway, Fishnet '75 began what was to be a yearly pilgrimage for many Americans to Front Royal, Virginia. Elsewhere that year, Jesus '75 Midwest was held in St. Louis, the Sonshine Festival in Ohio, Lodestone in Vancouver, B.C., and the Road Home Celebration in Colorado Springs, in the shadow of Pikes Peak.

In California, the Maranatha Nights continued at Knott's Berry

Farm. At the Joyland Amusement Park in Wichita, Kansas, the first Jesus Festival of Joy drew around three thousand people. In Texas, the Hill Country Faith Festival featured Terry Talbot, Liberation Suite, Jamie Owens, and Children of Faith.

As each year passed, more and more ambitious promoters and would-be promoters attempted to program festivals of Jesus music. Some succeeded; some failed. The events were held at stadiums, mountain glens, orange groves, amusement parks, fairgrounds, race-tracks, rodeo arenas, campuses, and beaches. Most of them featured musicians and ministers offering praise, worship, and learning experiences. Communions, baptisms, and altar calls were often included.

The festivals should have been the envy of thousands of ministers across the country who saw the free interchange between people of so many varied faiths. In some cases, that was the feeling. However, in other instances church ministers refused any support for fear that the youth would be "caught up" in someone else's religion.

The fears of proselytism could not be ignored. Some churches had lost their youth to the Jesus movement, and the Jesus festivals became about the only spiritual nourishment some youth ever got. Over the years, however, many of the skeptical churches began sponsoring busloads of their youth to go to the festivals, providing adult supervision and guidance. Such church efforts resulted in a melting of many barriers, as the adults were able to explain to the young people the differences which existed in the varied faiths and persuasions. The interdenominational fellowship was invaluable for youths in understanding other faiths. People who attended the festivals testified to the life-changing experiences they encountered:

At Jesus '74 I had my first encounter with God's love. Boy, was I surprised! Everywhere I went, there was love shining forth—in our camp, in many long lines, and in problems. "Praise God!" was on the lips and faces of those near me. I just had to know the source of this love and joy. So I asked Jesus to fill my heart and become Lord of my life. He did. Praise the Lord!

Last year at Jesus '75 the Lord's love and power was also manifest in many ways. Even through rainstorms, mud and all the resulting difficulties, He showed His love and power. In love He taught us to look only to Him, put our trust in Him and to praise and thank Him in *all* circumstances. It really works! He used the mud in a very special way, to help my mother to come to see and know His love and to become her Lord.[1]

Memories such as this helped one forget the sunburns, the poison ivy rashes, the cut feet, the bugs, and sometimes rain and mud to boot. The adversities were of little import when one was being saturated with Christian love, fine music, Bible teaching, new friendships, great fellowship, and often, changed lives.

13/ Let Us Be One

KYMS, "The Orange 106," was a small FM station located in Santa Ana, California. The music was "underground" rock, and the owners were having problems competing with seventy-seven other radio stations in the Los Angeles/Orange County area.

KYMS was one of four stations owned by Southwestern Broadcasters, Inc. The president of Southwestern was on the verge of giving up in the battle to win enough of a loyal audience to show up in the ratings books. About that time someone suggested that KYMS could become a religious station.

Orange County was reported to have one of the highest ratios of Christians in the nation. It would seem that a contemporary religious station concept would have become reality for that area much sooner, but there had been none, except for one or two Jesus-music radio shows. Since May 10, 1974, John Styll had broadcast "Hour of Praise" on KGER in Long Beach, a traditional religious station which carried back-to-back preaching programs, much like most other religious stations in the country. John's show was on each afternoon at 3:00 P.M. He would go into his studio in Newport Beach at ProMedia Productions, usually after lunch, and record the hour show on a ten-inch reel of tape. Then the rush was on.

The scene was somewhat reminiscent of an old Tom Mix cowboy movie, when the star literally jumped onto his horse and rode off to save the train. Except in this case John ran out into the parking lot with his 10″ reel of tape, literally jumped *into* his Mustang, and drove through the traffic-filled streets from Newport Beach to KGER's Long Beach studios via the most direct route possible.

More than once John and the tape arrived as the closing comments were being made on the taped show leading up to "Hour of Praise." The on-air announcer had long before learned to have an album of contemporary music queued up in case John didn't make it. But, as he is proud to admit, he always made it!

" 'Hour of Praise' ran on KGER for exactly one year," John explains. "It was both a vanguard show and an avant-garde show."

Just before "Hour of Praise" ended its year run on KGER, speculation began about what was happening at KYMS in Santa Ana. Finally the news was announced: KYMS was going to change from secular rock music to contemporary Christian music—one of the first stations in America to do so.

On March 15, 1975, KYMS, "the Orange 106," became the "Spirit of 106." Arnie McClatchey, station manager for KYMS in its first several years, recalled the public's reaction. "The sound on the air excited the young, Christian populace of Orange County," he remembered. "KYMS quickly became *their* station, freely playing the Jesus music which had been impossible to hear on radio before, except for an hour or so each day."

Some of Calvary Chapel's concerts were broadcast live on KYMS, almost immediately drawing the attention of the young people. Also a remote radio studio was built at Maranatha Village, the Christian shopping center located in the original Calvary Chapel building, which had been sold to businessman Jim Willems when the Calvary crowds outgrew the facilities.

Only nine days before KYMS' debut as a contemporary Christian radio station, Larry King and several associates had introduced KBHL-FM, "The Sound of the New Life," to Lincoln, Nebraska.

KBHL went on the air at 6:00 P.M. on March 6, 1975. "We're on the air! Thank you, Lord!" Those were the first words heard at 95.3 FM. In the next few weeks the station was deluged with calls of approval from all over the Lincoln listening area. Local businesses, including the A & W restaurant, distributed KBHL bumper stickers, which proclaimed that KBHL was "*Kept By His Love.*" Automobile bumpers all over Lincoln spread the news of KBHL's arrival on the scene. Brilliant orange T-shirts emblazoned with KBHL's call letters and a frosty mug of A & W root beer told the people that both were "Thirst Quenchers." It wasn't long until the station began sponsoring contemporary Christian concerts by 2nd Chapter of Acts, Barry McGuire, and other well-known artists.

KBHL's activities in promoting the new Christian music marked a major step forward, as did those of KYMS. Enlisting top-name business establishments for major promotions of Christian radio stations had been done before, but never for Jesus music.

Contemporary radio was a medium very much akin to Jesus

music. Like Jesus musicians, the main goal and desire of these contemporary broadcasters was to enable everyone to make their faith a part of their daily life. They wanted to present radio as part of a Christian lifestyle, one which was not ostentatious. The new Christian lifestyle would allow teenagers an opportunity to witness to their friends without being excessively verbal. Their music witnessed, but was not a turn-off, because it so closely paralleled pop music in style. A person could keep his radio on the contemporary Christian station without being ashamed of it in front of his peers.

The Apostle Paul stated, "I am not ashamed of the gospel, for it is the power of God for salvation to everyone who believes . . ." (Rom. 1:16, NAS). Likewise, the young people of the 1970s were not ashamed of the gospel, but they were embarrassed when they had to couch it in what to them was an antiquated music style or broadcasting style. For these youth, life in Christ was as exciting and real in the 1970s as ever before, and they needed to convey that as well as live it.

So, the solution to them was to take the venerable gospel message and run it as a thread through the fabric of their lives. Contemporary music and contemporary radio provided the necessary atmosphere. Listeners could tune into KBHL, KYMS, or one of several other new contemporary Christian stations and "participate" in radio as they did with the secular stations. News, weather, sports, music, personalities, and even contests provided the Christians with a companion—a Christian alternative.

The new contemporary stations usually didn't limit their programming to Jesus-rock music alone. In fact, a fairly strict hand was kept on how "far-out" the music was. Moderation was the rule. To balance the music and the audience, the station programmers generally played music which could best be described as MOR (middle-of-the-road). In one deejay's words, it had to be "not too rocky and not too hokey."

The result of this MOR approach was best described in a letter to the editor of the *Lincoln Star*. In part, it read:

> Anyone who is a Christian and hasn't yet discovered KBHL has been missing a very delightful and spiritual experience for over a month. If one is not yet a Christian, he should find out what this "new life" sounds like. There is nothing to lose, and everything to gain.
>
> Those within the age group of one to one hundred will find themselves participating happily in the worship of our Lord and Savior, Jesus Christ. The youth begin to

listen to those old favorites that have been passed down through the years, with new regard and appreciation. The not-so-young among us soon begin hearing with a new attitude those newer contemporary hymns of praise to God.[1]

Houston, Texas, was another city to be served by a contemporary Christian station in 1975. Benton White, who along with Scott Campbell, Rod Hunter, and Dewey Boynton helped to create the new contemporary format, experienced varied reactions of KFMK listeners.

"When the Houston station went on the air with the new format," recalls Benton, "there was nothing else like it there. The company, Crawford Broadcasting, wanted something new and exciting. They wanted to pioneer. So, when the opportunity came, they took it.

"KFMK went totally music from 6 A.M. to midnight, with mainly contemporary Christian music. Because of our lack of enough Jesus-music records in our station library, we really were fairly moderate to start with, kind of middle-of-the-road music.

"Being at the age I was, which was twenty-two, I was looking for something which spoke to a young age group. To see the possibilities of the Word of Christ being spread in that way, was something I wanted to be a part of from the ground up."

Jesus-music activity was on the increase. Residents of Santa Ana, Lincoln, Houston, and a few other cities could now experience contemporary music more than ever. One major problem still existed, however. People at one end of the country still didn't know what was happening at the other end. Things had been that way since the beginning of Jesus music.

Singer Danny Taylor, whose early years in Jesus music were spent in the Northeast, recalls how little he knew of the activities in the western U.S. "In 1969, we really had no models," Danny says. "For example, there was Scott Ross, myself, Larry Black, Charles McPheeters, and Mike Johnson. Mike was with the Exkursions out of Pittsburgh. The Exkursions were just about the earliest group out of the eastern U.S. to perform Jesus music. Anyway, all of our paths would cross doing different things.

"We weren't really aware of what was going on, until the Faith Festival at Evansville, Indiana, in 1970, when I did the concert there with Larry Norman, Bob MacKenzie, Thurlow Spurr, Crimson Bridge, and a group which was very heavy for the time, called 'e.'

"We had the feeling on the East Coast that we were primarily doing the whole thing as far as radio was concerned. 'The Scott Ross Show' was becoming a model for the East Coast at least. But in reality things happened slowly. The East Coast had traditionally been quite conservative, and it was a lot harder to break through there. It was in 1971, when we became aware of Love Song, that we became more aware of what was happening elsewhere. We started hearing stories of Costa Mesa, the Church on the Way, and other places."

Meanwhile, Californian Tom Stipe was working as a young minister at Calvary Chapel in Costa Mesa. "In the early days," he remembers, "there was such a personal, central movement in Southern California, in terms of incredible spiritual activity, there was little awareness of what was going on everywhere else. There was such a rush of media attention, every time we'd turn around the TV cameras would be set up at church, telecasting pictures of all the kids raising their hands in praise. It was an oddity for the press.

"As soon as a Jesus-music group got together, they would begin thinking, 'Well, this is nice but I wonder if we could go play someplace outside of California.' Then they started realizing some of the things that were going on elsewhere in the country.

"As the groups got together and we felt like we were being used sufficiently in Southern California, we began to turn our attentions outward. This came in about 1972, when Love Song did their first national tour with Ray Johnson. Ray booked the tour from Houston, and everybody was amazed! They went as far as Texas!

"Love Song would come back from their tours and tell all of us in California what was happening in the rest of the country. I remember the guys coming back describing how contemporary music was being played on the radio. They told us about Scott Ross, and spoke of his earlier days at Shea Stadium emceeing the Beatles concert. That was our first impression that someone in the professional world was stepping in and taking a stand for the Lord and utilizing his talents to the glory of God.

"Later there was considerable interest from Atlantic Records in New York City. Ahmet Ertegun, the president of Atlantic at that time and producer of top groups like Crosby, Stills and Nash, offered Love Song an incredible deal to be on Atlantic Records. It was the same time the group members were in final negotiations with Good News Records in California. At this point, we realized that all this was going to spread out. We realized it *was* spreading out!"

Meanwhile, Phil Keaggy, who had played guitar and sung with a Cleveland rock group, Glass Harp, recorded his first solo album in

1973 as the debut recording on New Song Records. It was titled *What a Day.* New Song Records was an outreach ministry of the Love Inn comunity in Freeville, where the "Scott Ross Show" originated.

"When guitarist Phil Keaggy had a short stint with Love Song around 1973," Tom Stipe recalls, "I remember the incredible excitement of having Phil walk in the door from a completely different part of the country, and it blew us all away at Calvary Chapel. Pastor Churck Smith still remembers the Monday night that Phil played."

Many people agreed that the Lord was busy with both the East Coast and the West Coast, and the main tie between them was the musicians and their relationships. To improve national intercommunication, twenty men from across the country and from various branches of Christian work met in Fort Wayne, Indiana, in April 1975 to discuss a change. Paul Craig Paino, Jr., a minister at Calvary Temple in Fort Wayne, called the meeting, which resulted in the formation of the Fellowship of Contemporary Christian Ministries (FCCM). According to Paul, "The FCCM was born out of a desire to see the segmented ministries of the contemporary outreaches brought together under a common mode of communication and fellowship." "Let us be one in you," one song had prayed, and the FCCM was undoubtedly part of its answer.

The organization of FCCM was a milestone in Jesus-music history, for the communication between the East Coast and the West Coast would improve, it was hoped. Also, beginning in 1976, the FCCM would sponsor annual summer conferences. These three-day retreats allowed musicians, concert promoters, coffeehouse ministers, theater groups, record company representatives, broadcasters, artists' managers, recording studio engineers, and anyone else who took contemporary Christian ministries seriously, to participate in a yearly fellowship with the brothers and sisters in common ministries throughout America.

An official newsletter was circulated among new members as a form of network, designed to facilitate communication between ministries. The newsletter was more or less a collection of epistles between members, sharing failures as well as successes.

Lou Hancherick, one of the twenty charter members of the FCCM who attended the Fort Wayne meeting in 1975, had a vision to keep not only FCCM members informed as to what was happening in the world of Jesus music, but to keep the general public informed as well. Lou announced his intentions to publish a magazine titled *Harmony.*

There had been a Jesus-music magazine before. In 1971, *Rock in Jesus* had been created. A total of five issues of *RIJ* were published, but the readership was much less than *Harmony* would later enjoy. *Rock in Jesus* was married with *Right On!* in January 1973, and continued for awhile as a middle section of the Berkeley Jesus paper.

Except for *Rock in Jesus,* Jesus music had received very limited specialized coverage in secular or Christian publications. Most of the Christian press which ran any articles ran antirock and anti-Jesus-music stories. The stories were written for the traditional clientele of those publications—people who were already against rock music.

There were a few exceptions. Cheryl Forbes in *Christianity Today* gave critical but generally positive reveiws of Jesus-music album releases. Occasionally *Campus Life* magazine, the top Christian teen magazine, would feature an article about or by Jesus-music artists, but to no regular degree.

So, in May 1975 the first issue of *Harmony* was a sight for sore eyes—a cause for celebration among Jesus musicians and contemporary Christians. Now fans had an opportunity to read a magazine from cover to cover and keep on top of everything happening in Jesus music.

Dan Hickling, the editor of *Harmony*'s first issue, had worked with publisher Lou Hancherick since August 1974 in preparing the magazine. Dan edited *Harmony* during a layoff from the Buffalo Ford Motor Company plant. The layoff was very timely for the *Harmony* project, but it meant tight times for the Hicklings.

"It was almost a full-time job," Dan related, "just trying to find out what was happening in Jesus music. Until 1975 we had hardly any communication from the record companies. I wanted *Harmony* to be a forum for information and exchange of ideas between artists and others involved in contemporary Christian ministries. My position was in the ministry of helps, especially helping people to establish contact with other people it was necessary for them to know."

Harmony's first issue appropriately featured Randy Matthews, one of Jesus music's pioneers, on the cover. Inside were an interview with Bob Hartman of Petra, a "Tuning Up" column authored by Danny Taylor, reviews of six new Jesus-music albums, assorted news releases, and the first part of "Brand New Song," a history of Jesus music, which would later be the starting-point for *Why Should the Devil Have All the Good Music?*, the forerunner of this book.

Harmony, KYMS, KBHL, KFMK, and the FCCM all contributed in making 1975 a milestone year for Jesus music. The year marked the beginning of a stupendous growth period for *all* forms of gospel music. But the most dramatic increase would be noted in *contemporary* Christian music.

14/ *Superstar*

The amazing growth of Jesus music in 1975 continued all over the country in 1976, as Jimmy Carter introduced Americans to the term "born again." Virtually unknown before his presidential candidacy, Carter testified to his faith and brought about a new interest in evangelicalism. In the tradition of *Look* magazine, whose writers in the early seventies had invented the term "Jesus movement," the press labeled this new consciousness the "born-again movement." Plenty of Christians already knew the meaning of the term, but it was new to people outside the church.

Well-known personalities began verbalizing their faith in Christ as Savior, and in many cases following dramatic changes in their lives: Chuck Colson and Jeb Stuart Magruder of Watergate infamy; Susan Atkins and Charles "Tex" Watson of the convicted Manson Family; actor Dean Jones of Walt Disney fame; actress Lulu Roman of "Hee Haw"; Eldridge Cleaver of the Black Panthers; and Roger Staubach of the Dallas Cowboys.

The same renewal seemed to be taking place in the musical entertainment field. Singers who once rocked and rolled for fame and fortune changed their tune as they got a better grip on their lives. Though there seemed to be a rash of such testimonies in the late seventies, the changed lives had been occurring throughout the rock and roll years. But it wasn't as easy in the earlier years for entertainers to admit publicly that they were Christians. During the sixties, the popular trend of youth was away from the churches, the Christian religion, and Americanism. For an artist to declare "I am a Christian" was a bold move with plenty of complications for his or her public life.

Pat Boone was one of the first rock performers to proclaim Christ when it wasn't the popular thing to do. He was chided by critics as being square, milquetoast, the epitome of blandness. Yet, the number of lives positively affected by Pat Boone's work and witness was definitely nothing to scoff at.

Frequent visits on national television talk shows were an excellent example of this witness. He was not pompous with his religion, and prior to each show he would carefully pray and ask the Lord whether it was the time and place to speak of Christ verbally, or whether it was more important for him to be a *living* example, while sparing words.

Because between 1955 and 1969 fifty-eight of Pat's records reached the top 100 charts, *Rolling Stone* featured a cover story on Pat in their January 29, 1976 issue. Author John Anderson stated that he had expectd Boone to be a "Rasputin-like character." By the conclusion, Anderson mused that he had not found Pat to be the "greedy, money-grabbing hypocrite" he had set out to discover: "Whatever Pat does, he does in response to the voice which calls out to him with a reality he can bank on."[1]

In 1972 Pat formed his own record company, Lamb and Lion Records, on which numerous gospel-music and Jesus-music performers were given their starts. The work Pat has done in getting the word out about Jesus has been unparalleled by any other pop entertainer.

Pat's daughter Debby carried on a family tradition of hits when she recorded "You Light Up My Life" in 1977. The song became the biggest pop record hit in twenty-three years, and remained in the number 1 position for ten weeks. "You Light Up My Life" had a special meaning for the twenty-one-year-old Debby. The song was the theme from a movie, which she admits she "didn't even agree with." (*Her* recording was not in the movie, nor did she see the movie until after "You Light Up My Life" was #1.)

"I sang it to the Lord, and that's all!" she added. "The first time I heard the song, I thought it was just an okay song. But when I started listening to the words and saw how it really applied to my relationship with the Lord, then the excitement came!"

With the hit came Debby's opportunity to perform on "The Tonight Show," plus an endless string of other network shows. On such occasions Debby didn't hide the fact that she was a Christian, especially if the question came up in an interview situation. But she didn't tout her faith on every stage on which she performed. She viewed her function in the Lord's work as being something similar to that of the Ark of the Covenant in the Old Testament—that is, a container of the Holy Spirit.

"I should just be who I am. Debby Boone—container of the

Holy Spirit," she explained in a private interview. "I don't have to get in a 'good one for the Lord' each time I appear on a TV show. The power of the Holy Spirit will come across and it will do the work! I don't try to hide it, but I don't try to force it either. It's just amazing when I get a letter from someone who says, 'I heard your song on the radio and recommitted my life to the Lord,' or 'I was going through such a difficult time in my life and I heard that song and it pulled me through.' And *I* wasn't even trying! I was just singing to the Lord!"

Debby's faith in the Lord was no secret, nor was that of her three sisters—Laury, Lindy, and Cherry—with whom she recorded Jesus-music albums on her father's record label. The sisters' upbringing in a Christian atmosphere made the Boone family the object of heavy scrutiny from the sensationalist press, ready to pounce on them for any wandering from that faith or its lifestyle. But each of the daughters, along with parents Pat and Shirley, withstood such criticism and continued to be strong in their Christian witness.

While John Lennon, Paul McCartney, and George Harrison were singing as "The Quarrymen" in church-hall dances and "beat clubs," a young man named Harry Webb made his first record. In August 1958, Webb took on the professional name of Cliff Richard, and with his group the Drifters recorded "Move It" and "Schoolboy Crush." The records catapulted Cliff Richard into national prominence as a rock singer.

The hits continued, at a rate of about five a year, and Cliff Richard became Britain's top performer. Even when the Beatles exploded with their hits in the early 1960s, Cliff continued his hold on the charts of Britain, as well as in Europe and Asia.

Thus, in 1966, when Cliff stepped up to the microphone on Billy Graham's podium at a London Crusade where over twenty-five thousand people were present, the whole nation listened. Though he was one of the nation's best-known and most popular individuals, he was nervous.

"I have never had the opportunity to speak to an audience as big as this before," he began, "but it is a great privilege to be able to tell so many people that I am a Christian. I can only say to people who are not Christians that until you have taken the step of asking Christ into your life, your life is not really worthwhile. It *works*—it works for me."[2]

Cliff's announcement hit the pages of every London paper the next morning. Would he end his career and go into "religion"? Just what would become of Cliff Richard was the gossip of the music papers. In a 1972 *Rolling Stone* interview, some four years after his public profession, Cliff expressed a frustration he shared with many other Christians. "When I came out for Jesus, most people said, 'Well there goes a good career,' When it didn't end, they said, 'Oh what a gimmick.' "[3]

Cliff also said in the interview that he challenged the " 'popularity' of Jesus Christ and some of his (Cliff's) contemporaries for going along with it." Cliff added:

> Everybody (is) able to record "My Sweet Lord" and "Oh Happy Day," except me. If I did anything like that everybody would say: "Oh here comes the religious bit." But everybody else could do it. As a Christian I felt that where they all missed out, although they were great records, was that they didn't know exactly who Jesus was.[4]

In 1976, rock superstar Elton John signed Cliff to a contract with his Rocket Record Company. Cliff recorded "Devil Woman," and the song reached #6 on the *Billboard* charts, the biggest American hit of his nineteen-year recording career. Those people who remembered Cliff's statements of his faith back in 1966 were taken aback by such a song as "Devil Woman." Cliff defended the song, stating that it was a warning against occult practices rather than an endorsement.

Cliff's continued testimonies for Christ in pop concerts around the world at least indicated his strong faith. His popularity as a singer enabled Cliff to experience awesome opportunities at witnessing. Not long after his American hit, Cliff was sharing Christ with nearly seventy thousand people in—of all places—Leningrad and Moscow.

Noel Paul Stookey met Jesus in an Austin, Texas, motel room. Stookey had been touring for years as the "Paul and" of Peter, Paul & Mary, one of the top vocal groups in the United States during the troubled 1960s. Noel's success as a performer had failed to give him the satisfaction of being a whole person. His friend Bob Dylan had advised him to read the Bible, so Noel was somewhat ready when a young man came up to him at an Austin concert to talk to him about Jesus.

"We got to rapping," Noel recalls. "I had been reading the New Testament and looking for some kind of a moral way to live my life—something more fulfilling than what I had. I had no idea I was gonna get 'smote!'

"It was terrific. I went back to my hotel room and I asked Jesus to come into my life. I cried, and oh! What a fantastic time we had that night! It was just a very cleansing experience."[5]

Noel's acceptance of Christ as Savior led to the dissolution of the Peter, Paul & Mary trio after ten years of many hits together. The three were still friends, but Noel felt it was time.

"I began to see my life as a paradox. I mean, I loved being on the road in terms of the people I met. I was talking about love, togetherness, home and family, and continuity of spirit, but I wasn't living it, because I was on the road four days out of the week. I had a child in school and it just seemed logical after accepting Christ and reading the New Testament that I should get me back to where I belonged."[6]

Noel did just that. He ultimately moved himself and his family to South Blue Hill, Maine (population 1,200). He began singing in the Congregational Church Choir. His twin daughters and older daughter began to see more of their father than most musicians' kids did. Noel's wife, Elizabeth, took up operation of a greenhouse, and the whole family benefited from Noel's revelation of "how much better it is to live near God."

Noel didn't say farewell to recording, however. He began his own eight-track recording studio and animation studio (he's a cartoonist, too). In 1977 he began releasing albums on his own Neworld label.

In 1978 Noel announced that Peter Yarrow, Mary Travers, and he would reunite as Peter, Paul & Mary for a concert tour and a new recording.

By late 1975, B. J. Thomas's record sales had reached thirty-two million copies. He scored high with "(Hey Won't You Play) Another Somebody Done Somebody Wrong Song" in early 1975. The singalong hit reached #1.

But just while everything seemed rosy for B. J. in the eyes of the record-buying world, the bottom had fallen out for him. He was a drug addict; his cocaine alone cost $3,000 a week. He was separated from his wife and daughter and could hardly get through a recording session because of his incoherency. He developed a reputation among musicians as being extremely hard to work with and creating havoc in the studios.

"In 1975 I began to realize that I was either going to die or I was going to make a decision to put the drugs down," B. J. recalls. "I couldn't put them down, so I resigned myself to the fact that I was going to eventually kill myself. On many occasions, I would take over fifty pills at one time and I would say 'B., this is going to kill you.' And then I would say, 'Well, who cares?' "

Later in the year, B. J. was scheduled to do a concert in Hawaii. After taking more than eighty pills that particular night, B. J. told the audience he couldn't sing. He left the stage and went back to his hotel room.

"Somehow," B. J. later explained, "my road man got me to the airport. They noticed I wasn't breathing very much. My fingernails turned black and my lips turned black. Then, as I got worse, they put a mirror under my nose and couldn't get any breath. For all intents and purposes I had died."

They got B. J. to a hospital and immediately hooked his body up to machines in an effort to revive him. "I woke up the next day and asked them, 'Well, how close was it?' They said I had been gone. Only the machines kept me alive."

Coincidentally, B. J.'s record company had released another single off his current album. The title, "Help Me Make It (To My Rocking Chair)," said more than anyone on the outside world could imagine.

B. J.'s wife Gloria kept imploring him to come home. Gloria had become a Christian, and she saw light at the end of the tunnel for her husband. By early 1976, he was no more than a hollowed-out shell of a man. He finally conceded to return home to Hurst, Texas.

Shortly after he came back, Gloria's witness, his daughter Paige's love, and some friends' prayers led B. J. to accept new life in Christ. He was healed of his drug habit in those intense moments that night in January 1976. "It was such a miraculous thing for me," he later recalled. "When I received the Lord as my Savior, I just knew I was gonna go through some withdrawals. I knew I was gonna lose my mind. But I never had one shaky moment, one sleepless night. Nothing bad ever happened."

The next few months were spent pulling his family back together, straightening out finances (including declaring bankruptcy), and generally making plans for a new future. B. J.'s contract with his record label was terminated, and one of his first moves was to do an album of songs relating his love for Christ.

"I just wanted to cut Christian music, but I think that happens so many times with new Christians. If they have a certain career going, they think that God wants them to quit it and do only religious things. I talked to my pastor about it, and he reminded me that a lot of people's ministry is not in a church. I began to realize that if I would just give my testimony at the end of my show, and just as God would have me say it, what a ministry that was!"

So B. J. signed with Myrrh Records to record Christian music, but he also secured a contract with MCA Records to continue singing pop music, too. His first Myrrh album became one of gospel music's all-time best-selling albums, and his first post-Christian pop single, "Don't Worry Baby," became #17 in the nation in 1977.

B. J. had become a *true* success. Not by his thirty-two million-plus records, he would remind you. It was his yielding to Jesus Christ that gave him a new lease on life. Like other big-name entertainers, he became stronger in Christ, but his strength would continue to be taxed as he ministered in the world and to the world. His entire life became a stage, and people were watching every move.

"I don't wanna be a super star. All I want to do is shine with the light of Jesus," a Christian hit of that era, well summarized the goal of B. J. and other born-again musicians.

Along with the new "acceptability" of Christianity, Christian music began to flourish at an even more astounding rate in 1977. The world was beginning to take more notice of the music as a result of increased product, promotion, publicity, and the people's genuine search for spiritual values in their lives.

An aggressive push by Christian record companies finally began to get record albums to the *front* of Christian bookstores instead of "back behind the greeting cards." Some Christian bookstores became known as "book and record stores."

Likewise, the availability of good Jesus-music albums increased at an amazing rate. At Word, Incorporated, in 1975 about 5 percent of the recorded product sold was contemporary. Only three years later, the amount had increased to 60 percent.

As record companies began producing more product, more radio stations were able to go on the air with full-time contemporary Christian music—stations such as WINQ in Tampa/St. Petersburg, KBRN in Brighton/Denver, KFKZ in Greeley/Ft. Collins, KQLH in San Bernardino, KBIQ in Seattle, WYCA in Hammond/Chicago, and numerous others who joined the Jesus-music radio pioneers. There were more and more newspapers and magazines giving attention to contemporary Christian music, too. *Gospel Trade, Singing News, Harmony, Cashbox, Record World, Billboard,* and *Contemporary Christian Music* all featured articles and charts on Jesus music.

In 1977, Myrrh Records kicked off a sales promotion campaign which would bring Jesus music into greater prominence than ever before. The $75,000 campaign was run with all the noise and glamour of a movie premiere in Hollywood. Giant posters, sample records in magazines, radio commercials, and special displays prompted Christian book and record store operators to carry more Jesus music. "The music is today, the message is forever," the banners announced. It was Jesus music's biggest advertising boost in its nine-year history.

By the time of the Myrrh campaign, the label had the largest roster of contemporary Christian artists in the country, including many musicians who had been major contributors to Jesus music's history: Malcolm & Alwyn (two of the first British musicians); Michael Omartian (respected Hollywood record producer and keyboard artist); B. J. Thomas; Honeytree; the 2nd Chapter of Acts; the Pat Terry Group; Randy Matthews; Limpic & Rayburn; Bob Ayala; Chris Christian; comedian Mike Warnke (more or less the chaplain of the Jesus-music world); David Meece; Lilly Green; and several other artists and groups. Myrrh and the labels distributed under its banner provided some of the best opportunities for musicians to communicate the gospel via Jesus music on record.

Myrrh also distributed several independent labels' recordings: Solid Rock (Larry Norman's label); New Song (Love Inn's label); Good News (pioneer Jesus-music label); Messianic (Lamb's label); and Seed (Paul Clark's label). Word, Myrrh's parent company, also distributed a good deal of Jesus music on Light, Lamb & Lion, and NewPax Records. Even the more traditional Word label fared well with contemporary Christian music fans through artist Evie Tornquist. Evie's music, like that of the Imperials and Andrae Crouch, tended to break down the barriers between "traditional," "inspirational," and "contemporary" Christian music. Some people of all ages found some of their music uplifting and enjoyable.

Word, Incorporated was not the only company pushing hard to promote Jesus music. Billy Ray Hearn, who had been with Myrrh Records since its inception, had left Myrrh and Texas to begin the new Sparrow record label in California. Most notable of Sparrow's early releases was Keith Green's first album, *For Him Who Has Ears to Hear*, which became one of the top three contemporary religious albums in 1977 and 1978. Also joining the Sparrow roster were Annie Herring, brothers John and Terry Talbot, Barry McGuire, Janny Grine, Danniebelle Hall, the 2nd Chapter of Acts, and Scott Wesley Brown. Sparrow also distributed Birdwing, Spirit, and Neworld Records.

In Nashville, Benson Publishing Company, whose Impact label had reintroduced Larry Norman's *Upon This Rock* and other albums to Jesus-music fans in earlier years, had reentered the contemporary music scene via Greentree Records in 1976. By 1978, their release schedule picked up radically, with everything from Reba Rambo Gardner's Streisand-style albums to Dony and Joy McGuire's Christian disco music. Greentree also released albums by Tim Sheppard, Dallas Holm & Praise, and others.

In Kansas City, Tempo started a contemporary label, Chrism, featuring music by a long-time Jesus music group, the Hope of Glory. In Pasadena, Texas, Star Song Records was born. In Costa Mesa, California, Maranatha! Music continued adding more artists to its roster. Likewise, other independent labels began springing up all across the country, providing more and more Jesus music for the masses. Jesus-music fans had never had it so good.

15/ We Need a Whole Lot More of Jesus and a Lot Less Rock and Roll

The summer sun was taking its toll in Denver. The mountains disappeared into a smoggy atmosphere reminiscent of Los Angeles, and Denver residents apologized, saying it was usually not so bad. I had longed for the weekend when I could head for the mountain peaks and breathe in some cooler and more refreshing air.

I stayed in the Denver area for a few days in July 1978 to reminisce with Tom Stipe and Danny Taylor about the past eight years or so—where Jesus music had been and where it was going. I'll never forget our enjoyable conversations at Tom's home near Boulder and at the park where we picnicked high in the Rocky Mountains. Much of what was discussed in those hours has been shared in the earlier chapters of this book.

During one of those afternoons in Colorado, Danny, Tom, and I had lunch with evangelist Bob Larson, whose headquarters are in Denver. Bob's reputation had been that of a notorious antirock preacher who broke and burned rock record albums by the hundreds during his crusades. His books were no doubt the objects of burnings themselves by some devotees of rock music.

We were invited to lunch with Bob and his wife at a restaurant on the outskirts of Denver. Thousands of questions were bubbling inside, as the three of us wanted so much to get to know this evangelist who in years past had been so vocal concerning rock music—including Jesus-rock music.

Bob told us of his ministry of spiritual warfare. In his crusades around the world, Bob speaks on the sinfulness of the occult, drugs, and numerous other pastimes and practices. He is an outspoken preacher, pulling no punches in delivering warnings to his audiences of the sins of the world.

Because of his outspokenness on so many subjects popular to

the world (yoga, drugs, marijuana, alcoholism, pornography, and the occult, as well as many others), Bob explained that he had what he called a "lonely ministry," a description which especially applied to his views on rock music.

But talking to the Bob Larson of 1978 and reading the Bob Larson books of the early seventies were two different matters in many respects.

"The book *Rock and the Church* should be looked at in the proper perspective," Bob explained to us. "When it was written, and even now, my stand on rock music was not a major part of my ministry. It is one night's sermon in a week crusade. But people like to categorize someone and simplify his personality into what they want. With me, it was my preaching on rock music."

Of course, Bob's earliest books were all to some degree devoted to his views of rock music: *Rock & Roll: The Devil's Diversion* (1967), *Rock and the Church* (1971), *Hippies, Hindus and Rock & Roll* (1972), and *The Day the Music Died* (1973). After 1973, Larson's books centered on other subjects, but the scar remained to be healed.

Referring to *Rock and the Church,* Bob told us, "The tone of the book was very defensive, and to a certain extent condemnatory, because I was a young preacher, and I was emotionally involved. I hadn't been out of rock music long myself." (Larson has been a pop musician before becoming a minister.)

"Also," he continued, "I did not know the state of church music, because I had not come out of a church background. So, I did not know how truly archaic it was."

Jesus musicians who plodded through the formative years to spread the gospel were greatly upset at any ministry which would seek to destroy what they were convinced the Lord had wanted them to build. So Bob Larson was seen as a man making money off antirock books, and very little more.

"*Rock and the Church* was written in 1971," explained Bob. "That was before there were any Jesus-music groups. There's hardly a day that goes by in which someone doesn't write to me and lash out at me for my anti-Jesus-music views. The first thing I ask them is, 'Did you see when the book was written?' I ask them to put the book into historical perspective.

"In *Rock and the Church,* I was criticizing the shallow, superficial attempts at copying the sound of the world's music in some sort of vague frame of reference. The book was written before I knew of Love Song, the 2nd Chapter of Acts, and other more solid musicians like that. I did not perceive that a truly authentic and spiritually mature statement of faith and expression of faith would come out of the contemporary field. All I saw was a copy of what the world was doing.

"The second point I try to make to those readers of *Rock and the Church* is to read for basic principles. I still stand by many of its principles today. But the music has matured to a depth that I would not have ever anticipated. What *has* developed in some quarters is an authentic idiom that isn't just a copy of the world. The one thing that does impress me is, even though I still find some musical elements objectionable, the lyrics are not of the sort of throbbing substance they originally were. They now really say something of depth. The change has come from musicians who developed their talents as Jesus musicians, not older musicians trying to copy the sound of the young. In the past six to eight years, musicians have developed Jesus music which is saying some profound things."

But Bob cautioned that his comments did not indicate a blanket endorsement of all Jesus music, and certainly not all rock music. He believes that a rock beat can be a dangerous thing when it brings with it erotic response or even mental response.

"I still believe that music has the power to transcend one to a spirit plane, and the really super-heavy stuff I see as portending that possibility, to the extent that I don't think the Holy Spirit is pleased with being expressed in that frame of reference. That's obviously a subjective line that I'm drawing, but I'm still drawing some lines."

Bob also said he had picked up a copy of an album by Maranatha Jesus-music group Bethlehem, and was especially impressed by a song entitled "Dead Reckoning," one of the hardest rock selections on their album. "There's an example of a song that musically I don't feel comfortable with, not totally. I can understand why that sort of hard, raunchy style had to be used, because the sort of spiritual sarcasm they're using in speaking to the old man does fit it. I agree that the whole mood created is necessary to an extent. But if it had been me producing the album, I would have laid it back. But I think the song does prove a point. In other words, musically it doesn't fit into my frame of reference. But the message is so deep, it has to be genuinely born of the Holy Spirit."

Bob then cited instances when certain Jesus-music songs had been instrumental in even *his* work with people. He cited the Pat Terry Group's song, "I Feel Free" as an example. The lyrics of the song helped in Bob's ministry with a woman heavily into witchcraft. He recounted with joy the anointing that song carried.

In another instance, he remembered how "Abraham," a song written by Buck and Annie Herring and recorded by Phil Keaggy on the album *Love Broke Thru,* likewise ministered to a person with whom Bob was counseling. "That particular individual had been involved in the occult. The Lord used the song in a supernatural way to show us the steps we needed to take in our counseling procedure.

"There are two things I look for in any Christian song," Bob added, "the motive behind it and the ultimate intent. Some of the earliest forms of Jesus music were only meant to be entertaining."

I asked what advice Bob would give to aspiring Jesus musicians. He replied, "I would tell them to let the Holy Spirit do something unique and authentic through them, that would be born of the Holy Spirit, and that it would genuinely say something that would cause reflecting and rejoicing." (A popular contemporary Christian song expressed a similar thought: "We need a whole lot more of Jesus and a lot less rock and roll.")

Finally I asked Bob about the current explosion of popular Jesus-music artists, with some almost reaching a superstar status among Jesus-music fans. Is he fearful that it would get out of hand?

"I am just as fearful as ever," he answered. "It's a natural evolution, bound to happen. I'm very disturbed by the commercial overtones of it all. My advice to any 'fan' of any Christian music would be to read Psalm 101:6—'My eyes shall be upon the faithful of the land, that they may dwell with me; he who walks in a blameless way is the one who will minister to me.'"

Bob informed us that his upcoming book, *Rock,* would give parents positive ways to prevent their youth from selling out totally to rock music. "I want to give parents positive ways to handle it, other than going in and smashing all of their kids' records."

One of those positive ways which Bob suggested was through "Jesus music which genuinely glorifies Christ."

16/ Gospel Light

1978. Thirteen years since Ralph Carmichael's song "He's Everything to Me" set the Christian music world alight.

Ten years since Baptist preacher Arthur Blessitt opened His Place at 8428 Sunset Strip to reach out to the runaways, dopers, alcoholics, and lonely people.

Nine years since "Oh Happy Day" put Jesus on the charts.

The gigantic Jesus festivals were held for another year: "Jesus '78" in Florida, Pennsylvania, and Ontario; "Fishnet '78" in Virginia; a tremendously successful "Jesus Northwest" festival in Oregon; and scores of other smaller events which drew people together in fellowship. Not so small was the Fourth Annual Christian Artists' Music Seminar in the Rockies, more elaborate than ever as the guest roster grew to new lengths and more people planned their summer vacations around the Estes Park camp and the nightly concerts.

It was a sort of "two steps forward, one step back" year for contemporary Christian radio, with five top contemporary stations dropping their Jesus-music airplay to assume other formats. That in itself left several cities without a contemporary Christian voice.

However, all the radio news wasn't bad. The number of stations playing at least some contemporary music increased. Likewise, more and more independently produced, syndicated Jesus-music radio shows were initiated, providing decent Sunday programming for the thousands of secular radio stations in America.

It was also a year of shifting. "The Larry Black Show" moved from Freeville to Nashville, Jerry Bryant moved his "Jesus—Solid Rock" from Carbondale to California, Dale Yancy's "Rock That Never Rolls" rolled from Vermont to New York, and "A Joyful Noise" was transferred from Texas to Colorado.

With the widely expanded variety of Christian music, the distinctions between Jesus music and other contemporary Christian music had all but faded. Ralph Carmichael, in a magazine article, tried to explain the different types of Christian music and came up with eleven. Traditional artists began recording more contemporary songs just as the secular "traditional" artists had done at least fifteen years earlier. Even singers such as Tennessee Ernie Ford and Ray Price were recording songs by Randy Stonehill and Pat Terry.

Also noticeable around 1978 was a tremendous improvement in the quality of Jesus-music recordings. The world had seen Christian music as music of poor quality, and a lot of Christian recordings had provided ample fuel for that fire. Some well-meaning Christians who wanted to jump from knowing four guitar chords to having the top album on the charts in one easy step, or those who regardless of their talent wanted to record an album to please their own egos, made a mockery of gospel music. (In fact, the differentiation between "Jesus music" and "gospel music" was originally the result of the Jesus people's desire to create a new and more professional form of gospel music.)

But alas, even some of the Jesus musicians fell into the same trap. Often they would go into a recording studio before they were ready musically and spiritually. The results were albums of inferior quality. However, through their burning desire to "live up to" the standard set by the world's top rock musicians, the contemporary music makers forced the religious record industry to improve their standards of quality.

Budgets were a great part of the problem. While the Elton Johns of the world had recording budgets in the $100,000 figures, Jesus musicians were lucky to get more than $10,000. A record company could sell a million copies of an Elton John album even before its release and recoup the album's entire production budget overnight. The Christian record companies would have to wait for a year or so to recover even the lowest of expenditures.

It is possible that the artists who recorded albums of Jesus music were "pressured" into being better artists through working under extremely modest budget conditions, and thus completing albums in considerably less time than their secular counterparts. This extra pressure under which the Jesus musicians worked may have purified their music in some cases.

Through all this recording activity developed a strange irony. Christian musicians and record companies, when producing their albums, began hiring top studio musicians—the same ones who appeared on hundreds of pop recordings each year. The combination of a talented artist or group, a competent producer, and expert studio musicians would often yield a top-notch recording—one not only compatible with the top pop hits, but sometimes even better. After all, numerous Jesus-music artists had had #1 secular hits and million-selling records. In fact, they had amassed more than a dozen #1 hits, and the sale of probably over 200 million records through 1978! Yet, the Jesus-music songs by these same artists (by no means hasbeens), done in the same studios, performed by virtually the same musicians, and often written by the same people, never even touched the top hit charts in America! The problem still exists.

Prejudice against religion hardly seemed a justifiable reason for the pop music world to turn down fine music by fine musicians. But prejudice was a main reason. The Bible makes it very clear that the world will not necessarily look on the Christians (or their music) with favor. "For unto them the preaching of the cross is foolishness, but unto us who believe it is the power of salvation."[1]

The Jesus musicians' challenge to the world's prejudice was the added dimension which contemporary Christian music offered. It was mainstream rock music, on par with many of the world's hits. It was music which, without being overly preachy, was uplifting and positive. It was music with answers, not problems. Hope, not despair. Love, not lust. Life, not death. As a Terry Talbot song said, "Sing with your own voice . . . Don't you try to hide that candle. It's burnin' in that word you're feelin' inside. It's that gospel light." The twentieth-century world had never seen, heard, or experienced anything like it.

There was an awesome responsibility before those people involved in contemporary Christian music. Their music had to be professional and something the world would listen to, but it had to exude the truth with every word. That obviously didn't mean each song had to have "Jesus saved me, this I know" repeated over and over. It *did* mean, however, that each song should be conceived, written, performed, and recorded under absolute direction of the Holy Spirit. Christian musicians and their record companies had to be cautious not to compromise their music to get it into the secular marketplace.

With the extremely rapid growth of Jesus music, the momentum had occasionally bordered on frenzy. Vestiges of the world's star-oriented society had at times crept into the promotion of Jesus-music artists. Madison Avenue-type ads describing so-and-so as "a new star in gospel music" bordered on the outer limits of where Jesus music should go. In fact, such promotion prompted one group to print T-shirts with the message "Jesus Christ is the only star." They were seeking to reestablish priorities.

There had always been a secret dream of Jesus-music fans to see one of the artists break through the national charts with a giant "Jesus hit." Plenty of musicians had set that as their personal goal, too. But it showed a limited knowledge of how God could work.

Jesus Christ Superstar and *Godspell* ignited controversy and popularized the man Jesus at the same time. Some Christians recalled how *Superstar* first interested them in Jesus. Others were still repulsed at the brazenness of the production, years after its premiere. *Godspell* entertained millions of people, but no one could tell how many people became Christians as a result of enjoying the play or movie.

"Put Your Hand in the Hand," "Jubilation," "Jesus Is Just Alright," "Jesus Is a Soul Man"—all of the big Jesus hits of the seventies may have kept making Jesus "impressions" on the minds of the hearers, but they didn't bring the country to repentance.

What did make a difference was Jesus music, teamed up with a critical ingredient—witness. The big Top 40 Jesus hits were recorded mainly as a part of the "fad" created by the Jesus movement. It was "in" to sing about Jesus. Thus, there were hits.

But the *real* Jesus music most often was the music by the non-"stars." Music by minstrels whose daily bread was often their only pay. Music by singers whom nobody understood, but who believed in what they were doing for the Lord. Singers who traveled tens of thousands of miles while their spouses sat at home missing them. Musicians whose love for their Heavenly Father stripped away any star image they might have had when they publicly cried on stage in response to what the Lord had done for them.

The living witness of the musicians spoke as loudly as any of the songs they sang. Debby Boone's testimony of her faith in God spoke clearly to all the fans of her smash hit, "You Light Up My Life." B. J. Thomas' vivid testimony in each of his pop concerts spoke of the Lord to the audiences. But, the witness of Christian musicians had to remain as strong and as important as their music, for the public watched and heard both.

So, perhaps in God's infinite wisdom He did not see the necessity of putting a Christian artist with a Jesus song at the top of the charts. The Lord could use stars. He could also use unknowns. The Lord could even use has-beens in his work. But a musician should never strive to be anything else than what his Lord wanted him to be. The goal should never be to be a "star" for Jesus unless the person is already a star. Gaining "star" status brought with it inherent problems. Personalities change, priorities change, purposes change. The performer's goals should be to please the Father, whether it meant singing in one-night stands, or appearing on national television. For, as one Scripture proclaims, "Promotion comes neither from the east, nor from the west, nor from the south. But God is the judge: he puts down one, and exalts another."[2]

17 Time We Returned

During three August days in 1978, the Fellowship of Contemporary Christian Ministries had its third annual retreat, this time in the wooded environs of the Agape Force Ranch near Lindale, Texas. Since the FCCM's formation with charter members in 1975, the membership had grown to more than three hundred and fifty.

Following the three days of fellowship and worship, the topic of discussion was "Where is Jesus music headed? What's the next step?" Talks by ministers Tony Salerno and Winkie Pratney had been calls for return to holiness for all Christians.

One of the people who privately shared his thoughts on the subject was Terry Talbot. In the late 1960s, Terry and his brother John had performed as secular rock musicians in the group Mason Proffit, who had an excellent following through their numerous albums. In 1974 the liner notes on their album, *The Talbot Brothers,* gave hints of their new faith in Christ. Two years later both of them began recording Christian albums for Sparrow Records.

My wife Debbie and I joined Terry on the porch of the guest house, seeking some relief from the sweltering August sun. I asked Terry how Jesus music and the Jesus movement had affected him over the past ten years.

"For those of us who were not involved in it," Terry replied, "the Jesus movement was incredibly small. When I was in the world, I didn't know anything about it or the music. The whole thing to me was a bunch of kids in California who went to the beach every Sunday to be photographed by *Time* magazine. That's all I knew about it. It amazes me in retrospect that that's all we nonbelivers heard about it. I know it was magnificent to be a part of it, but that magnificence never reached me or a lot of other people."

As Terry recounted how small the movement seemed back

then, I recalled the startling number of people I had recently talked to who never even opened a Bible or read a Bible verse until they were well into their twenties. It's so easy to fall into a trap of believing *everyone* knows about the Bible if you do yourself. The truth is, they don't.

"Where were you in 1969 when the Jesus movement was really starting?" I asked.

"We were cutting the first Mason Proffit album."

"None of you were Christians then?"

"No," he replied. "We were brought up in church and I would defend Jesus philosophically to anyone who thought another way was better. I always knew he was the only way, but I didn't know any way to walk with the Lord. I didn't know how.

"When I first came to the Lord, when I was on the road with the Eagles, I still had never heard of the 2nd Chapter of Acts or Larry Norman or Word Records or any of that. And that was only a few years ago! The thing that's amazing to me is that John and I were doing what all of these young Jesus musicians are trying so hard to do! 'Let's go out there, get on a secular concert bill. Then let's go for it and preach the gospel.'

"That's all we *knew* to do! You make a record and do a tour with a major group and you go for it. We'd never heard of all this. We didn't know that Jesus music was called that! It was just more of our music!

"Then I began to hear Jesus music, and to be quite honest, I wasn't real impressed with it. But the Lord dealt with me on that, that not matter how bad it was technically, it still blessed the socks off a lot of people.

"Then I heard 'Easter Song' and I got blown away. I just wept when I heard it."

I asked Terry to share his opinions of where Jesus music was headed. He responded by again referring to the early days of the Jesus movement.

"As the Jesus movement grew, so did a new danger," he said. "I think of what happened in 1969 and 1970. The movement was really made up of the salt of the earth. But it seems the salt stayed in the shaker in many ways. The Lord poured more salt in the shaker, and the cap was put on by the church itself in some cases, and most of the holes were plugged up. Nobody turned it upside down and gave it a shake so that we could fall out. And that's what we need now. The church needs a good shake, and it's happening!

"We've become so introspective, so narcissistic, that we just turn inward and begin to examine ourselves and stop reaching out. I can remember back before I knew the Lord, I was dying! I *needed* someone to reach out!

"I think we're taking the first step toward a revival," he added, "and a return to a genuine desire to walk with Jesus. I think that there are a lot of people in Christian music who don't belong there. God is calling them someplace else and they ought to be there to do whatever it is. I think it's gonna get real big real fast and contemporary Christian music is going to be the harp that heralds the endtimes, the Second Coming.

"David or the musicians would play before the prophets would prophesy. We're in that position. We've taken upon us that office in the body of Christ. So there is that call to a real tight walk with the Lord Jesus. It is heavy! I know in my life right now the Lord is calling me. It's time to take the garbage out and minister, and I don't want to do anything if I don't minister Jesus."

The conversations with Terry Talbot and other seasoned musicians, promoters, broadcasters, even Christian record-store operators, revealed a few disturbing facts by the late seventies. First, there were many people who saw the urgent need for renewal within the Jesus music industry. Just the fact that it was called an industry, and the various cities where the musicians played and recorded their records were by then called "markets," exposed far more than some people wanted to see. The ministry had become a business, and many musicians saw their only way of getting to their goals as succumbing to the "system" which was rapidly being defined. For "success" you needed to be "popular." To be popular you needed "hits." To get hits, you needed more "exposure." For exposure, you signed "contracts." Your songs had to be "commercial."

In his book *The Worldly Evangelicals,* Richard Quebedeaux warned that "Historically, since the time of Constantine, whenever the church has become 'established'—too popular, too respectable— corruption and secularism have become rampant within its ranks."[1] This was too important a warning to treat lightly, because Jesus music, in fact the entire "contemporary gospel" industry (which had overshadowed Jesus music by the late seventies), was vulnerable in the same way as was the entire evangelical church.

The vulnerability wasn't so much a threat that big business would discover Jesus rock and exploit it; they tried it in the early seventies and would again in the early eighties. Each time it lasted only a year or so. The concern needed to be for a vulnerability from *within* the camp. Priorities could be forgotten in the roar of the crowd. And in many cases, the musician had come to worship and serve the Jesus music rather than Jesus. That attitude had encouraged Jesus-music fans to do the same.

As the year 1978 drew to a close, and the first edition of *Why Should the Devil Have All the Good Music?* was being put to press, these were the cautions for the future:

Expert musicianship and sketchy training in the Word doth not an excellent witness make. There is a brand new generation of modern-day Christian "minstrels" now arriving on the scene. They are stepping into the world of contemporary Christian music with no knowledge of the battles fought to keep Jesus music alive during the past ten years, nor any recollection even of why and how Jesus music came about. Meanwhile, the youth of the early Jesus movement are now parents themselves, and I'm sure that it won't be long before even newer and more innovative musical styles will be introduced which will raise *their* eyebrows. Even, heaven forbid, Christian punk rock. (Already certain magazine ads and covers for Christian-rock artists feature photographs of the artists in a somber, grimacing mood very similar to those used in promoting secular punk-rock groups.)

Though the *styles* of the music may shock the fainthearted, they are not the major cause for worry. *Leadership* is— rather, the lack of it. A great number of the new, potential "ministers" of the Jesus-music genre lack any leadership at all—from the churches, but probably worse, even from their peers.

There remains an alarming apathy on the part of many youth ministers and church-music ministers, through which they fail to encourage, nourish, and guide the churched or unchurched youth in their chosen line of endeavor, even ministry. Quite frankly, in all too many cases, there is no one in the church to turn to if a young person's interests lie in communicating the gospel through rock music. Either that particular church categorically denounces rock, or the interpretation of the term "contemporary Christian music" is the stumbling block. The youth minister, music minister, or pastor views all "contemporary Christian music" as being large choral groups of twenty or thirty youth, maybe more, singing middle-of-the-road Christian music which in reality may communicate mainly to the elder members of the congregation. The young person who sees the validity of a Christian *rock* ministry has a completely different type of music in mind. The difference in interpretation ends there, at a stalemate, and the youth's creativity is quite possibly stifled. A potential "music minister" may thus channel his ambitions and energy elsewhere, though he was receiving a genuine call of the Lord in Jesus music.

Church-oriented ministers *must* begin widening their horizons when it comes to youth and their music. Rock music is *not* going to fade away as many adults predicted and hoped. It's here for a long time, like it or not, and the number of people affected by it is constantly growing. *How* they are affected by it can in many ways be determined by the church. Whether or not rock music is to the liking of the leaders, there *are* ways of using it for the glory of God.

Newcomer Jesus musicians also need the expressed concern and the encouragement of their brothers and sisters in the ministry. In conversation with the more established musicians, I have seen a general lack of interest on the part of the "professionals" when it comes to nurturing the younger musicians, and guiding them.

Quite frankly, many of the older Jesus musicians, having been in the "business" for anywhere from four to ten years, are getting tired. Tired of traveling to one-night stands (and trying to keep their families together, too). Tired of leaving behind young audience members who will receive no follow-up after their concert (such as witnessing, invitations to a specific church, or even friendship). Tired of the rejection of their music by so many churches (such as church leaders who never offer the youth of their church a ride on one of their buses to attend a local Jesus-music concert, mainly because someone *else* is putting it on). Tired of trying to serve their Lord in music while they see some trite, "plastic gospel" albums with "commercial" value wedge them out of a recording contract.

No wonder they're fatigued! It's been an uphill climb. And ten years later the problems haven't been solved so much as they have been made more complex. Unfortunately, some of the veteran musicians are about to give up, when the victory could be just around the corner if they would just "press on toward the mark." They are sapped of energy and will, though, and they need renewal.

The tired, established Jesus musicians would probably benefit from a Paul/Timothy relationship with younger musicians. The vitality and the zeal of the young is refreshing, and could well engender a more optimistic view of things. Don't the veterans remember that that same vitality *was* the Jesus movement in the late sixties and early seventies? And far be it for the older ones to *discourage* the younger. Paul, training Timothy for the ministry, *encouraged:* "Let no man despise thy youth, but be thou an example of the believers, in word, in conduct, in love, in spirit, in faith, in purity."[2]

In my work with the Fellowship of Contemporary Christian Ministries, I have received an alarmingly high number of letters from young people wanting advice on their music, their aspirations, and their callings—young people who complain that there is no one who understands them. They are even willing to "submit" themselves as Peter challenged: "Likewise, ye younger, submit yourselves unto the elder. Yea, all of you be subject one to another, and be clothed with humility: for God resisteth the proud, and giveth grace to the humble. Humble yourselves therefore under the mighty hand of God, that he may exalt you in due time: casting all your care upon him; for he careth for you."[3]

But where are the leaders for these "younger" to turn to? On one hand, the church ministers most often seem too busy to involve themselves with someone or something that does not happen within the total confines of their "church program," and the related lack of compassion, or at least understanding, is depressing. On the other hand, many of the Jesus musicians are either run down with no real hope, or they are so occupied with their own music and their own work that they are never even aware of what fellow-musicians are doing, writing, or feeling; much less do they take time to encourage or exhort the newcomers.

Thank God for the preachers, youth ministers, music ministers, musicians, teachers, parents, and others who are taking the time to care—to extend the hand of Christian fellowhsip to these musicians of the eighties and the nineties. The original strength of the Jesus movement didn't come from radio, television, records, or magazines. It came from one-to-one confrontation and one-to-one caring. A great number of the Jesus musicians mentioned in this book were won to the Lord by a face-to-face confrontation with one person. For Noel Paul Stookey, it was someone in a motel room following a concert. For Barry McGuire, it was a Jesus freak on a Hollywood street. For B. J. Thomas, it was his wife. The work of individuals, meeting with and having compassion on these performers, changed their direction and indirectly resulted in thousands of people coming to know Christ as Savior. The work of countless young Christian musicians now seeking to begin their ministries will be just as important in the future years.

Though the observations made in this chapter are somewhat negative, the spirit of the early Jesus movement is still alive today in hundreds of contemporary Christian musicians and likewise in thousands of nonmusicians. The electricity can be felt. Our concern is that this tremendous energy is not stifled.

And it's time we
    returned
    to our call
Otherwise the children
    gonna fall
And it's time we
    returned to
    simplicity
The simple job of
    settin' people
    free. . . .[4]

In its early years, Jesus music was rough on the edges; more or less a jalopy in appearance, but with an extraordinarily dynamic engine within. All the parts worked together quite well, with positive results—especially countless changed lives.

Contemporary Christian music has come a long way since the jalopy days. Recordings sound more professional, and there are more and more of them available. The Christian bookstore operators, once wary of Jesus music and the musicians themselves, are now carrying complete lines of contemporary Christian music. Radio station programmers are gradually widening the limits of musical styles featured, and more and more secular broadcasting outlets are featuring Jesus music on Sunday mornings. Contemporary gospel albums are showing up more frequently as nominations for Grammy and Dove Award-winners. (The Dove is the gospel counterpart of the Grammy.)

But we must make sure that "contemporary gospel," as the industry itself has tagged it, doesn't become a sparkling new show car with a jalopy engine. We've polished the outside until it's starting to gleam, but there is a lot of maintenance on the inside that is being forgotten. Some of the parts of that originally well-tuned engine have become frayed or rusty, through ordinary wear, through misuse, and sometimes through outright neglect. Once we get those inner parts renewed, we'll be truly roadworthy again!

Part II

1979–1984

18/ Hits and Singles

The first and second editions of *Why Should the Devil Have All the Good Music?* ended with the preceding chapter. It was the most difficult of the chapters to write, for it dealt with a tremendous challenge ahead for an art form and ministry which had taken on much of the color of a full-fledged industry not unlike its secular counterpart. Though the growth and the increased availability of Jesus music was definitely worth celebrating, there was a fear that the industry aspects would overshadow the original, ministerial purposes behind the music.

Except for the veterans who had been with it pretty well from the start, Jesus music was no longer called Jesus music by the end of the seventies. It had gradually been absorbed into the more all-encompassing terms of "contemporary gospel" or "contemporary Christian music," which included everything from middle-of-the-road music to the hardest rock. Those terms proved to be more favorable and less exclusive in the marketing of the music. But the spirit of Jesus music was still found on the cutting edge, in songs of the performers who continued to encourage Christian-music reform and experimentation.

There is a certain irony in the fact that the term "Jesus music" was coined in order to avoid the use of the term "Christian," at a time when the established church was being criticized for complacency and hypocrisy. Now, a brief decade later, the term "Jesus music" has faded from the vernacular, because it might prove to be "too exclusive" or "too smug" to the outside world. The term "Christian" was once again preferred.

By 1979 contemporary Christian music—no matter what the tag put on it—was, as a whole, becoming much more tolerated and even accepted within the church. Many church bodies were opening up to many forms of music to which they had been adamantly opposed only a few years prior. As had been the tradition, many churches had gradually (if not reluctantly) followed behind the world's patterns of style and expression by several years. (By the late seventies, the hair on the deacons' heads, and the shirts and ties they wore, more closely paralleled the fashions of the Beatles of 1964 than most would want to admit.)

Folk music and occasional jazz masses continued to be the contemporary music of the Catholic church in America at the end of the seventies. In the evangelical churches, contemporary Christian music had finally begun making its way in, not so many years after groups as righteous and evangelistic as the 2nd Chapter of Acts had been criticized at theaters such as the Baptist Baylor University's auditorium because they dared wear bluejeans onstage. Ironically, a few years later 2nd Chapter of Acts would upgrade their dress, while the college students, in many cases, settled into jeans—designer jeans, at least.

As the number of musicians involved in the penning, production, and performance of contemporary Christian music rapidly increased and the family grew, many songs began to take on a hybrid character, influenced by church music, street music, and pop music. The lines of definition between Christian-music styles continued to blur, much as had already happened in secular pop music.

By 1979, when President Jimmy Carter invited Christian singers and musicians to participate in "Old Fashioned Gospel Singin'" at the White House, there was a fascinating diversity of talent represented under the gospel-music banner. In Washington to represent the contemporary branch of the gospel family tree were Larry Norman, the Archers, Barry McGuire, Reba Rambo, and others. This appearance further entrenched contemporary Christian music in the gospel-music camp, and added further respectability to a music form shunned only a few years before.

Two major songs released on albums in the late seventies greatly contributed to the depolarization of Christian music, probably more than any others. One of them, written and performed by Don Francisco, was a dramatic account of Christ's resurrection, done in a storytelling style of music—folk in nature, but big on production. The soaring chorus of "He's Alive" was a triumphant restatement of the Christian faith, taken up by evangelicals en masse. Some radio stations would report in 1980 that even after being there for more than a year, the song was still in their Top 10 popularity charts, based on listener requests and sales.

Francisco, who had already been writing his folk-style music for ten years, was taken aback by the extreme popularity that came to him as a result of recording such a dynamic song as "He's Alive" and touring with the Bill Gaither Trio, themselves great contributors to the expansion of Christian music tastes.

"I was taken from my own crowd of a few hundred people and put before ten thousand," Don recalled in a 1981 interview. "The first time I got up to sing in front of them, I was terrified! I tried to tell myself I *wasn't* terrified—that I was gonna do this for the Lord. I was *still* terrified!"

Francisco had committed his life to the Lord in the summer of 1974, after living a prodigal life which took him through Eastern philosophies, drugs, and the other, all-too-usual entrapments of the sixties and seventies. After a period of spiritual and physical healing and study in the Word, he began to write Christian songs. Noted producer Gary S. Paxton was impressed by Don's music and produced the first Francisco Christian album, *Brother of the Son*.

But it was the stunning "He's Alive" on a later album which not only made Don Francisco a popular name, but also introduced a singing style unique to contemporary Christian music. Further, it helped popularize the crescendoing, elaborate production style which would later be further utilized in songs by artists such as Sandi Patti and the Imperials, as well as the other innovators of that style, the Bill Gaither Trio and Doug Oldham.

The other song which most helped to break down the barriers between Christian music styles was "Rise Again," recorded by Dallas Holm & Praise. They were a Texas-based group, an active part of David Wilkerson's crusade evangelism. Much like Francisco, Holm in no way expected his composition to be one of the first "smash hit" songs in contemporary Christian music. As he said on their *Live* album, where the song first appeared on vinyl:

> This one came to me in a real special way. I couldn't really describe or explain how it happened. Some songs that I've written I've just maybe sat down and decided, 'Well, today's job is to write a song. . . .' But there's other times that . . . (comes) just a special kind of inspiration—something you can't put your finger on, but it happens. And this was one of those times when this song came to me. It's really what the Lord was saying through me.

As with "He's Alive," Holm's portrait of Christ's crucifixion and resurrection was a victorious Easter song around which believers rallied. Though perhaps not as overtly contemporary as "He's Alive," the song managed to attract fans of both traditional and contemporary Christian music. Both songs became anthems for much of the contemporary body of Christ, much as "Easter Song" by the 2nd Chapter of Acts and "Alleluia" or "The King Is Coming" by Bill and Gloria Gaither had become earlier.

Though there obviously had been other popular Jesus-music songs before 1979, the proliferation of contemporary Christian radio gradually turned the concept of "popular" gospel songs into "hit" gospel songs. If enough stations played a song such as "Rise Again" or "He's Alive" regularly, the concerted buying power of the consumer began to be realized in the record sections of the Christian book and record stores and at the record companies themselves. Not every city had stations playing contemporary Christian music, but where they were, sales followed, such as in Denver and northern Colorado in response to KBRN and KFKZ.

It was partly through such an effort that the *Live* album by Dallas Holm & Praise ultimately sold more than five hundred thousand copies and would earn gold-record status by 1984, only the fourth on a gospel label to do so at that time.

The record companies began paying more and more attention to selecting single cuts from albums and putting them onto 45-rpm singles, to help target radio airplay on specific songs. By doing that, they reasoned, the play would be more concentrated, and the album would have longer "shelf life." As the first hit waned, they could press a second 45 single and send it to the radio stations in order to sustain the interest in the album.

If that reasoning sounded a bit like the pop music industry, it was no coincidence. Leaders in the gospel music business admitted that much of what they did was patterned after the secular. It was the only effective model they had.

Gospel music did present a challenge that differed from the secular industry, however. The life of some albums on what sales charts there were for gospel music at the time indicated an admirable staying power not often experienced by secular recording artists. The same went for single songs on the radio airplay popularity charts. The longest a normal secular song could survive on the hit charts was about twenty-three weeks, while some gospel songs remained for more than a year.

The gospel labels thus reasoned that they could get even more mileage out of the albums by focusing on one single at a time. Some of them eventually went a step past pressing singles for radio play: they began releasing *only* singles to the radio stations (and not the album), even after the album was available to consumers in the stores. By this method, they reasoned, play on the specific song would be insured, and that would help bring about a more successful, unified hit across America. Some programmers balked at the method, complaining that this left them little latitude in programming their own particular stations.

"That's right," the labels responded, citing their own justification for the strategy. Only in recent years had there been Christian-music radio stations. Sadly, Christian radio did not have the grandest reputation for knowledgeable music direction. Though there were some music directors who knew very well how to program the music, there were an equal number, or perhaps more, who didn't. The latter would receive an album and play all or several of the cuts on it right away, rushing to be the first.

The record companies argued that the result was no concentrated play, hence no staying power, and the album was spent prematurely. The programmers would retort that if a song was good enough to be a hit, it would be chosen on its own merit and get that desired concentrated airplay—in other words, rise to the top on its own.

In the programmers' defense, the supply of quality contemporary Christian music had been greatly limited over the years, and often picking just one cut at a time from an album was too prohibitive to the programmer and to the station's listeners. After all, if an artist had recorded an album, didn't they want it played? More perturbing was the embarrassment the programmers faced when the consumers could get records at stores before the radio stations had them.

Unfortunately, even as late as 1984, the system would not be worked out to everyone's approval. In the words of one record company spokesperson, "It's all being fussed about in the secular side of the business too." Conferences held for the benefit of secular broadcasters experienced the same debate between radio station programmers and record companies.

There was one difference, however. Christian radio had the added dimension of *spiritual import* in the lyrics performed by Christian artists. Songs were intended to minister as well as entertain. Going for the most commercial song on an album did not necessarily mean going for the most valuable one from a spiritual perspective. Was holding back on these songs quenching the Spirit? While commercial-sounding, hookish songs got radio exposure, how many edifying and ministering songs never got nationwide exposure because of the system?

Thus the debate continued, gradually moving on to less heated diatribes and more helpful and constructive discussions at seminars, workshops, and conferences across the country. Both sides had good points; the challenge was to work them out for the good of all concerned.

Perhaps the greatest irony of the gospel singles "market" was that there was, even as late as 1984, no market. Singles, sent to radio stations to concentrate airplay, were used only as promotional tools to direct listeners to albums. But, with only one or two exceptions, the singles could not be bought. (Word released an "Ageless Medley" by Amy Grant on a 7-inch, 33⅓ disc for promotion of one of her albums, and PTL Records successfully marketed a Christian version of "Up Where We Belong" and a Pat Boone single in several regions in the early eighties.)

Many Christian bookstore proprietors didn't want to carry singles, citing that they were "too much trouble" to display or handle. Record companies didn't want them for virtually the same reason, plus they had more interest in long-term albums.

In other words, gospel music was an album market, and both the record labels and the stores liked it that way, evidently regardless of how the consumer felt. Though there were many times when certain popular Christian songs would have sold well as 45 singles, the few major labels nixed the idea, perhaps because a "hit" still did not constitute enough sales to merit selling singles. Thus the majority of inroads were closed, except for small, independent labels selling their singles by mail or in a very limited number of outlets. If a song was a "hit," the consumer had to buy the albums to get the song. (The booming blank-cassette business helped remedy the problem to thousands of radio listeners anyway, who just taped their favorite songs from the radio instead of being obliged to purchase an entire album from which it came.)

This put the young, radio-listening (or jukebox-listening), record-buying consumer at a marked disadvantage if he or she preferred or switched over to Christian music. Such a consumer was already usually hit with full retail record prices, which most stores charged. The stores' special prices, when they had them, were on special "albums of the month," or new budget lines for records which started in the early eighties. The other major way of buying records and tapes in the stores at a discount was through bonus clubs, in which the consumer could buy a certain number of albums and then get one free. These were a beneficial service extended by the record labels to the consumer.

But when it came to singles, the gospel music industry had the dubious honor of having national popularity charts of hit single songs which were not available to consumers as single songs.

Helping to establish a gauge of popularity (or at least sales) of specific albums or songs were the song charts appearing in various publications over the years. They included, at one time or another: *Harmony*, which folded after its twelfth issue, in 1977; *Gospel Trade*, a relatively short-lived Nashville publication; *Singing News*, an influential southern-gospel newspaper which by the early eighties was at least accommodating some contemporary-music news items and charts; *Bookstore Journal*, the most respected monthly journal of the large Christian Booksellers Association; *Christian Bookseller*, which premiered their "Music Makers" section in May 1978; *Foreversong Journal*, a 1978-79 radio-oriented worksheet published by Dan Hickling; *The Radio Report*, originally edited and published by John Taylor; *Contemporary Christian Music*, which debuted in July 1978; and *MusicLine*, the 1983 offshoot of *Contemporary Christian Music*, begun when the latter became *Comtemporary Christian Magazine*. *Contemporary Christian Music (CCM)* quickly became the most influential magazine for that branch of gospel music.

CCM undoubtedly helped to focus widespread contemporary music efforts into a more unified industry, much like *Harmony* had done earlier on a smaller scale. Such a publication was definitely needed to create a "team effort" in further developing Christian music. Not only did it help the industry to expand, but it also created an accessible forum where the technical and spiritual aspects of current Christian music could be discussed.

CCM began as a trade newspaper, more or less an offshoot from *Contemporary Christian Acts*, a general interest tabloid aimed at the Christian consumer, especially in Southern California. When *Acts* announced they would have to begin charging for the publication instead of distributing it free, support waned and the paper folded. Out of those ashes came *CCM*.

Later the magazine would be changed from a trade tabloid into a type of Christian *Rolling Stone*, becoming an alternative publication which unabashedly defended Christian rock and sought to further all types of contemporary Christian music. Its design was sleekened over the ensuing years, going to a large, glossy format much like the secular international music newsweekly *Billboard*. In late 1981 *CCM* was again modified, into a more compact, standard, newsstand-favorable size. Newsstand distribution was a long-range goal in publisher John Styll's mind.

In 1983, at a circulation of close to forty thousand, enjoying the position of second-best-selling magazine in Christian bookstores, *CCM* again reformatted, this time to become a contemporary Christian, general-interest magazine. The editors sought to give more indepth attention to nonmusic news and issues, while preserving the music slant to much of each issue. Renamed *Contemporary Christian Magazine* in 1983, the publication began showing a marked increase in reports on where contemporary Christian music was making inroads into the secular music and entertainment scene, or at least where Christian music makers were being seen in secular company. The new *CCM,* skewed toward the California music and entertainment industry, also included reviews of secular movies such as *Footloose* and *Gremlins,* secular albums such as one by the Police, open quotes from known antichristian performers such as Ozzy Osbourne, photos of Christian musicians in the company of movie and recording stars, and the like.

Though *CCM* contained meaty, issue-oriented articles and interviews with Christian leaders and with newsmakers, the inclusion of the entertainment-slanted material bothered some purists, who felt that the magazine of contemporary Christian music in general should not fraternize so freely with the world or seek to be so "hip." These conservatives felt that the magazine should have stayed within the Christian community entirely. The change in emphasis also left the gospel labels less opportunity for articles and items on their artists, including cover publicity.

In May 1983, CCM Publications premiered *MusicLine,* more or less the early *CCM* revisited. *MusicLine* took on the trade-oriented features and articles which had earlier been a part of *CCM.* Thanks to its newspaper-type layout and production, it provided the gospel trade news in a much more timely fashion than the more polished and preplanned *CCM* could do.

MusicLine offered first-class mailing of its issues to subscribers (a first for gospel music), and provided a vehicle for prompt dissemination of trade information and news. Such a service helped to jettison the gospel-music trade into the information age.

There were a few other notable magazines published in the late seventies and early eighties which carried substantial news on the contemporary gospel music industry. *Cornerstone* continued its insightful articles about music, as well as advertising and reviews about records. *Progressive Pacer,* published in Minnesota, was a Jesus-rock music magazine. *Motif,* published out of Georgia, was a Christian arts magazine which included some music coverage. *Windstorm* was a short-lived, full-color, glossy publication predominantly about contemporary Christian music. *Sounds of Triumph* was a newspaper published as an adjunct to a Jesus-rock radio program hosted and produced by Gord Driver in Toronto, Ontario, published in the late seventies. *Firewind* was another Canadian newspaper, edited by Chuck Clements, and filled with news about contemporary Christian music, published in the late seventies. *Concert* was a music-oriented publication out of the northeastern U.S., the last region of the country to get a solid hold on contemporary Christian music.

Magazines such as *Campus Life, Group,* and a few others occasionally ran features on musicians or the music, but their coverage was limited. By the mideighties, there was a definite gap needing to be filled. The big, national publications put much more emphasis on the well-known and well-promoted musicians and singers, the ones usually with major record labels to push for coverage in the press. In a situation similar to the plight experienced by Jesus music in its infancy, the local, regional, and less-hyped musicians had virtually nowhere to go to inform people of their whereabouts or their ministries. There were only a few exceptions: self-published papers or newsletters; paid ads in the national publications; the FCCM National Newsletter; or the *Christian Activities Calendar,* published in Southern California and in Chicago for those respective areas, with listings of all known concerts. For effective communication between *all* ministries and the people served by them, there was a definite need for much more extensive work and coverage.

19/ Music and Mammon: Entertainment or Ministry?

As the gospel music industry got more sophisticated in the eighties, there was constant dialogue behind the scenes regarding how far was "too far" in building an industry and paralleling pop music trends, not just in music style, but in publicity, promotion, glamorization, and exploitation. On the positive side, the recordings had improved in quality of sound over the years. The album art, such as on the covers of Christian rock group Petra's albums, was easily on par with secular cover art. The advance in getting the records and tapes to the front of the stores was a most notable step forward, as was the never-ending search by the record companies to find new outlets to sell the product.

However, sometimes advertisements for the product boasted clichéd phrases and slogans which resembled, too closely, slick Madison Avenue and Hollywood sales jobs. An uncomfortable majority of artists were being portrayed as being "one of the finest in Christian music," a claim which quickly lost any meaning through its overuse.

One artist's contract for concerts required that fresh roses be given to her onstage following each performance, presumably to further an image-building campaign for her. In some cases, prices asked by artists, agents, and managers for concerts escalated radically, taking concerts virtually out of reach for many churches and promoters. Awards and competitions such as the Doves and gospel Grammies became more publicized and sought-after as goals rather than honors incidental to the work of spreading the Good News and building the Kingdom of Christ.

Thus, the historical tracking of the growth of gospel music became increasingly based on standards and milestones constructed by the industry to further itself: songs of the year, albums of the year, artists of the year, and so on. Having the best-selling album was mistakenly equated with having the greatest and most effective ministry.

There developed two distinctly different contemporary Christian mindsets. The questions kept coming up over and over: Is the music a ministry, or is it entertainment? Can it be both? Should there be such a thing as Christian entertainment? How far was too far in becoming like the pop-music industry? At what point came the change from the Christian musicians using the tools of pop music, to the tools of pop music using the Christian musician? Was it possible to build a widespread gospel-music voice which would be heard without resorting to the tactics of Madison Avenue or the world? On the other hand, was it such a sin to use those tactics to win the world to Jesus? Would Jesus have done the same thing?

Needless to say, these questions and other similar ones made for lively forums and discussions. Opinions were as varied as the people expressing them. One fact must be brought out, however. The motives, on both sides, were nearly always sincere and well-intentioned, rarely malicious. There appeared to be only a few musicians and contemporary Christian music industry people who did their work solely for their own gain. Any entrepreneurs of that cut were usually quickly found out and did not survive the contemporary Christian music scene for long. On the whole, motives were spiritually based. There were just myriad ways of approaching the ministry and the entertainment provided through music. Each person had to make an individual decision whether to go with the flow or fight it, whether to be a leader or a follower, radical or conservative, minister or entertainer. That's what made contemporary music so interesting but controversial.

There were some musicians who chose to shun what they perceived as the trappings of the music "business." Keith Green was the most vocal about doing so. He recorded his first album of Jesus music, *For Him Who Has Ears to Hear,* for Sparrow Records in 1977. It was very well received. Over the months and years to follow, Green's music became increasingly searing in challenging the church to holiness without compromise. His songs, though often exhortative, rapidly gained favor with music fans and increased the fervor of many to evangelize. He thus carried on the tradition of the early Jesus musicians.

In 1980 the twenty-seven-year-old writer and singer took the music community by surprise when he announced that beginning with the release of his album *So You Wanna Go Back to Egypt,* his albums and tapes would no longer be sold for any listed price.

Instead, his product would be *given* to anyone unable to get them because of lack of money. The maverick musician said that too many people were missing out on the music and the message for that reason.

Several predictions came forth as a result of the announcement. Some critics said he would quickly go bust, that all the Christians would swamp him with freebie requests and he wouldn't be able to support the method for long. Others said the newness would wear off, reality would set in, and Green would return to a more universally accepted form of marketing. A few artists were even perturbed at the move, which created an undercut of their own album prices, constituting what they considered to be an unfair competitive edge. But they weren't able to say much because of the altruistic nature of Green's decision.

Most, however, watched with a mixture of awe and fascination, curious to see if Green's Pretty Good Records (the label name) would succeed in "bucking the system." Green's bold step of faith was quite respected by many. The effort evidently was a success, and the revenue from the record orders sustained the system. While some people requested the albums for free, others paid more than what the list price would have been, and the plan worked fine. Because of the great continued demand for his albums, the policy would later be modified to allow retail stores to carry the records and tapes too, but only with a variable price option.

Several other artists, some without as much fanfare, would gradually modify their methods of selling their records and tapes, at least in concerts. Such a policy was only feasible for many artists on commercial labels if they carried it out at concerts, where the artists could establish their own prices. In retail stores the price structure was out of their hands, unless they were on their own labels.

Another move which proved as controversial as Green's record policy was that of some artists deciding to change from ticketed to offering-only concerts. The subject was hotly debated in several places, including the 1977 national conference of the Fellowship of Contemporary Christian Ministries (FCCM). The disagreement there and elsewhere fell mainly between artists and concert promoters.

To some musicians, "offering" concerts were viewed as more in keeping with traditional Christianity, and ticketed concerts were more related to the secular entertainment world. Thus certain artists, such as 2nd Chapter of Acts, opted for the former. This frustrated certain Christian concert promoters who felt the Lord had led them into concert promotion, but had no guarantees to pay the bills necessary in putting on an offering concert, with no budgeting possible. Promoters said faith was okay, but the money for procuring and guaranteeing the halls and advertising the concerts had to be paid up front, constituting a gamble for the promoter. After the offering money was divided following the concert, what if there wasn't enough to pay the bills? Who lost? The dialogue continued.

A similar type of discussion ensued when some churches began sponsoring free concert series featuring contemporary Christian artists, while certain promoters continued to put on ticketed concerts in the same cities. In some cases the churches and the promoters worked at odds with each other, a vestige of the old "street vs. church" arguments of earlier days. One of the greatest dangers in these situations was the potential for overbooking an area with concerts or scheduling concerts too close together for either to maximize their draw.

The choice of going the nonticket route may have been the result of a guilty conscience in some cases. Some musicians found they were pricing themselves away from the very people they were supposed to reach, much the same problem expressed by Keith Green in regards to album pricing. However, others felt that paid entertainment was not evil in and of itself, and they preferred to continue entertaining the body of Christ, charging for it, and not feeling guilty about it. Their concerts, they reasoned, were excellent alternative entertainment for people who would otherwise be spending their money on raunchy rock concerts, questionable movies, or staying at home watching TV. And with current pop music, rock especially, the cost of putting on a concert and traveling with personnel and equipment from city to city had become exorbitant as prices for equipment and travel increased.

More and more artists ultimately helped to foot the bills for their travel and equipment (and paying off their album production expenses) through the sale of items at concerts. Albums, tapes, sheet music, book music, T-shirts emblazoned with some Christian sentiment or the name of the artist or group, and other various souvenirs often brought in the necessary revenue. Album and tape sales in the foyers were, in many cases, quite hefty, but several artists laughingly conceded that T-shirt sales outstripped the sale of their recordings at concerts. Many of the musicians finally realized that the "trinket tables" of the southern-gospel groups which they had derided not so long ago somehow made more sense now.

The trend toward "love offering" concerts would become even more pronounced in 1984, when two major concert groups announced they were going the free concert route. Truth, a group of ever-changing personnel born out of a motive similar to that of the Continentals and the Spurrlows, had been founded in 1971. Thirty-one albums later, director and founder Roger Breland explained how Truth was seeing the importance of making changes. He stated plans to go back to churches, where many of their initial concerts were, rather than performing in so many auditoriums for paid admissions.

"I think that Christian music is only speaking to a handful of people in the world today," he said, "and there's a great big world out there. Our ministry has gone back to the basics. If Billy Graham's statistics are right, and 75 percent of the people who go to church are not Christian, there's a lot of work to be done right in the church. We feel we've come full circle, right back to where we started."

Dallas Holm & Praise also changed to "offering-only" concerts, because "God has told us specifically to do it," Holm explained in 1984. "It's not right for everyone. A lot of things have changed both in Christian music and in our ministry, and we just had to reevaluate.

"I think free concerts will bring in a lot more unsaved young people, the people we really want to reach. I think it's going to *enable* them to come in, whereas why should an unsaved kid spend seven dollars to come hear a Christian singer or musician? The bottom line is souls, and there's no question in my mind that more people will come for free, especially the type we want to reach. It really is healthy for us, because it really does make you rely on faith in the Lord more.

"Sometimes you can get too comfortable when you get where you can project things. You know what your income's going to be. You have a clear picture of your whole operation, but often that doesn't require a whole lot of faith."

Many of Holm's observations sounded very much akin to what Keith Green had expressed seven years earlier. Holm's driving motivation in 1984 became one taken up by several others in the eighties who felt a stronger burden than ever for reaching out with the gospel to as many people as possible.

20/ *Reaching the Young*

Dallas Holm and his group Praise based themselves in a small, rural community in east Texas. About an hour drive east of Dallas on Interstate 20, Lindale is nestled in gently rolling, wooded hills. The scenery is nothing like what most people think Texas should be; sagebrush, cactus, and desert are hundreds of miles away from Lindale.

The small community is somewhat overshadowed by nearby Tyler, a town well-known for its beautiful Tyler roses. However, Lindale became a flowering center of another sort during the seventies and eighties. In the wooded environs surrounding it, a surprising number of contemporary Christian ministries sprouted and grew to world-reaching proportions.

Among the first contemporary Christian music makers to settle there were Jimmy and Carol Owens, who moved from the California hills in the midseventies. They were composers of the landmark church musicals *Come Together, If My People,* and *The Witness.*

David Wilkerson, famed evangelist and author of *The Cross and the Switchblade,* also settled near Lindale to base his worldwide outreach there. Dallas Holm & Praise toured with and assisted Wilkerson in his crusades.

Keith Green moved his Last Days Ministries to Lindale from California, followed later by the 2nd Chapter of Acts singing group. Youth with a Mission also settled in the Lindale area. Nearby in Tyler lived Jerry Williams and Ed Kerr, the duo making up Harvest.

Though people had come from various parts of the country to settle in the Lindale area, the main trail seemed to lead from California, including the exodus of Agape Force Ministries, the group which had several years prior worked closely with singer Barry McGuire in his infant Christian years. Agape Force, led by Tony

Salerno, set up a training school for missionary work to be carried on especially in the streets of American capitals and college towns. The Agape Force Ranch, adjacent to the Wilkerson land, became a staging area for young street-workers.

The laid-back, sleepy east Texas countryside, complete with grazing cattle and placid ponds, provided a retreatlike atmosphere for the various groups to prepare themselves for the work to be done, much of it through music. But though the environs appeared tranquil, within the buildings on the grounds of these ministries the activity was never-ceasing. Music was being composed, books were being written, sermons were being prepared. Highly respected Christian teachers and thinkers such as Winkie Pratney and Leonard Ravenhill contributed their teachings, to be added to the work of Wilkerson, Salerno, and Green. And young people were being armed to minister whenever and wherever the Lord called.

Music was a major part of all the ministries based in Lindale. Within the Agape Force alone, there were several music outreaches, including Christian pop group Silverwind, praise group Candle, countrified trio Streetlight, and the carnival-type group known as Gingerbrook Fare, complete with clowns.

There was a great desire early on at the Agape Force to see young people reached not only with the story of salvation through Jesus, but also with the nurture that comes from learning God's precepts from his Word. While in California the Force sensed tragedy among children.

"As we worked with the young people on the street," explained Salerno in 1978, "we would see, passing by us, teenagers and children that were unsupervised, uncared for, able to do anything they wanted, and involved in horrible sin. It was quite shocking to us at first."

Salerno and the Agape Force workers saw that reaching teens wasn't enough. They had to work with younger children as well—the teenagers and adults of the future.

"Children that we saw," Salerno added, "were growing up in their important and tender years without any knowledge of God at all, except in their own consciences. But there was nothing to *reinforce* their consciences! They weren't going to church; they weren't hearing about God in school, unless it was something negative. We felt we *had* to get the message to them."

Salerno's observations were astute indeed. In the years to follow, the problem with unloved and undirected children would become a national blight brought to prominent attention. The Agape Force found that music and drama were the best ways to teach the children God's Word.

The Agape Force's first full-fledged children's musical, *Agapeland*, had been introduced in 1974. Many of the character concepts in that musical had come from the Force's work in the streets, in the ghettos, door to door. When their *Agapeland* record was complete, the sales of the album took the same route. Nearly eighty thousand copies were sold door to door by Agape Force members, remarkable movement for any gospel album at that time. The Force found that parents who might not be receptive to being preached to at the door were quite receptive to purchasing an album for their children, even if it was a Christian children's album.

Agapeland, however, took so much time to prepare and perform as a musical that Salerno ultimately decided to continue producing the musicals on record, but to leave the actual stage production of them to schools and churches. The Agape Force worked out an arrangement with the then-new Sparrow Records to distribute the albums for retail sales internationally (except the original *Agapeland* LP, distributed by Word). The Force team members would continue to sell records door to door.

To come would be a string of musicals based on the original Agapeland theme. Each was written and recorded to encourage better application of Christian principles in children's lives. Also, associated production aids and related curricula were devised and distributed from the Lindale headquarters.

In 1981 *The Music Machine,* one of the early Agapeland series, which taught about the fruit of the Spirit, became only the second album on a gospel label to reach certified gold status, signifying the sale of five hundred thousand copies. That half million only accounted for store sales, and not the ones sold door to door. In 1985 the album was predicted to reach platinum status, signifying the sale of one million copies.

Out of another musical, *Bullfrogs and Butterflies,* came the most popular of the Agapeland songs. The title song, performed by Barry McGuire, became a classic. The album was expected to reach gold status in late 1984 or early 1985.

The albums created by the Agape Force can be considered a most important part of the history of contemporary Christian music. They were a highly conscientious effort to present the gospel of Christ to children in a quality way. By utilizing all forms of contemporary music in the presentations, they successfully reached a generation which had been all but forgotten on many fronts. The younger people first raised on Agapeland musicals were in their teens by the time the eighties were underway, and in some cases the Agapeland musicals had been one of the few bridges of the generation gap which existed in Christian music itself.

It would be a mistake, however, to conclude that there were no other effective children's albums. Projects by Clark Gassman, Flo Price, Super Gang, the Rambos, the Gaithers, and the Maranatha! Music *Kid's Praise* series of albums all were highly important ventures into the world of communicating to children. The music from their albums would be sung for generations to come.

21/ Crossing Over from the Other Side

As discussed earlier in this history, scores of young Jesus musicians got their starts through Maranatha! Music and the associated record company started as an outreach of Calvary Chapel in Costa Mesa, California. By the end of the seventies, there were around fifty Calvary Chapels which had sprung up around the country, constituting one of the largest "nondenominations" in America. (The leadership shunned the classification which would lump all of the Chapels into the very category so many of its members had sought to escape: denominationalism.)

Each Calvary Chapel was different in its own way, but most of them based their work on ideas from home base. From a national perspective, though, the ministry of the Calvary Chapels continued to manifest itself especially in the excellent music pouring forth from Maranatha! Music and Records, A & S Records, and the related Ministry Resource Center (MRC). Their ministries continued to be very much a part of the cutting edge, daring to experiment in new forms of music, from praise choruses to rock, from the *Kid's Praise* children's albums to adult mood music.

The MRC was designed as a training ground and starting-point for new artists and groups. Though not exactly the same, some of the services of the MRC were similar to those offered through the Fellowship of Contemporary Christian Ministries (FCCM). However, the FCCM did not have the same financial base for development as did MRC, and the going was rougher. Since some West Coast ministries often showed little interest in working with organizations or churches from outside their own geographical region or jurisdiction, no strong bond developed between the two organizations.

In microcosm, such duplication of efforts and poor cooperation between individual fellowships was a problem which developed fairly early in the history of Jesus music and was not yet totally solved in the eighties. In spite of efforts to bridge the chasm, West Coast, East Coast, and Midwest Christianity often found difficulty in interrelating. As large as the United States was, sheer geographical separation made it tough in many cases.

In the FCCM, the least populated regions for membership were the Plains and Rocky Mountain regions and the West Coast. Cities in much of the Plains and Rocky mountain states were practically islands, they were so distant from each other. With gas prices leaping to way over a dollar a gallon, travel became more costly, and fellowship through regional and national conferences was more difficult than it had already been. Separated from the rest of the nation by a vast expanse of desert, the West Coast, particularly California, was pretty well an island unto itself, developing a unique lifestyle and form of regionalistic loyalty. In fact, one major West Coast concert promoter shied away from featuring artists from anywhere but California.

People traveling from one part of the country to another often noticed a distinct difference in the musical preferences among Christians, and just who the most popular Christian singers were. While one artist was considered the most popular in one region, he or she would be virtually unheard of in another.

In the Southeast, for example, contemporary Christian music was just beginning to show tremendous growth around the end of the seventies. The region was a latecomer in establishing itself thusly, but once the growth began, it became one of the most active regions for contemporary Christian music and work, especially on the less-publicized street level. Part of that slow start may be attributed to the generally charismatic nature of Jesus musicians, who were suspect in the eyes of the strong Southern Baptist churches of the South. For instance, some Baptist church leaders would not escort their youth groups to the large annual Jesus festivals in Orlando (such as Jesus '80), worried about their young people being proselyted by the charismatic speakers and singers.

East and West had been somewhat pitted against each other in other ways also. Nashville, long recognized as a gospel-music center, faced Los Angeles, where contemporary music developed and flourished. *Singing News* was published in the Southeast. *CCM* was published in California. *Singing News* highlighted southern gospel; *CCM* highlighted contemporary Christian music. The content of the magazines allowed for coverage of news and music from all parts of the country, but the prominent features generally followed regional lines of patriotism. And each explained that it was because their region was where things were happening the most. Whether the magazines caused such an East-West mentality or whether they only reflected what already existed is up for debate.

The mention of such problems as the East-West debate or ministry vs. evangelism might tend to make the reader assume that there were nothing but problems within contemporary Christian music, or that this book dwells on the negative. The fact is, the dichotomies existed and were very much a part of the history, though they were fairly well kept behind the scenes. But such a history as this would not be authentic if it did not observe the differences as well as the smooth-going side of the contemporary Christian music work. Such problems in and of themselves are not negative; in any growth there should be open dialogue and discussion of differences in order to improve upon the future.

On the positive side, there were several factors contributing to the bridging of regional barriers or gaps. Artists were hard at work touring, crisscrossing the country with their musical message. The extensive and commendable work of record companies in getting product out, as mentioned before, also helped. The increased interest among Christian booksellers to give records an honest try put music product in a more prominent position. As a result, music sales increased from 9 percent of total sales in 1976 to 25 percent in 1984, an increase of 250 percent. In the overall recording industry, gospel recordings accounted for 5 percent of the money spent in retail stores for albums and tapes.

Radio stations expanded their music hours, giving more exposure to the artists and their songs. Concert promoters endeavored to bring in artists for concerts which would minister to the public. Christian magazines covered more music topics. Record companies helped spread the music by appointing regional sales representatives who could feel the pulse of their own regions of the country and report local trends back to their home companies.

Perhaps one of the most important gap-narrowers on a national scope was the tremendous work done by Christian television. The advent of satellite broadcasts greatly lessened the distances between the various regions of the United States. Ultimately the space-age technology would mean immediate access in virtually every home in America to the best and worst Christian television programming, be it a house trailer in Searchlight, Nevada, a white frame house in Prairie City, Iowa, or a cabin in the Maine woods.

Nationwide radio accessibility showed promise with satellite too. In 1981 the Continental Satellite Radio Network took to the air from WXRI-FM in Virginia, sponsored by the Christian Broadcasting Network. Top-name personalities were enlisted for the continent-girding network, and high hopes reigned—for awhile. It was a fairly brief, ill-fated flight, however, as the Network failed to sign up enough receiver stations to make the venture financially feasible. Only a year or so later the Network, which featured music in a secular positive pop/Christian contemporary mix, went silent.

Satellite television was a different story. Though gradual, the growing use of video to broadcast the Good News via gospel music showed signs of promise. The PTL Television Network became the first all-satellite network, while CBN used the burgeoning cable possibilities to become a highly respected cable "fourth network." The Trinity Broadcasting Network, based in California, also began satellite broadcasts. Each of these three major Christian TV networks began to feature contemporary Christian musicians and their music for viewers from the Atlantic to the Pacific and beyond.

New horizons had been discovered and explored in 1979 with Hosanna USA, an extravagant concert performed at the Anaheim Convention Center in California, attended by ten thousand people inside and four thousand outside the building. What made this concert unique was its transmission live via satellite nationwide, a first for contemporary Christian music.

The concert, emceed by Calvary Chapel Denver's Tom Stipe, was sponsored by Maranatha! Ministries and featured Kelly Willard, Benny Hester, Leon Patillo, and Denny Correll. Pastor Chuck Smith delivered a "hosanna message" to conclude the concert.

Most of the artists featured in that satellite telecast were "crossover" artists, having defected to Christian music following dramatic conversions in their spiritual lives. Benny Hester had recorded a secular album previously, while based in Las Vegas; Leon Patillo had performed as keyboardist and singer with secular group Santana; Denny Correll had been part of the San Francisco Bay Area early-seventies rock group Blues Image.

The list of artists crossing over from the secular side of the pop-music fence was lengthening at a pace invigorating and exciting for Christian music fans. Many Christians followed secular pop music too, and they were overjoyed to see some of the musicians they had already watched closely add new dimension to their music.

The strongest reaction came when news filtered out, first through fast-traveling rumors, that Bob Dylan had become a Christian. Viewed by many observers and musicologists as the most influential single lyricist of the sixties, Dylan had evidently brought his long-time spiritual odyssey to the cross of Jesus, according to the rumors and later news reports. After talking with pastors of the Vineyard Fellowship in Tarzana, California, Dylan had reportedly prayed to receive Jesus Christ as Savior. Or, as the secular press was wont to explain, he "got religion."

Dylan, always the enigmatic one, so stunned the music industry by this revelation that the occasion even prompted a rushed book entitled, *Dylan—What Happened?* It was released immediately following a series of concerts in late 1979, during which Dylan seemed to remove most doubts about his conversion, except for those expressed by the most skeptical critics.

In his concerts, Dylan incensed many of his longtime fans, not so much by changing his tune, but by changing his lyrics. A concert review in *The Denver Post* was typical in its sarcastic tone: "Now that Dylan's enamored of religion, a charitable review would be 'Christian,'" it read. His fans were evidently quite content with his continuing his spiritual search and sticking with his old hits in the meantime, rather than settling on something as "ordinary" as born-againism.

Dylan appeared on the popular "Saturday Night Live" TV show, performing what would become his Grammy-winning song, "Gotta Serve Somebody." That song was chosen to be the first single off Dylan's controversial *Slow Train Coming* LP, heavy with Christian symbolism down to the cover art, and recognized by some Christian music people as one of the finest rock statements of the Christian faith ever recorded. The vibrant selection of songs on the LP was full of bumper-sticker slogans, which Dylan seemed unmatched in creating. The title song put it as blatantly as could be for a searching world: "It might be the devil, or it might be the Lord, but you gotta serve somebody."

When reporters tried to get to him for interviews, Dylan was just as elusive and reclusive as ever, prompting some Christians to begin doubting him, further questioning stories about his conversion. Finally in 1980 he consented to an interview with the *Los Angeles Times*. In it, he freely spoke about his belief in Christ.

Dylan repeated in the few interviews he gave that the music said everything about where he was and how he felt. Even Columbia Records, his label, couldn't seem to get a handle on the new Dylan. How do you market a stern rocker singing about Jesus? It had been a question they had encountered before on a small scale, but never with a giant like Dylan. Seeing his conversion as a sure slice in record sales, it appeared that they more or less let rumors fly unabated about Dylan's rumored subsequent return to practicing Judaism in 1982, following Dylan's attendance of his son's bar mitzvah. He was also reported to have visited the Lubovich Hassidic sect, noted for its work in drawing alienated Jews back into the fold.

To some, it evidently appeared that Dylan's odyssey wasn't over yet. To others, the speculation was that Dylan was just choosing to keep silent, as usual, rather than grandstanding his religion.

Finally, in 1984, after three postconversion albums—*Slow Train Coming, Saved,* and *Shot of Love*—Dylan granted an interview with *Rolling Stone.* He was quoted in giant, headline-style letters: "I never said I was born again." However, the startling quote was taken out of context. The article, though salted with less-than Christian language, confirmed in Dylan's own words his high respect for the Bible and his literal belief in it, especially the Book of Revelation. His confession of never having said he was "born again" could have been typical semantical sparring, his true feeling, or somewhere in between. The mystery continued in a sort of Howard Hughes avoidance of the truth.

Regardless of where he stood in 1984, Dylan had helped in the early years of the eighties to add considerable momentum to a crossover movement in pop music. In accepting the Grammy award for "Gotta Serve Somebody" in 1980, after singing it on the show with remarkable clarity of lyrics, he added: "I didn't expect this, and I want to thank the Lord."

Few words, but in that rare televised utterance the 1980 Grammy show took on an unprecedented "religious" air. During the first hour of the telecast, there seemed to be an endless procession of people expressing their gratitude to the Lord, giving one the impression that God was alive and well in the music industry. Andrae Crouch and the Disciples and the Mighty Clouds of Joy gospel group brought the audience to their feet when they performed. Later, when Dionne Warwick accepted her Grammy, she gave God the glory for endowing her with musical talent. Several other performers, each in their own way, gave the awards show an unbelievably gospel air. In addition, several personalities who were Christian celebrities were shown on camera, seated in the audience.

One of them was Donna Summer, who had also recently found spiritual renewal through faith in Christ. On her 1980 pop album *The Wanderer,* the woman credited with perfecting the sultry, sexy disco song had made efforts to clean up her dirty-girl image. One cut on her LP was "I Believe in Jesus," an exuberant song which tended to give more credence to the rumors of her conversion. Later she would appear on Christian talk shows and share more about her faith, while continuing her secular work.

Hot on the heels of the Grammies in 1980, it appeared as if there might be a return to the spirit of the seventies, with songs about heavenly things hitting the charts at a pace unparalleled since the days of the Jesus movement. "Gotta Serve Somebody" had hit the top in many cities. "All Things Are Possible," a double-entendre song recorded by Dan Peek, formerly a member of the pop group America, stayed on the hit charts for several weeks. (This double-meaning music was tagged "positive pop" by its proponents, but the term never really took off.)

Paul Davis, the son of a Methodist preacher, scored with a big hit in "Do Right," which began with an unmistakeably clear Christian message for pop music: "I know that He gave His life for me; set all our spirits free." Keeping close company with Davis' hit was Bruce Cockburn's "Wondering Where the Lions Are." His first American hit after ten albums in his native Canada was part of an LP project titled *Dancing in the Dragon's Jaws*. Cockburn was inspired to write much of his poetic, esoteric music by British novelist Charles Williams, a friend of C. S. Lewis. Williams wrote a series of horror stories with spiritual themes.

Other religious and quasi-Christian music on the pop charts in the early eighties included songs such as "The Good Lord Loves You," sung by Neil Diamond, and "With You I'm Born Again," performed by Billy Preston and Syreeta. The latter was a sexy, secular double play on words, using the religious buzzword of the seventies. Preston had always included a gospel song on each of his rock albums, and in 1978 recorded his first of two gospel albums for the Myrrh label. Preston's popularity as a Christian performer was limited among evangelicals, due most likely to his double-meaning hit with Syreeta and a controversial performance in a rock movie.

Christians also had a hand at producing several hit secular recordings in 1980. Michael Omartian, Freddie Piro, Bill Schnee, and Chris Christian all contributed their talents in producing hits.

More specifically within the Christian music industry, there was a roll call of sorts developing—a *Who's Who* of rock and pop artists who were making the crossover in their lives and on the stage.

Not all of the fairly new Christians chose to stay in the secular music business. Many of them determined that too much compromise would be demanded of them that way, or already had been. So they devoted their time to recording and performing Christian music exclusively.

Dion DiMucci, who began singing professionally with a Bronx street-corner oo-wee group named the Belmonts in 1958, gave a poignant testimony in his words and on his album *Inside Job*, recorded on Word's DaySpring label. Later, during an appearance on a Dick Clark TV special, Dion got his say out to the millions watching.

"They asked me the same question they asked each performer," Dion later recalled. "It was, 'Where are you now?' I looked directly at the camera and said:

" 'I started out in this business in 1958, and I've seen people reach the top, yet die of miserable, broken lives. By the grace of God I'm sitting here just born. I feel like I've just started. I've never lived! I feel like the Apostle Paul said in Philippians: I count it all rubbish, I count everything I've gained rubbish, for the sheer joy of knowing Jesus.' "

Dion's enthusiasm was indicative of the spirit of many of the artists who crossed over into the Christian music scene as the result of their personal encounters with Jesus. "On that show," he continued, "I had the chance to say it's not in the gold records, it's not in the next party, it's not in the next record contract, it's not in the next relationship, or the next sports car you've got, or the next house you buy, or the next this, or the next that, or your position. I said, 'Your serenity depends on your relationship with God. Your peace of mind depends on God. It doesn't depend on your feelings or your circumstances.' "

Gary S. Paxton, whose early rock career included working with the Hollywood Argyles of "Alley Oop" fame and Skip & Flip, had a similar testimony on one of Dick Clark's "where-are-they-now" TV specials. Other legends of early rock and shoo-bop music shared their testimonies on other occasions. Little Anthony Gourdine, who had been lead singer of Little Anthony and the Imperials in the fifties and sixties, was one. "He's polishing me up and putting me through the faith," he said in an interview in 1980, the year he recorded a Christian album called *Daylight* for MCA Songbird Records.

From the more recent rock scene came Richie Furay, whose recording history included Buffalo Springfield, Poco, and the Souther-Hillman-Furay Band. In 1982 he turned down a recording contract with a major secular label by refusing to soften the evangelistic tone of the songs on the album he was to do. "I am a servant of the Lord," he responded. "He has given me the reason for being who I am, what I am, and what I'm able to do. I will not compromise." After recording a new album of Christian music for Myrrh, he settled into pastoring the Rocky Mountain Fellowship in Boulder, Colorado.

Maria Muldaur, whose big hit, "Midnight at the Oasis," brought her fame in 1974, encountered salvation through Christ as a result of listening to Bob Dylan's *Slow Train Coming* album. "The album played over and over in my mind," she recalled, "from beginning to end. The words just pointed to one thing: God."

After twenty-two gold and platinum albums earned as drummer for Paul McCartney and Wings, Joe English still wasn't satisfied with his life. It was the miraculous healing of his wife following an automobile accident that convinced Joe to accept the Lord.

Added to these musicians and performers were: T-Bone Burnett and Stephen Soles of the Alpha Band and Bob Dylan's Rolling Thunder Revue; Jeff Pollard, originally with the southern pop band LeRoux; Roger McGuinn, originally with the Byrds; Rick Cua of the Outlaws; Philip Bailey of Earth, Wind, and Fire; Beeb Birtles and Graham Goble of Australia's Little River Band; Reggie Vinson, formerly of Alice Cooper; Bernie Leadon, formerly with the Eagles; Teri DeSario, whose "Yes, I'm Ready" and "Please Don't Go" duets with K. C. and the Sunshine Band in 1979 made #2 and #1 on the pop charts respectively; Phil Driscoll, who had left gospel music in the sixties to work with Joe Cocker, then returned to a new gospel career in 1978; Deniece Williams and Donna Summer, who both performed gospel cuts on their secular album releases; and others, including three members of Irish rock band U2, and members of British rock band After the Fire.[1]

Kerry Livgren, keyboardist and co-founder of the rock band Kansas, was one of the more well-publicized crossover stories in the early eighties. Through Jeff Pollard, Kerry learned about Jesus in a new way in 1979 in the rear lounge of a touring bus, on the road between concerts.

"At that point I was very frustrated," Kerry recalled later, "but I didn't realize I was frustrated. Maybe consciously I didn't realize the length I had come looking for something I could really believe in and latch onto as an absolute truth.

"Jeff presented me with some of the basic truths of Christianity, and he was very well-learned in defending Christianity and Scripture. But I simply had never heard it. I found that most of my objections and excuses for not believing in Christ and Christianity evaporated. The Holy Spirit was drawing me into being a believer, and I felt it happening. The sinful part of me wanted to reject it, but I simply surrendered. Just like in warfare, I surrendered, gave up, put up the white flag, and said, 'Okay, you win!' "

The music Livgren composed for Kansas from that point on showed clear evidence of the changes in his life. In 1980 the song "Hold On," from the Kansas *Audiovisions* album, referred to the return of Jesus Christ. It was referred to even more boldly in "Ground Zero" and others of the seven songs he put on his own album, *Seeds of Change,* featuring secular rock vocalists singing Livgren's lyrics.

Next would come an autobiographical book, co-written with

Kenneth Boa, also titled *Seeds of Change*,[2] then a Kansas album called *Vinyl Confessions,* continuing a pervasive Christian tone. By that time three of the Kansas members were reported to be Christians: Livgren, Dave Hope, and the new lead singer Jon Elefante. But, as in other performers' situations, Livgren finally found too much pressure within his own group as he continued his outspokenness about his faith. In 1984 he and Hope would leave Kansas to be the nucleus of a new band, Kerry Livgren A.D., and record a new album for CBS, *Timeline.*

The new band made their concert performance debut at Cornerstone '84, a Midwestern Christian rock festival which drew some eight thousand people for its finale.

22/ Penetrating the Secular Market

While Kerry Livgren and others were crossing over into gospel territory, there was not much movement in the other direction, though it was still dreamed of. Christian musicians still pondered the same question which they had for years: Why can't we get a hit on the pop charts?

One obvious answer was, no perceived need. The secular was quite happy with the music it was pumping out, and there was no desire for preachy songs and singers. The attitude of the secular was evidenced at a radio programmers' meeting at a *Billboard* magazine-sponsored conference on gospel music. The truth cut like a knife, but it was the truth: Unless it was *sellable* music, Christians were told, unless its quality was on or above par with secular music, no matter how sincere the intent of the artist, they didn't want it. In other words, there was very little sympathy or tolerance as was the case in the gospel-music work on the inside.

John Young, as early as 1976, was telling Christian broadcasters at the National Gospel Radio Seminar that they were going to have to stop comparing themselves with and competing with each other and using their success in that as a gauge of effectiveness. In order to make an effective impact in the secular marketplace, whether it be for ratings, advertising, sales, or recognition, it would have to be done so extraordinarily that the secular moguls and business leaders would *have* to take note and act, or at least react.

Likewise, in the Christian music field, the albums and tapes, the songs, and the artists would have to excel in talent in such a way as to almost catch the secular industry off-guard, with its defenses down.

Pehaps it was the conversion of Dylan, the abundance of "born-againism" in the press, the crossover of other artists such as Johnny

Rivers and Kerry Livgren, or the God-oriented hits of Paul Davis and Neil Diamond which began to spark that interest. Maybe it was the Grammy show of 1980, which was so pregnant with gospel influence. It could have been the wooing of the gospel record companies in an attempt to get noticed by the secular record industry and be treated more fairly. Whatever caused it, there began to be an increased secular interest in gospel music by the early eighties.

Gospel music was being touted (by the gospel industry) as "the next frontier" of music, paralleling the growth of country music a few years earlier. Figures on the sales of gospel music as a piece of the music industry pie showed an increase in its share. The Gospel Music Association produced a film to draw attention to the potential of gospel music as a growth industry. Major network TV programs and investigative reports dealt with the ringing cash registers at Christian bookstores (*still* not called book and record stores except in a few cases). Articles in the major secular trades started looking hard at attractive dollar figures representing gospel music sales potential in the midst of a financial crisis for the overall recording industry.

All the hoopla and somewhat evange*la*stic dollar reports on gospel music managed to draw the attention of several major secular labels for either teaming up with gospel record labels or starting their own.

It wasn't the first time it had been done, though. The initial try at secular distribution or production of gospel recordings on gospel labels, other than in black music, had come back in 1974, when the American Broadcasting Companies organization purchased Word Records in Waco, Texas. When that buy was made, both critics and supporters of the move watched with interest.

In the long run, however, those involved in the secular end of things showed little or no interest in promoting the newly inherited product. In all honesty gospel music, as late as the midseventies, was nothing short of laughable in most secular minds. It still evoked stereotypical visions of poorly produced, backwoods recordings not fit for distribution, even though Word, Light, and a few other labels had made considerable inroads in upgrading the sound of gospel music.

Thus, getting distributors within the secular companies excited about gospel music was an uphill battle. Gospel records were generally left at the bottom of the promotion stack when records were pitched to radio, and the great Christian hope of crossovers into the secular realm flashed brightly only on a few occasions, usually with generic songs which could be considered religious or otherwise.

Word ultimately found out that the best way to handle things was to distribute their own product. While Word stayed under the ownership aegis of one of the ABC divisions, they were given the freedom to handle the distribution through channels as they saw fit. Their success in doing so was quite notable, and Word maintained a strong profile in the gospel-music field.

MCA Records was the next company to have a go at recording and selling gospel product. The secular company reestablished the old Songbird label (which in earlier years had carried mostly black gospel acts) and set up its offices in the Universal Tower in California. Artists signed to the MCA Songbird label included B. J. Thomas, Fireworks, Dan Peek, Roby Duke, Little Anthony, B. W. Stevenson, and several MCA country artists who would record gospel albums for the Songbird side.

One of the most noteworthy and memorable albums to come from MCA Songbird was *Brand New Start* by Mylon LeFevre and Broken Heart, which marked his return after more than a decade away from Christian music albums. TV entertainer Barbara Mandrell, who gave gospel an extra boost in the marketplace by featuring a regular gospel-music segment on her weekly television show, was the last performer to have an album on Songbird, *He Set My Life to Music.* Upon its release, news reports were issued announcing that the fairly young label was being shut down. In an article about the closing featured in *CCM* magazine, Jim Fogelsong, the president of MCA Records Nashville Division, said, "We have found that gospel's a totally different record business than the record business MCA is in, and we haven't found a successful way to make it tick."

In spite of the MCA Songbird closing, a distribution agreement made with Sparrow Records for swapped distribution of certain MCA and Sparrow product was kept, assuring that the MCA Songbird albums would still be available, at least until stock ran out or demand was down.

The year before Songbird's demise, CBS Records had entered the gospel-music field by establishing Priority Records. First gleaning gospel product from their existing catalog, it wasn't long before considerable new product was being recorded for the label. The lineup would ultimately include B. J. Thomas (his third gospel label), the Cruse Family, Cynthia Clawson, rock legend Johnny Rivers, Bob Bennett, Patrick Henderson, jazz fusionist James Vincent, Carman, and others. Priority showed great promise for the future, with high-quality, well-packaged product.

In a surprise move Priority's doors in Nashville were closed in July 1983, some eighteen months after they were opened under the direction of the CBS management. The explanation for the sudden shutdown came in the form of a press release from CBS/Records Group. "We just weren't selling enough records," it said, citing the move as "a matter of sheer economics."

There was speculation that the move came when Dick Asher, a man instrumental in the establishment of the gospel label, left the CBS company. After that, some people theorized, there was little or no interest at CBS in continuing what had originally been proposed as a four-year project.

Buddy Huey, who had headed up the Nashville operation for Priority, said later in a private interview, "I was saddened that there wasn't a way to keep Priority going. It didn't make sense because we had far exceeded our expectations." After the closing, the artists, just as in the case of MCA Songbird, had to go in search of a new label on which to record their product.

In one other experiment in secular/gospel joint distribution, Light Records, Ralph Carmichael's label, also announced a pact with Elektra-Asylum Records for distribution of certain Light product to secular outlets. The agreement, however, was short-lived. By 1984 the only secular/gospel distribution agreement still in effect was between Sparrow and MCA. Other labels got their product into the secular outlets through large distributors of recorded product.

Part of the reason for the dismantling of secular gospel labels and dissolution of distribution pacts was probably a disenchantment experienced by the secular executives. The reports given to them about gospel music had signaled a lucrative future, in the midst of a waning record market. But by their own admission gospel-music sales were foreign to them. Or perhaps the market just wasn't big enough to capacitate so many labels.

If there was any prime candidate for crossing over into the secular market as an artist, it was Amy Grant. Her career history was a remarkable one. When only fifteen, she took a tape of some songs she had written and recorded for her family and a friend to her Sunday school teacher, Brown Bannister, who played the songs for Chris Christian, a producer and talent scout for Myrrh Records.

"I was completely shocked," Amy admitted a few years later regarding her signing to the label. "I was flattered that Chris liked the music, but I never expected to get a recording contract as a result."

While still in high school, Amy spent much of her fifteenth year working on her debut album, which included seven of her own songs. The "recording thing" was all new to her, to the point that her embarrassment about singing before a studio microphone led her to request that the studio be darkened during some of her album vocal sessions.

After the album was released, Amy's popularity quickly flourished, mostly on her own strength and merit, without the help of much initial extraordinary publicity. Most likely it was because of the lack of many young, new influences in Christian music at that time that she was received so well. The musicians of the late sixties and early seventies were maturing, more or less taking their music styles along with them. Ironically there had developed a sort of generation gap *within* contemporary Christian music. There was little new music for the younger teens and adolescents.

The Nashville teenager provided that music. Not only did she please the young people, who could readily identify with her; her wholesome, clean image also hit well with many older parents who had always been somewhat suspicious of any of the new contemporary Christian music.

It wasn't long before Amy's personal management and her record label began plotting a well-orchestrated career, ironically even before she herself knew for sure whether music was indeed in her long-range future. But within a few years the course was clear. Through her extraordinary ability to reach virtually all ages of gospel-music fans, and through the continued promotion and sales strategies of her management and her record company, by 1983 Amy had become probably the most popular Christian female vocalist in the country. Her *Age to Age* album stayed at the top of the album sales charts for twenty-two months consecutively, replaced only by her own sequel, *Straight Ahead,* released in the spring of 1984. By that time, *Age to Age* had sold more than five hundred thousand copies and had earned a gold record. In the same year, as sales soared toward platinum status for one million copies sold, she packed out concert halls during her album-preview tour, which included two sold-out performances at the famed Universal Amphitheater in Hollywood.

As her remarkable career continued, rumors began circulating that Amy was considering going secular, crossing over where other Christian musicians and singers had only dreamed of going. Many of the musicians who had previously eyed crossing over into the secular, though, had changed their attitude by 1984, either viewing such a crossover as unattainable or spiritually compromising, or at least having the potential of being so. Many of the secular musicians who had come from the other direction couldn't understand why someone would *want* to get involved as a Christian in the pop-music business. There was even some speculation as to whether or not the secular music business would even *allow* it to happen to any measurable degree. Christians performing in their own territory of music was okay, but when a Christian started making noise in the secular, would it be allowed?

But the idea was still toyed with by some Christian musicians, whether in pipe dreams or as tangible goals. Gene Cotton had crossed over in the seventies and had had a few hits. Andrae Crouch had recorded an album for Warner Brothers. The question still taunted and frustrated some Christians in music: Why can't we have Christian music on the pop charts? Why can't we have Christians record pop hits for the pop charts, even though the songs are not religious in and of themselves? If the lyrics are *true,* if they're about truth, aren't they really Christian?

As her management continued to plot her career, with one gold record and two more gold and a platinum on the way, Amy was about as close as anyone to finding out if it could be done.

23/ *Aerobimania and Fallen Warriors*

The year 1982 was one of the most eventful in the history of contemporary Christian music. Unfortunately there was as much bad news as good in that year.

Attendance at the annual Christian Booksellers Association Convention in Dallas was down slightly, signaling a cautious attitude among booksellers and record-sellers waiting for a sluggish economy to show true signs of picking up. But with a recession in full swing, the casualty list was uncomfortably long. One of the first Christian all-record stores (if not *the* first), The Praise Company, operated by Robbie Marshall in Denver, closed its doors. Distribution by Dave, a major supplier of recorded Christian product to Christian retailers, also closed. Sonshine Artists, which had appeared to be a rapidly growing concert promotion firm, went belly-up in Tulsa, following an elaborate "gospel cruise" to the Bahamas which failed to pay for itself. In Nashville, New York, and Los Angeles the offices of *Record World*, a major secular trade magazine which also carried some gospel news, closed permanently. As mentioned earlier, Continental Radio, based in Portsmouth, Virginia, signed off its satellite radio network after less than two years on the air.

While the industry adjusted itself, most album prices went up another notch to $8.98, matching cassette prices. The cassette tapes were approaching the point of surpassing record sales, while 8-tracks faded into tape history, where they belonged.

Other than the new reign of Amy Grant as the top-selling artist in gospel music as the result of her *Age to Age* album, the most notable trend in contemporary Christian music was Christian aerobics-mania. Led by *Aerobic Celebration* on the New Pax label, a string of at least ten other Christian alternatives to Jane Fonda and Richard Simmons would be released in the following year.

Among the leaders in sales were *Aerobic Celebration, Firm Believer,* and *Believercise.* Not since the days of the folk musicals had there been such a glut of thematic albums, with every label getting on the aerobiwagon; and not since the days of the early Christian coffeehouses had so many inventive, punnish names popped up. By March of 1983 there were four aerobics albums in *CCM*'s Top Album Sales chart, indicating there was a definite demand.

The most common justification heard for the albums was from women who wanted to exercise, but preferred not to do it to secular disco music, as was the rage. The aerobics albums from the gospel labels used current contemporary Christian artists and their songs for the workout backups, and later Stormie Omartian recorded *Exercise for Life,* which introduced original music for alternative aerobics. Also on her album was an up-tempo medley of familiar hymns, arranged and performed by her husband, Michael.

Another facet of music and ministry that showed strength in the midst of a recession were the Jesus festivals and conferences, most of which were well attended in 1982. Even the lights of Broadway and Hollywood marquees helped to brighten the picture with religious themes, much as they had in the early seventies, but this time perhaps a bit closer to the gospel truth.

The outstanding success of *Chariots of Fire,* for instance, a motion picture about 1924 Olympic runner Eric Liddell, an outspoken Christian, had stirred new feelings of respectability among Christians. The Christian lifestyle *could* make a difference, it proved, and a new courage seemed to develop in believers who watched the success of the film. It won four Academy Awards that year, including Best Picture. The music from the film, especially the title song, was equally well received. It was played both on secular and Christian radio, providing an interesting and unusual fusion of two audiences.

In New York, *Joseph and the Amazing Technicolor Dreamcoat* was successfully playing off-Broadway to decent reviews, some fourteen years since its creation for a boys' school in England. On Broadway, the Reverend Al Green, soul-singer-turned-gospel-singing preacher, took to the stage for a lead role in *Your Arm's Too Short to Box With God.* The show proved a short run for the Memphis music maker.

At the Lamb's Theater in Manhattan, an important location for Christian gatherings in a secular environment for several years, *Cotton Patch Gospel* debuted in late 1981. The play was an adaptation of a book called *Cotton Patch Version of Matthew and John.* The sprightly one-man show (with assistance from a musical trio called the Cotton Pickers) drew good-sized audiences, partly because the music was composed by Harry Chapin, a pop singer and songwriter who had been killed in a fiery auto crash in July 1981. The death had been mourned by pop-music fans and performers alike. *Cotton Patch Gospel* would later be staged across the United States by various touring groups before very receptive audiences.

Somewhat ironically, in the same month only one year later, as audiences were listening to Chapin's *Cotton Patch* music in New York, the Christian music world would experience a comparable feeling of loss in mourning a respected singer and composer. On July 28, 1982, Keith Green and two of his young children, along with a family of friends visiting Green's Last Days Ministries complex near Lindale, Texas, left for a short sightseeing plane flight that ended in tragedy.

The Cessna, designed to carry six passengers and a pilot, was loaded with a total of twelve people instead. At takeoff, it couldn't get enough altitude to clear the treetops, and it crashed, exploding in flames on impact with the ground, killing all on board.

Green's wife, Melody, pregnant with their fourth child, was thereby left to carry on the work of Last Days Ministries with the help of other members of the Christian community there. Outreaches of Last Days Ministries included extensive mission work, distribution of Keith's albums and tapes, publication of the widely read *Last Days Newsletter*, and the dissemination of literally millions of tracts for evangelistic and Christian growth purposes, including ambitious antiabortion literature.

Green's sudden death stunned the gospel music community, especially those involved in the contemporary side. His songs, though searing, were an ongoing example of what contemporary Christian music could be without falling into commercial trappings and limitations. Much of his music was labeled as prophetic—literally the voice of one crying in the wilderness, a voice which moved many people into changed and recommitted lives.

But the sad news for contemporary Christians did not end with Green's death. On the day of Green's funeral, Charles McPheeters, whose most recent activity had brought his Holy Ghost Repair Service back to the Hollywood streets where he had worked years before with Teen Challenge and then Arthur Blessitt, succumbed to a battle with stomach cancer. He had known of the condition only a brief six months or so before.

The passing of Green and McPheeters in the same summer week in 1982 showed that death didn't claim just the elderly, and that sometimes it claimed warriors for Christ in their prime. The old hymn, "Work, For the Night Is Coming," took on new meaning for some. There was work to be done right away, and two of the leading officers in at least the music and street-level divisions of God's army on earth had been taken. Thus grew the immediate need for other bold, daring Christians who would do the work without argument and, more important, without compromise.

McPheeters had recorded two lively, sometimes hilarious albums characteristic of his infectious humor, but mixed with compassion and an underlying urgent plea for people to see the glorious light of Jesus' salvation. His two albums were released on custom labels, with no nationwide distribution and no chart action. He never became a big name in Christian music. But not having a hit album never fazed him or deterred him from the serious work at hand, ministering to the people of the Hollywood streets who virtually no one else seemed to care about. His wife, Judy, carried on the leadership of the Holy Ghost Repair Service after Charles' death, with the same intensity and courage as was shown by Keith Green's widow at Last Days.

Keith Green's albums, conversely, *were* hits. He was well-known because of his music. But rather than get carried away with the fame, he used it for the work God had called him to, even when it wasn't the easy or popular thing to do.

The examples set forth by Green and McPheeters undoubtedly spurred other musicians to carry on the work. It would be several years before the tremendous impact of their ministries would even begin to be measured.

24/ Coping with Burnout

The extensive growth of the contemporary Christian music industry had lent tremendous odds that sooner or later some "dirty laundry" would be exposed to the press, and then to the scrutiny of the public. This happened in 1982 when a well-known gospel artist was arrested for possession of cocaine in California, and the story went out on national news wires. The serious charges were dropped, however. (The national press did not pick up that story as readily.) The singer insisted that the night in jail had been the result of a series of misunderstandings—a not-so-funny comedy of errors, a case of more or less being in the wrong place at the wrong time.

The reports during that summer in at least one Christian magazine told of tiffs between two major Christian performers, evidently onstage and offstage. Brought on by personality clashes, the war of nerves between the two artists was evident on some double-bill concerts where they shared the stage.

In addition, one of the artists, a major crossover singer who continued to perform his secular hits along with gospel music at his Christian-billed concerts, drew heckling from individuals in various audiences where he performed. Though well meaning, perhaps, the shouted criticisms fired from that direction were untimely and came across as sanctimonious and merciless, not to mention rude. The pressure of those hecklers, as well as the tension created by performing on both sides of the entertainment fence, ultimately led to verbal exchanges which would have best been left unsaid. The artist went through what could only be described as severe burnout, and in later interviews was quoted in ways which would lead one to believe that things had changed considerably in his spiritual life.

On several of the occasions mentioned here, it appeared as if maybe the gospel-music industry had lost its way and things were getting a bit chaotic. But these occurences of that year may have helped to get those involved in the pop Christian music industry and ministry to reassess their own goals and through introspection determine just why they were in the business of music in the first place.

Such embarrassing events again brought to the forefront the need for living out Christian attitudes and precepts on and off the stage. The musician, by virtue of his trade, was a public figure and was being watched in both scenarios. Though the Christian public was harsh and overzealous at times, such as in the disruptive heckling, they deserved to know if the artist was walking his talk. The role of the musician often bordered on that of a preacher, and if the musician took that position, he should back up his words with an active witness in his own behavior.

As the contemporary Christian music scene matured more, some private admissions of closet sins began to surface. (Public admissions were slow in coming, though.) A few musicians admitted privately to toying with, or even indulging in, marijuana use over the years. Several Christian artists developed reputations behind the scenes—founded or unfounded—of having homosexual leanings. Marital infidelity reared its head in a few situations, as people gave in to their passions.

Mention of such rumors and realities in a history such as this would be viewed by some as unnecessary, tasteless, overly judgmental, and better left unsaid. Likewise, they might provide fuel for critics of contemporary Christian music or Christianity in general, choosing to be blind to the fact that instances such as these are found in all types of Christian music and in all types of Christian bodies.

However, yielding to the view that such problems were better left unsaid would further a prevalent attitude of many in the church of the eighties—that of mutual tolerance to the point of hiding each other's gross negligence of scriptural principles. Rather than confront and exhort privately, any such move was considered as negativism in a period famous for its "me" generation: "You let me sin, and I'll let you sin."

Thus it would be improper to ignore a few unfortunate problems which existed within contemporary Christian music circles—not just among musicians and singers, but in all levels of the body, down through the concert promoters, deejays, and office workers. Though those in the Christian music and ministry communities needed to have an empathy for their fellow-workers who were toying with worldly trappings, the tolerance of such behavior continuing without confrontation was a serious blight on the entire work at hand, one which in the early eighties began washing back upon the industry as a whole. Tolerance instead of exhortation was a sin in and of itself, of which quite a few people "in the know" were guilty. Complicity had the potential of undermining the work of the Kingdom.

This all happened in a period when there was no "covering" in many cases, no eldership or church body to be responsible to. At times the only advice or confrontation came from peers who also had no eldership or covering. Thus, there were casualties.

As a body, churches had been reticent to support any musicians who did not fit their stereotypes of what a Christian should be. Likewise, Jesus-rock musicians doggedly defended their music and refused to bend. Thus, they often went out alone, without the discipleship and prayer support from a church or group which they so desperately needed. Some of these independent minstrels sped head-on into burnout from literally spinning their wheels due to the demanding, solitary life on the road.

In addition, there was often no church-backed follow-up provided for the conversions at the altar following the musician's concert. Thus many young people and adults who went forward the night of the concert soon slid backward toward their old ways. This put a further burden on the musicians' hearts.

"For the last five months," said Russ Taff in an interview published in the August 1984 issue of *Christian Review* magazine, "I've given my best to one-nighters, and there would be a real outpouring of the Lord, and the kids would come forward." After four years with the gospel group known as the Imperials, Russ struck out as a solo performer, backed up with his own band.

"I would turn to James (Hollihan, a member of the band) and say, 'I would give anything if I could stay one more night.'" Taff decided to go into a city and stay for several days of concerts and interaction with the people in the audience, thus establishing what he hoped would be an effective follow-up. "I believe we are going to see tremendous things because of that," he added. "If we get people excited, they will want to hear the message."

Russ told *Christian Review* that rather than finding the travels on the road as tiring, he and his wife, Tori, who traveled with him, considered it as a retreat, looking forward to the new faces, and leaving much of the "business" at home. The Taffs had thus apparently licked the problem of burnout which several musicians had had to deal with in their lives.

Around the end of the seventies, as the FCCM and some other groups began calling out for reassessment of priorities, some of the early, pioneering Jesus musicians who had been diligent for a decade began to lose the steam which they had pretty well generated on their own. In some cases, they saw other, newer artists get the promotional pushes from record companies they themselves had striven for, but had never quite reached. They had struggled for years to create music with soul-searching and soul-cleansing properties, and they watched as commercial-sounding, hookish songs were promoted and played on the radio instead of theirs. Some of the veterans, once in pivotal roles in Jesus music, were overwhelmed by the sudden, tremendous growth of the industry they had helped to develop, and sometimes felt that the industry and the audiences were passing them by.

Their families were affected too. Touring schedules, spotlighted personalities, and tension between artistic value and lucrative commercialism put a tremendous strain on many, especially in the case of musicians who had been out on their own without fellowship or church covering.

Burnout often hit in the form of broken marriages. The word *divorce* reared its ugly head more and more often, sometimes in the least expected circles. For other musicians, burnout came in the form of alcohol or drugs. Working in Christian music was sometimes as stressful as working in secular music, and the temptations of alcohol or drugs proved too great for some to handle.

And lest any branch of Christianity get haughty about the problems of the contemporary Christian musicians, they need to be reminded that the same sins and burnout dilemmas hit in all parts of the church, music and otherwise. It was a sign of the times, and the strength of the church seemed to be seriously endangered because of the radically individualistic trends of the seventies and eighties and the correlative lack of accountability.

Artists, driven by a desire to stay in the mainstream rather than be passed by, rounded off what they knew were the ever-important barbs of conviction in much of the music. The result: for a long time there were tiring numbers of songs written to be hits on the Christian charts. They were often innocuous, "formula" hits which were here one day, gone another. For a few years, double entendre was in fashion, with complete albums of some artists naming the subject of their songs, Jesus, only once or twice, but giving exhaustive lists of recording information, including names of singers, musicians, songwriters, producers, executive producers, conceptualizers, their friends, their parents, and so on, ad nauseum.

By no means should this imply that there were no convicting, thought-provoking albums on the record labels in these years. And many in the industry would argue that formula or not, if the songs widened the audience for gospel music, and if the songs had to be hookish to catch their attention (after all, fishers of men should be able to use hooks), then there was no harm in a commercial Christian song.

But more than one artist, being told by a record label that his or her songs were not "commercial" enough to put on record, either moved from label to label seeking a more acceptable contractual arrangement, or started their own labels for their product and that of other musicians who had burned out in trying to express themselves in their music freely. On the other hand, some labels were initiated by the record companies to allow the more progressive and less commercial music to have a testing ground. And in some cases the larger labels agreed to distribute albums on smaller labels which strived for such artistic freedom.

Among the established artists who recorded on their own custom labels by the early- to mideighties were: Chuck Girard, who spent a two-year hiatus from recording in study of the Word before he released *The Name Above All Names* on his own Seven Thunders label; Nicholas, a contemporary black gospel group from Los Angeles who started Message Records and experienced considerable success with their *Words Can't Express* LP; Glenn Garrett, who formed Zoe Records for his *Back Where Love Begins* album; Mickey & Becki, who recorded all their albums on their own Maiden Music label; and Candi Staton, former rhythm and blues recording star whose first gospel album, *Make Me an Instrument,* was the initial release on her own Beracah label.

Candi Staton, Chuck Girard, and other artists, though veterans in the recording business, both secular and Christian, formed part of a new cutting edge in the eighties. Whether on big labels or small, they expressed on their albums and in their lives a new call to holiness. This was their antidote for burnout, and showed a very positive upward move in Christian music in general.

"Especially in the past year," said Dallas Holm in late 1983, "we've really delivered a message on dealing with holiness and separation from the world—counting the cost, what discipleship's really about. It's been a very strong challenge to the body, to really rethink what we call Christianity and what the demands of the gospel really are. It's a strong challenge to get people to open themselves up to radical change.

"I think the one Scripture that really started it all was 'Be holy, even as I am holy.' How is that accomplished? What does that actually mean? The Scripture before that one says, 'Like the Holy One who called you, be holy in all your behavior.'

"Quite frankly," he continued, "as I look at a lot of contemporary Christianity, I don't see too much that I would define as holiness. On the contrary, I see a very disturbing trend of people seeking to be accepted by the world, applying the world's methods and standards to Christianity, rather than the other way around."

Holm's words got even tougher. "I see a lot of letting down of the standards, a lot of permissiveness, and a lot of watering down of the gospel, especially in the field of Christian music. People writing shallow songs, or shallow magazines, or preaching shallow sermons. I think the thing I'm most challenged about at this point in my life is that as I read the words of Scripture, and as I take them and apply them literally to my own life, I realize that I have to undergo a revolutionary, radical change in my whole way of thinking.

"Like author Anthony Campolo says, we basically have made Jesus a middle-class, white, American Republican. That's how we perceive him. But the fact is that he was an incredibly radical individual who called us into incredibly radical relationships, and that's what I'm challenged with at this point in my life.

"Likewise, I want to challenge the body to rethink and reread and reapply literally the true principles of Jesus and of Christianity. I think one of the main points where this starts is the concept of holiness; that God has not only asked us to be, but actually has commanded us to be a holy, separate, peculiar people. None of those words do we like! We all want to be a popular people, but Jesus, to the contrary, said, 'The world hated me; they'll hate you.' We need to quit endeavoring to try to be accepted by the world and try to sneak Jesus in, because it was never meant to be that way."

Don Francisco, upon the release of his album *Holiness* in 1984, said that burnout had hit him for awhile, like so many other artists. "I'd been on the road ministering a long time, since '75 or '76. I was getting really burned out. I was getting to the point where I was saying things on the stage that I knew I believed, but I knew they weren't a part of my life anymore. I was just getting so busy, I was beginning to lose my daily relationship with the Lord. So over the last seven or eight months I've been getting things straightened out.

"The Lord has said," Francisco continued, "as He destroyed the temple—and He had to, because it was keeping people out of the *real* sanctuary—that He is going to destroy every ministry that does not bring people to His sanctuary. And this is a sanctuary of the heart. It's a heart relationship with the Lord Jesus. And every ministry that directs people's attentions to other things, and is consequently gonna keep them out of that really deep relationship with Him, He will destroy."

But Francisco's perspective was positive. "Revival is going to come," he added. "The Lord is going to do it, on an unprecedented scale. I want to be part of it when it happens."

Instead of speaking her mind, Candi Staton sang it, in a song from her album *Make Me an Instrument:*

> This body of mine is His temple,
> His home away from home;
> I must keep it spotless for Him,
> It must stay ready for His coming,
> Swept clean with truth and love;
> That's why Sin Doesn't Live Here Anymore.
> We can't afford to let sin reign in our mortal
>   bodies,
> To obey the lusts thereof;
> Our bodies are the only temple
> That the Holy Spirit can dwell in
> Until Jesus comes back.
> And He said, 'Behold I come quickly
> And my reward is with me,
> To give every man accorded as His work shall be.'
> And He's coming back.
> And every eye shall see Him
> And every tongue must confess
> That He's Lord of Lords
> And He's King of Kings
> And He'll reign forevermore.
> Sin Doesn't Live Here Anymore
> Sin Doesn't Live Here Anymore.
> God's temple, oh it must be holy,
> I must stay ready to meet him and greet him,
> That's why Sin Doesn't Live Here Anymore.[1]

25/ *Praise and Worship*

"Praise and worship" became a key phrase in much of the mainline Christian music of the eighties. As the line between contemporary and inspirational/M.O.R. became increasingly diffused, contemporary praise and worship music provided a comfortable middle ground, much as the praise/Scripture choruses of the sixties and seventies had done.

The victorious praise music—vertical music—took on a whole new style in the eighties. There was a contemporary flair to much of it, enhanced by advanced recording techniques, synthesizers, and larger recording budgets. The music wasn't limited to choir and congregational performances; solo artists also did well with the new "hallelujah" music, as did groups.

Each year there had been a few worship and praise songs introduced which would become long-lived classics. If the song adapted well to congregational singing, it had an even better chance for a long life.

Some of the classics came via Andrae Crouch's masterful writing. "The Blood Will Never Lose Its Power," "Jesus Is the Answer," "Bless the Lord," and "My Tribute (To God Be the Glory)" were a few which would long be sung and remembered, in churches and in homes. Bill and Gloria Gaither also had been reliable sources of praise music for more than a generation. "Let's Just Praise the Lord," "Alleluia," and "There's Something About That Name" were a few of the classics from their pens which managed to cross age barriers and establish themselves in the churches, as well as on radio.

Songs by Crouch, the Gaithers, and several other noted composers became new hymns for the seventies and eighties, to be added to the very popular Maranatha praise choruses such as "I Love You, Lord," "Sing Hallelujah," and "Let's Forget About Ourselves." Even before the beginning of the eighties decade, hymnbooks such as *The New Church Hymnal* from Lexicon Music included songs such as Kurt Kaiser's "Pass It On," Mylon LeFevre's "Without Him," Andrae Crouch's "Jesus Is the Answer," Karen Lafferty's "Seek Ye First the Kingdom of God," John Fischer's "All Day Song," and even Larry Norman's somber last-days lament, "I Wish We'd All Been Ready."

There were other compositions and records which managed to carry a spirit of praise and worship in a more contemporary vein, by using more contemporary arrangements, recording techniques, or rhythms. One of the genre was "The Victor," recorded first by Jamie Owens-Collins (the composer), then Keith Green, and much later, in 1984, incorporated into a musical of the same name by Jimmy and Carol Owens. "The Victor" employed much of the same musical style as had the extremely popular "Easter Song" by Jamie's friends, the 2nd Chapter of Acts: a light, rhythmic ballad, building in 6/8 time to a rousing anthem which would stir hearers to their feet in grand finale. The influence carried through on an even more elaborate note when Michael Omartian, who arranged for both 2nd Chapter and Jamie, recorded "Here He Comes" on his *Adam Again* album.

Glad, a Pennsylvania-based group of musicians, some of whom were trained in classical music, often performed harmony-based music which occasionally gave rise to contemporary anthems of praise. One of their compositions, "Sing," was another harbinger of praise songs to come from contemporary Christian songwriters and singers in the eighties. First recorded on their own 1980 album *Beyond a Star*, it was also picked up by Debby Boone for her *With My Song* album in the same year.

Boone's album of modern praise and worship music was a landmark recording, as she introduced a new genre of songs to many contemporary-music fans. "I really prayed and sought the Lord for what kind of music He wanted me to do," she explained in a private interview. "I wanted it to be something that would bring glory to Him and would please Him as a sacrifice of praise and be unlike anything I'd ever done before."

With My Song, released on Lamb & Lion Records, was produced by a man who, in the coming years, was to have considerable influence in contemporary Christian music, especially as a producer. There was a certain sound, a certain formula, which producer Brown Bannister managed to hook on to and would become more or less a trademark and a trend in Christian recording for several years to come.

In addition to Glad's second album (*Beyond a Star*, co-produced with Ed Nalle) and Debby Boone's *With My Song*, Bannister produced a considerable number of other contemporary albums. His crowning achievement came in 1982 when he produced Amy Grant's *Age to Age* album, a marked departure for the young singer from her earlier records, which Brown had also produced.

The opening song on the Grant album closely resembled much of the song style and production of Boone's *With My Song*. "Sing Your Praise to the Lord" ushered Amy into virtual stardom, and it also firmly solidified the trend toward rousing, building, fully-orchestrated, contemporary, neo-classical praise songs. This song, and the many others like it to follow, bridged generation gaps and pleased nearly everyone but the most traditional of the traditionalists.

"Sing Your Praise to the Lord" was written by Richard Mullins, one of several young songwriters of a new breed which greatly contributed to contemporary Christian music in the eighties, including the songs of praise and worship. Quite a few of the most prolific composers and lyricists were based in Nashville. The decision of several record and publishing companies to hire staff writers, or at least to sign on more exclusive writers, drew new, contemporary composers to a city which had previously been best known for its country music. Companies such as Meadowgreen, Paragon, and Word Music helped to establish a foothold for the contemporary writers in Music City, USA.

Much of the music conceived by the songwriters who made up the new Nashville genre was of the contemporary praise variety, relying heavily on Scripture passages for their inspiration. Writers such as Michael Card, Michael W. and Debbie Smith, and others helped determine a new direction for much of the contemporary Christian music in the eighties.

At least one man traced church music back through the years and worked at fusing its forms with the current trends. Rather than living in Nashville, he resided and wrote on the grounds of a monastery in Indiana and later a retreat in Arkansas. John Michael Talbot, who along with his brother had been part of the seventies country rock group Mason Proffit, took new directions in 1980 when his spiritual convictions led him to join a Franciscan order in the Catholic church. Talbot delved deeply into the early musical heritage of the church and out of those studies came a steady stream of simple and melodic guitar music and singing with an ethereal, almost mystical feel to it. Due to his earlier affiliation with Sparrow Records, his Catholic music was released through the same company, resulting in an unusual crossing over of Catholic music into the Protestant market.

As early as 1979, after nearly a decade of creating their own hymns and Scripture/praise music, Maranatha! Music started showing indications of a renewed interest in the standard hymns of the church, as well as a continued interest in creating new ones, usually based on Scripture. In that year, their album *Hosanna* featured several California artists performing slightly contemporized versions of old faithful hymns of the church, such as "Fairest Lord Jesus," "Great Is Thy Faithfulness," and others.

Four years later Tom Howard and Bill Batstone teamed up to create a *Psalms Alive!* album of original songs based on Scripture verses performed by a full orchestra and chorus, and utilizing synthesizers, drums, and other more contemporary instruments and instrumentation usually associated with pop music. The second *Psalms Alive!* album followed in 1984.

On the whole, the Maranatha Singers albums, originally called Maranatha's Praise Series, began skewing more toward an easy-listening, M.O.R. sound, though away from the folky Jesus-music feel of the first praise albums of the early seventies. The records became progressively more polished, better adapted to the new traditional audiences of the eighties.

"There's been more of a praise/worship feel to much of the contemporary Christian music in the past two years," confirmed Billy Ray Hearn, president of Sparrow Records in 1984. "That's a trend that's at its peak right now." Hearn had experienced considerable success with his *Hymns Triumphant* albums, and he noted the possibility that new record buyers for such product were being found in the *book* sections of the bookstores. "Maybe the people who go into bookstores and buy books have all of a sudden discovered that there are records over in the record department."

But Hearn noted that he had seen a surprising mixture of musical tastes. "I know a lot of kids and adults who like contemporary music but are also giving me comments like, 'I loved your *Hymns Triumphant!*' The same people that are buying Praise Strings are also buying the new-wave music of Steve Taylor. They go to church and hear the hymns and they go Saturday night and hear a jazz group like Koinonia. It used to be separate, but no more."

On Hearn's label, Steve Green, a tenor who had first sung with an excellent Christian rock group known as White Heart, and then performed with The New Gaither Vocal Band, released a 1984 album which bridged the stylistic gap with contemporary praise music.

Indeed, as Hearn said, the popularity of the contemporary praise songs seemed to hit an unprecedented high in that year. Consider this list of just some of the songs released and charted in popularity in 1984: "Hosanna," by Michael W. Smith; "Hosanna," recorded by Karen Voegtlin; "Hosanna Gloria," by Farrell & Farrell; and "Sing the Glory," sung by Stephanie Boosahda. Equally popular in that year were songs focusing on the many names and characteristics of God, a trend probably started by the popularity of Michael Card's and John Thompson's "El Shaddai," featured on Amy Grant's blockbuster *Age to Age* album. Some of the 1984 songs included: "Jehovah," recorded by Grant; "You Are Jehovah," by Glenn Garrett; "Jahweh," written by Gloria Gaither and contemporary Christian singer Carman; "Baruch Hashem Adonai," by Kelly Nelon Thompson; and "Y'shua Ha Mashiach," sung in 1984 by Scott Wesley Brown. Also recording some memorable tracks of more traditional music with a contemporary flair were Twila Paris, with "We Will Glorify" and "Leaning on the Everlasting Arms," and Kelly Willard, whose 1984 album on Maranatha! was filled with *Psalms, Hymns & Spiritual Songs,* including "Nothing But the Blood" and "Washed in the Blood." Even the Rex Nelon Singers, long known for their southern-gospel flavor, crossed over into contemporary radio with a beautiful, original chorus entitled "O For a Thousand Tongues."

Sandi Patti was a singer who greatly helped in the continuing diffusion between contemporary and traditional church music styles. Her extraordinary voice mesmerized radio listeners, record buyers, and churchgoers alike. Her wide vocal range astounded listeners as she carried audiences to new heights of ecstacy and inspiration. Perhaps such a description sounds more like a prepared press release, but it is exactly the effect Sandi had on most of her audiences.

Her musical career began when she sang with her father's Ron Patty Trio. While attending Anderson College in Indiana, she continued her singing. It was during and after her touring with the Bill Gaither Trio, and appearing before those massive audiences, that her career really took flight, much like Don Francisco's had before her. During those performances on the road, the singing of the Dottie Rambo composition "We Shall Behold Him" thrust her into a new high in popularity.

By late 1983 Patti had become another sweetheart of Christian music, much like Amy Grant, though their respective labels, true to form, would have preferred that such a comparison be left unmade, each proud of their own favorite daughter.

Sandi's fame first hit in her native Midwest and then in the South, spreading from there to a national recognition which would in 1983 win her three Dove Awards. Her album *Live More Than Wonderful,* co-produced by Sandi, David T. Clydesdale, and prolific producer Greg Nelson, edged its way to the five hundred thousand sales mark in late 1983. Thousands of young, aspiring singers dreamed of singing Sandi Patti songs in their churches: "We Shall Behold Him," "Upon This Rock," "O Magnify the Lord," and the duet she performed with Larnelle Harris, "More Than Wonderful," written by Lanny Wolfe.

The Benson Company, for whose Impact label she recorded, took those young singers one step closer to fulfilling their dreams by recording and selling Mastertrax, the original instrumental backgrounds used in the actual recording of Sandi's hits. The Mastertrax tapes, recorded on high-quality chromium dioxide cassette tape, featured the songs of the most popular artists on the Benson labels and their most popular recordings. The series proved so popular that Word Records introduced a similar series in 1984, called Studio Series. These original background tapes joined the list of thousands of other tracks which had been sold by Lexicon Music, Christian World, and other companies for years, bringing the full presence of professional musicians into the smallest of sanctuaries. They became as common as the organ and piano in many of America's churches.

26/ Common Ground, New Controversy

While praise music and contemporary music often found a common meeting ground by the eighties, there were even encouraging signs that southern-gospel advocates and musicians and contemporary supporters were becoming more tolerant of each other and mutually less antagonistic. One of the groups to pioneer the crossing of southern gospel into contemporary and vice versa was the Imperials.

As early as 1976, the seemingly ever-popular male quartet began contemporizing their music, while they maintained vestiges of their southern-gospel heritage. Producers Chris Christian, Michael Omartian, and Bill Schnee helped carry the Imperials into high standing with contemporary music fans.

Up to a certain point their music got progressively rockier, and the sales of their albums continued to be healthy. In 1984, however, in the year of their twentieth anniversary, they wisely recorded an album of modern-day standards in a middle-of-the-road vein. *Classics* rapidly became a hit and possibly reestablished their contact with the more conservative listeners, although not southern-gospel music.

From the other direction, rock group Petra successfully crossed over from contemporary into southern gospel with their recording, "The Coloring Song," which showed up on the contemporary, the inspirational, and the southern-gospel popularity charts, an unparalleled feat.

Other artists and groups dabbled in fields ordinarily foreign to their expertise, and the audience didn't seem to mind at all. In fact, by 1984 there were many albums of music released which defied description due to their wide variety of music styles. Artists such as Petra and Sheila Walsh continued to put a softer cut or two on their otherwise rock albums, thus increasing the chance for airplay on the traditionally conservative medium. This caused a bit of confusion when listeners purchased a favorite song they had heard on the radio station, then found that the rest of the album contained other styles of music. On the other hand, it introduced music to people which they otherwise wouldn't have tolerated, and more than a few people found themselves liking the varied styles.

There is no doubt that some of the tolerance for varying styles of gospel music and a new, peaceful coexistence between factions came as the result of the efforts of the Gospel Music Association. The GMA opened new categories within their annual Dove Awards, allowing the various facets of gospel music to be recognized and highlighted in their own right. Gospel music was no longer lumped into one category. Nor was it all southern gospel, as had been the original domain of the GMA. As gospel music grew, so did the number of categories.

By 1983, however, questions surfaced regarding the hybridizing of gospel music. Many of the questions came from people whose own favorite styles of gospel music had been somewhat eclipsed by the rapid burgeoning of contemporary Christian music.

"Why do the Christian rockers look down on traditional and southern-gospel music?" one leading publisher asked privately in a candid conversation in 1983. The query was an ironic reversal of questions asked by Jesus musicians in the early 1970s, such as, "Why is everyone ignoring or criticizing Jesus music?"

Sitting next to the writers for a major southern gospel publication at that year's Dove Awards in Nashville, one could sense their chagrin over the increasing dominance of contemporary music evidenced by each consecutive award. A year later, the discontent grew in the form of a scathing editorial in that publication from a southern-gospel performer who lashed out at the GMA for supposedly neglecting his type of music. As more contemporary influence grew in the GMA, the debates continued.

Meanwhile, onstage it was almost the sixties and seventies revisited, at least in a few cases. In one southern town the lead singer of one of the top southern-gospel groups in the nation stood before a large audience and ridiculed Christian rocker Mylon LeFevre for his long hair and his hard music, the same ridicule that had sent Mylon off onto a prodigal trip which took years to repair before he returned to the fold and to Christian music in the early eighties. Yet, only a few weeks after the critical remarks were derisively made in the downtown concert hall, Mylon appeared with his band, Broken Heart, in an Assembly of God church across town, with young people kneeling at the altar after the rock concert, yielding totally to Jesus Christ after hearing the message in Mylon's music.

While these flareups showed that some distrust and discontent existed among the various types of Christian music, the majority of the performers and workers were getting along fine. There was enough room for all types of music, they reasoned. They saw the caustic remarks and intolerant attitudes as an embarrassment for a field of music which should show the greatest unity of all.

Much of rock music had always been experimental, explosive, and progressive, preaching a message and trying to win concerts. One of the great differences between secular and Christian rock was what the music preached, and the lifestyle it supported or represented. In secular music, hard-core rock often (though not always) promoted licentiousness, violence, anger, despair, and self-centeredness. There is hardly any dispute of that fact, even among the rock performers; the only question is perhaps how much is dominated by those philosophies and mindsets.

Christian rock, on the other hand, though a musical relative by nature of style, preached a totally different message: moderation, peace, love, hope, and selflessness. If there was a true core of contemporary Christian music that was in the 1980s still "Jesus music" in the original, radical sense of the word, it was Christian rock. It was the experimental, cutting edge for gospel music, constantly looking for new styles, instrumentation, recording techniques—any new way to tell the old gospel story to a new audience. Of course, Christian rockers could do that job well or poorly, and they did both. Some hit the mark; others missed it by a mile.

The line of demarcation between secular and Christian rock, two similar but really vastly different music fields, was virtually ignored by many antirockers who in their written and spoken tirades against the evils of rock lumped all rock music—secular and Christian—together in one "evil" category.

Christians were even briefly implicated during the early eighties when a controversy developed over the use of backward masking, a technique which had actually been used in recording since around the midsixties. Backward masking involved the recording—in reverse—of lyrics, music, or sound effects, usually with (or on top of) music recorded in the standard, frontward direction. The Beatles, Black Oak Arkansas, Pink Floyd, Led Zeppelin, and other giant rock acts employed small segments of backward masking in their recordings, often creating otherworldly sounds.

What bothered Paul Crouch, Jr., and some other Christian observers was that in some cases the otherwordly messages apparently were in reality nether-worldly, satanic messages, being slipped into music and thus into young people's minds in reverse. Backwards or not, Crouch and others contended, the mind's subconscious can receive and interpret the satanic praises.

Other Christians countered that the concern about backward masking, though sincere and well-meaning, was a general waste of time, because much secular rock *frontwards* was enough to worry about. Why search for satanic messages in reverse, they maintained, when rock performers such as Ozzy Osbourne, AC/DC, Black Sabbath, and Van Halen did their antichristian damage blatantly frontwards?

During the controversy, even Christian rock musicians became suspect by the ultra-antagonists of rock. But Christian rock group Petra tried to allay the controversy (with their tongues in their cheeks) by inserting this phrase backwards in between two songs on their *More Power to Ya* album of 1983: "What are you lookin' for the devil for, when you oughta be lookin' for the Lord?"

To further confuse matters, by 1984 some of the backward-masked messages on secular rock albums had positive, even religious or quasireligious content. Prince, one of the eighties' most controversial rock performers, put in such a message on one of his albums.

A California representative went so far as to recommend a bill which would require record companies to print a backward-masking warning, similar to cigarette health warnings, on each album containing backward masking. Several ambitious dissertations and books were written on the subject, but by 1984 things had calmed down a bit.

The backward-masking affair in the early eighties did bring focus back on the true dangers of secular rock and roll, however. Rock had become increasingly and more blatantly blasphemous and contrary to Christian ethics, much as movies had done. The lyrics, the performances, and the lifestyle of many rock performers lived up to the charges leveled at them by many of the antirock evangelists. For many Christians, it further pointed to the desperate need for alternative Christian rock music for young people in the body of Christ.

Although by the eighties contemporary Christian music had the support of an increasing number of pastors and evangelists, such as Bob Larson, there were other speakers and writers who still maintained staunchly that all rock, Christian or otherwise, was of the devil.

During the late seventies, evangelist John Todd spread vitriolic venom against Jesus music, directing his most vicious attacks at Pastor Chuck Smith and the music ministries out of Calvary Chapel in Costa Mesa. Todd's impact, however, was lessened greatly when his ministry was proven to have serious, fraudulent credibility gaps.

Anticontemporary-music writer David Noebel continued to write and rewrite prolifically on the subject of rock music. "Christian rock is a compromise with the world," he accused in a 1980 personal interview. "They (the Christian rock musicians) are preparing the next generation to accept rock and roll when they think they're leading them to Christ." Noebel went further and said that the use of the term "contemporary" to describe the new Christian music was a case of "hiding under the term contemporary because they're somewhat fearful of (using the term) rock and roll."

Noebel authored an antirock (Christian and secular) book entitled *The Legacy of John Lennon,* an extension of his earlier, self-published diatribes against rock. In it he said, "We don't need more rock music—pagan or Christian."

On a more moderate level, national seminar instructor Bill Gothard continued to somewhat passively raise doubts as to the validity of contemporary Christian music, citing an instance he had heard about when someone from Africa testified that the contemporary Christian music was virtually the same as the music which the natives used to call up evil spirits. This recounting left a trail of questions after his seminar left whatever town he was in, sometimes reigniting dormant arguments about Christian rock in homes.

Evangelist Jimmy Swaggart created the most controversy there had been in a long time over the subject in 1980. In his *The Evangelist* magazine, he categorically denounced all contemporary music as sinful. (Ironically he himself had used instruments and arrangements on his own recordings which would have been considered heretical only a few years earlier.)

Swaggart's published views were quickly followed by those of Lowell Hart, a teacher at Prairie Bible Institute in Three Hills, Alberta, Canada, who authored a 189-page tirade against just about every kind of music short of classical, hymns, and Sousa marches. Christian music was included in his criticisms. Part of the notes on the back of the book said: "Like the hamburger-french fry diet of today (that has replaced the nutritious foods of Grandfather's day), frothy, candy-coated 'Christian' music is being substituted for the solid meat of Luther, Wesley, Watts, and Sankey."

In at least one area of the United States—Denver—the main Christian book and record distributor refused to carry the first edition of *Why Should the Devil Have All the Good Music?* because of its tolerance and endorsement of contemporary Christian music. The bookseller instead opted to stock bookstores and even grocery store book racks with the Hart book.

In 1982 evangelist David Wilkerson, who admittedly had serious misgivings about any rock music, became the second major evangelist, following Bob Larson's lead, to change his tune on Christian rock. In a pamphlet he wrote and published entitled *Confessions of a Rock Hater*, Wilkerson shared how he had felt in the past.

"As I saw it," he said, "(converted rock and rollers) should have forsaken everything from their past—rock music included. But I could not deny that most of them were sincere, deeply in love with Jesus, and God was blessing their efforts.

"In all sincerity," he added, "I preached against what I thought was compromise. I condemned a music style that was born in rebellion and idolatry. Looking back, I wonder how many innocent young converts I hurt—those who were giving to Christ the only talent they had.

"In the past few years, my battle with rock 'n' roll came to a head. . . . It began when one of my music associates started singing what I thought was rock in my crusades. I equated it with backsliding. A grieved young man had to part company with me, deeply hurt that I thought he had forsaken 'the old paths.' Some will think I have become too soft in my middle age—but we so desperately need to love one another and quit judging. I probably will never like 'Christian' rock and roll—but now it is not an issue with me. And I can truly say that I love all who differ with me."

In spite of Wilkerson's courageous adjustment, Swaggart remained one who differed and held the fort against contemporary Christian music. Once again in *The Evangelist* in 1984, he categorically threw out the proverbial baby with the bathwater, saying that contemporary Christian music was "incompatible with true biblical Christianity." He said it was "designed to mimic—as closely as possible—the fetid music of the world."

Throughout the same year, the battle against rock continued in several forms, including yet another book, *The god of Rock*, written by Michael K. Haynes and subtitled "A Christian Perspective of Rock Music." Jim Peters, one of the three Peters brothers who began nationally publicized antirock seminars in late 1979, released the fourth book to come out of that ministry on the subject.

"We became alarmed at the amount of time people were spending listening to secular music," Peters recalled of the early days of their ministry. "At the most, kids were maybe in church four hours a week, but there was a survey which came out and said that teens were listening to about six hours of music a day. We figured it had to be having some kind of influence on them. Since we got started, God has allowed us to see literally tens of thousands of young people accept Jesus Christ and get set free from the bondages of secular music and other things that have really hindered their Christian growth."

While touring for the various seminars and multimedia presentations, Peters' Gentle Touch Ministries utilized a contemporary Christian music group called Gentle Touch. "We've been in eight countries in the last two years," Peters explained in 1984, "with God allowing us to preach the gospel through music, plus sharing what is really going on with the major secular artists in rock 'n' roll and country music, and what they have to say about morals or the Lord. We talk about four aspects of music: the lyrics, the lifestyles and the intentions of the musicians, and the album covers themselves. The Bible says we should expose the unfruitful works of darkness by the light of God's Word, and that's what we try to do."

Al Menconi, an evangelist based in Southern California, used the same verse as quoted by Peters, Ephesians 5:11, to open up his first issue of *Media Update,* in which he discussed the question: Is rock music really the devil's music? His *Media Update* covered not only music, but also other forms of media, such as movies and television, covering it all from a Christian perspective. As his newsletters progressed into the eighties, Menconi began putting extra emphasis on how to listen to, criticize, accept, use, and encourage the use of contemporary Christian music, mostly as an alternative to secular music. Rather than accept or reject it lock, stock, and barrel (as Swaggart had), Menconi attempted to approach the subject with consideration of both the pros and the cons, encouraging his readers to do the same.

Thus, by the 1980s there were definitely two schools of thought among preachers and evangelists concerning contemporary Christian music. There were a growing number of ministers who had become its advocates, even though many opposed much of the current secular rock and pop music.

At home, parents who were raised through the early Jesus-music years had survived that sort of musical environment, including Christian rock, and they in turn for the most part saw that there was no good reason why their children couldn't be raised in the same way. Indeed, for younger families the music often served as a common point of fellowship, especially in places where contemporary Christian radio or concerts existed.

In fact, the parents were the first generation to have contemporary Christian "oldies" to reminisce around. In communities where contemporary Christian music was available on the radio or in concerts, people began growing up with the music, as an alternative to the normal secular pop music.

And Christian rock didn't invade church services as some had feared in the earlier years. It found its place in home listening, in concerts, on car stereos. It was for the streets, for parks, for coffee-houses, for prison ministries.

For awhile, though, Harvey Jett agreed with the antirock arguments. Formerly the lead guitarist with the infamous raunch rock group Black Oak Arkansas, a band which helped rock get its bad name, he had left them in June 1974 after accepting Jesus into his life.

"For three years after I became a Christian," he recalled ten years later, "I was totally against rock music of any kind." As late as May 1977, in a private interview while at the Festival of Joy in Wichita, Kansas, he said, "There's just something about it I don't like. When I hear it now, it brings me back into the same mood, the same feelings that I used to have. I have to battle with that spirit of bondage, that lost spirit.

"I believe that I saw exactly what rock is," he continued, "right to the point of how it's being used of Satan—the actual beat and the chord harmonies and just the whole spirit of it itself, how it can affect the human body, mind, and spirit." At that time, Jett included Jesus rock in his admonition. "It does the same thing to me that secular rock does. It's the music itself that has a spirit with it."

Jett then went into the same story (the voodoo beat being recognized by the missionary's children in contemporary Christian music) that Bill Gothard was telling at his seminars.

Jett's denouncement of all rock, even Christian, ended only a few months after the above-mentioned interview. He was playing at a recreation center, where he had been invited to play his nonrock music for the "messed-up" kids. Some were on drugs.

"I told him if he'd get 'em to church, I'd play for 'em. He told me if he could get 'em to church, I wouldn't *have* to play for 'em!"

There were three hundred young people at the center that night. After the first song, he recalls, they started getting up and leaving.

"I'm just standing there, thinking, 'God, what did I do?' and he spoke to me, saying, 'If you do it for my glory, and not to glorify yourself, I don't mind if you play your guitar.'

"I walked over and picked up a guitar—it wasn't even mine—and I plugged it into an amplifier and started playing. The kids started packing back in. I could see that all of a sudden the guitar was my bait. I was a fisher of souls, but until then I had been losing all the fish."

Jett would from that moment on perform rock—Christian rock—with new resolve.

27/ New Frontiers

Jesus-rock music, when well done, often had an element which was missing in the majority of secular pop releases: spiritual relevance. So in most cases, in order to get the message clearly across, the lyrics were miked more "up front" than in conventional secular rock, in which singers' words were more occluded. The vital lifeline for Christian music remained the lyrics—gospel themes couched in familiar musical expression.

"But I can't understand a single word of what that Jesus-rock band is saying, so they're not of any use or value," would cry many older people in their criticism of Christian rock. What many of them failed to recognize, even into the eighties, was the phenomenon of what could be called "decreased lyrical perceptiveness," which seemed to be experienced by countless numbers of rock-generation parents and grandparents. The older they got, or the less interested they were in rock music, the less they'd hear of what was being sung.

But the argument against inaudible lyrics in many cases was no more than the persistent frustration of older people not being allowed into the musical world of the youth. When Christian new-wave music began to come on the scene in strength in the eighties, lyrics suddenly began to clearly stand out again. That would seem to have put an end to those arguments about indistinguishable words.

It didn't. Even though the lyrics were lucid, complaints against new wave and new music came in hot and heavy, this time challenging the dress, hairdos, and lifestyle of new wave, punk, and techno-rock. Once again the Christian rockers, though performing the music and patterning some of their dress after the secular, usually held the line on lifestyle. It confused the critics, but evidently reached the youth.

Christian new wave and techno-rock music's arrival in the early eighties seemed the camel's back-breaking straw for the opponents of Christianity and rock music getting together. Would this new breed of religious rockers bring a punk lifestyle with them? Even the first edition of *Why Should the Devil Have All the Good Music?* speculated on that question, and only partly tongue-in-cheek.

Instead of introducing a radical, deadly lifestyle, such as secular punk had done, Christian "new music" filled a serious gap in Christian music. The young people who just gave blank stares when told that Bob Dylan or Paul Stookey or Dion DiMucci was a Christian now lit up when they saw creative, eighties-clad people their own age playing a staccato song which got onlookers hopping.

The new Christian music was, like its secular counterpart, greatly influenced by early, garage-band rock, back in the days when virtually anyone with a Silvertone guitar and a lead vocalist had hopes of making a hit record. With the youthfulness came a vitality, a joy, and even a new sense of urgency. More important, the new music often carried with it a refreshing blatancy of lyrics—straightforward, simple, and often clearly evangelistic words, rather than hidden, double-meaning references to the faith. No one could charge those singing the new music with lyrics that didn't get to the point. Consider the song belted out by the California group Undercover at Knott's Berry Farm amusement park's Christian Music Night in 1983: "If you'll excuse us, we love Jesus." No hidden meanings there.

One of the most radical of the new-music writers and performers was also one of the quickest to catch on. An American Baptist "preacher's kid" from Denver, long, lean, and lanky Steve Taylor, formerly part of the Jeremiah People music/drama troupe, lifted the roof at the Christian Artists Seminar in 1982 with some of the most animated Christian music to date.

A quite remarkable thing happened during that historic Colorado performance. The audience, treated to top Christian talent, but not used to Christian new wave, got it square in the ears and eyes. There was laughing, cheering, and clapping in the audience, all at the same time. Taylor was pleasantly outrageous.

At a repeat performance the next year, on the same stage, the response was much the same. But this second time a disenchanted member of the audience went back to the sales table where Taylor's material was being sold and swiped her arm across the table, sending the material to the floor. Her justification: Taylor's music was revolting to her, definitely not of the Holy Spirit. Taylor's reason for singing it: he had composed and sung biting, concise lyrics aimed directly at a complacent church, rather than pacifying his audience with more soothing, "everything is okay" lyrics, which was characteristic of so much Christian music.

But by 1982 many of the audience members were evidently ready to hear such truths. As a result of the overwhelming reception he got at Estes Park—one woman excepted—Taylor was signed to a contract with Sparrow Records. His first recording, *I Want to Be a Clone,* was a mini-album featuring six songs. Produced by accomplished Christian record producer Jonathan David Brown, the mini-album became a moderate hit in spite of virtually no radio airplay to support it, due to its high rock velocity. Taylor's second album, *Meltdown,* also produced by Brown, would meet with even greater acceptance.

Topping off Taylor's good showing on the first time out, the singer/writer received a letter of commendation from noted Christian author and thinker Dr. Francis Schaeffer, congratulating Taylor for the lyric content of his songs, and reiterating the definite need for the church to hear such provocative lyrics.

Taylor expressed his exhortations with humor, which sometimes made his music tolerable even to those who didn't like new wave or rock. He administered "a spoonful of sugar to help the medicine go down." That sugar was something that only a limited number of singers—Taylor, Randy Stonehill, Daniel Amos, Carman, Gary Chapman, and a few others—had managed to effectively weave into their acts.

Thus, the new Christian rock of the eighties had at least two strong points: evangelistic lyrics which reintroduced simple songs of the type that had earmarked the Jesus movement of the late sixties and early seventies, and caustic, exhortative lyrics aimed at shocking the sometimes-sleeping church into new motivation and a cleaning-up of its act. Both attributes were early Jesus music revisited.

There was a third function of Jesus-rock music, too: alternative entertainment for Christians or for people in general who felt that secular performers had carried their music too far. Young people could opt for contemporary Christian music recordings and concerts rather than support secular music, Hollywood movies, or Music Television (MTV), which brought rock videos into millions of homes nationwide. All forms of secular entertainment showed increasing moral turpitude, hard to justify for someone seeking to live a Christ-centered life.

So Christian rock gravitated to the public auditoriums more often than churches, although their access to school auditoriums became greatly limited during the eighties, thanks to congressional legislation and hardening local laws less tolerant to Christianity. Skating rinks also turned out to be great gathering places for Christian young people, families, and Christian rock fans. Contemporary Christian music nights and church nights at rinks across America proved extremely popular.

The list of Christian rockers had grown by 1984 to an impressive variety of performers, the majority of which seemed to come from the West Coast. Maranatha! Music and their associated A & S and MRC labels stayed on top of the new music crest with releases by Undercover, the Lifters, the Altar Boys, and others. The Lifesavors were signed by Refuge Records. Leslie Phillips, who later signed with Myrrh, first appeared on A & S. Quickflight carried their techno-rock from the Canadian Tunesmith label to the Texas-based StarSong label. Myrrh distributed an innovative new label, Exit Records, which introduced the 77s, Vector, and other rock groups through Sangre Productions in Sacramento, California. (Later Word added the Broken Records label to their roster, featuring new-wave music groups.) Stryper, the most ostentatious of the groups in their appearance, released their hard-rock album on Enigma Records, a secular label.

TV celebrity Lisa Welchel, from the series "Facts of Life," delivered a young rock sound on her debut recording, *All Because of You,* on Nissi Records. Her LP producer, John Rosasco, also created strong, pop-rock recordings for artists such as Joe English and the Cruse Family.

Christian female rockers came in strong in the eighties, whereas in earlier days their main strength had been in folk songs. In addition to those mentioned earlier, several other women made their mark in Christian rock music. Sandi Brock often sang leads for Servant, an Oregon band whose sound varied between music reminiscent of Jefferson Airplane and the Go-Gos. In Barnabas, Nancy Jo Mann belted out strong leads following the style of the Resurrection Band's Wendy Kaiser. Of a softer vein, but still rock, was Michele Pillar. Kathy Troccoli added a soul touch to her rock.

Rock group Daniel Amos, one of the most creative of the bands to come out of contemporary Christian music, moderated their sound over the years from country rock to innovative, new Christian rock and concept music. Single artists producing noteworthy rock included, among others, Mark Heard, Pat Terry, Will McFarlane, Tim Miner, Paul Clark, Steve Camp, Kenny Marks, Darrell Mansfield, Rob Frazier, Randy Stonehill, Rick Cua, and others.

Bob and Jane Farrell and Dony McGuire and Reba Rambo

McGuire were husband and wife duos who delivered some solid rock in varying styles. Both Prodigal and DeGarmo & Key produced high-energy rock with provocative messages. Canada's Daniel Band added their own driving music to the eighties' rock roster.

Of the harder rock groups, there were three which probably could be categorized as the hardest-driving, both in miles logged and in enthusiasm for keeping the rock rolling. Resurrection Band continued an unimpeded effort in evangelism, with some of their post-rock-concert altar calls drawing young people by the hundreds to the stage for salvation or recommitment. Servant seemed to be on the road almost constantly, rocking out with hard-edged music and stage effects.

Petra, however, was the most persistent in Christian rock record sales. Three of their albums, *More Power to Ya, Not of This World,* and *Never Say Die,* had sold around six hundred and fifty thousand aggregately, with their three earlier albums totaling another one hundred thousand. They had performed more than thirteen hundred concerts by the end of 1984, their eleventh year. Out of their Nashville offices, Petra geared up for another year of performing for more than half a million people on stage, and probably more on record.

Though most of the young "new music" mentioned earlier was being created on the West Coast, many of the most memorable rock festivals were held in the Midwest, especially the Chicago area, which hosted the likes of the Illinois Jam, the 1982 Harvest Rock Fest, and Cornerstone '84, hosted by Jesus People USA (JPUSA), who also sponsored the veteran Resurrection Band.

While Christian rock seemed to be having a good sprint at the Christian music market, there were many contemporary artists who were more laid back, recording excellent albums of more mellow music. One of the most underpromoted but also most deserving of attention in that regard was Bob Bennett, whose two albums *First Things First* and *Matters of the Heart* helped to establish Bennett as a musician's musician. His second LP was ultimately chosen as Best Album of 1982 by the writers of *CCM* magazine. Bennett's music was largely composed of acoustical ballads, and Jonathan David Brown brought the songs out to their fullest as producer of both Bennett albums.

Some of the other artists keeping pretty well to middle ground in their contemporary music and developing followings included Wendy Hofheimer and Mary Rice-Hopkins (better known as Wendy & Mary), Cynthia Clawson, Pete Carlson, Steve Archer, Chris Christian, and others.

By the mideighties, a soft, easy style of jazz had finally gained acceptability among Christian music listeners after a rough and sporadic start lasting a decade or more. Secular jazz band Seawind's popularity in the early eighties trickled over into the Christian market, based on the fact that some of the members of the group were Christian and their songs often gave further credence to their faith.

While Seawind opened the doors from one side, Christian jazz artist Fletch Wiley and Christian jazz fusionist James Vincent helped them along. Wiley, also an album producer and former member of Andrae Crouch's group the Disciples, recorded for Star Song Records out of Pasadena, Texas. And Vincent came from the secular Caribou label to record his second album, the latter on Sparrow. Paul Clark, Phil Keaggy, Roby Duke, Bruce Cockburn, and a few others had all shown jazz leanings in their recordings, but it was late 1983 before a seemingly steady flow of Christian jazz recordings began.

Keith Thomas released an album of upbeat piano jazz. John Mehler and Kenneth Nash (the latter formerly with secular group Weather Report) created an album of jazz arrangements of Maranatha! choruses and a few originals, entitled *Light the Night*. Likewise, Nash produced his own album of "devotional moments in praise and spoken word," *Quiet Streams*. Omega Sunrise did Seawind-type music. Former Seawind members Bob Wilson and Larry Williams teamed up with Tommy Funderbirk and Dan Huff to form "The Front." Sparrow's Koinonia jazz group started out playing one night a week at a club in Southern California and had two albums out by 1984. Interestingly, three of the members of Koinonia—Harlan Rogers, Bill Maxwell, and Hadley Hockensmith—had been three-quarters of Sonlight, which recorded some of the first jazz-flavored Christian music a decade earlier on Light Records. The other member of Sonlight had been Fletch Wiley.

Koinonia and some other groups and artists also showed a distinct Latin American influence in their music; Abraham Laboriel, Alex Acuna, and Justo Almario, the other three of Koinonia, hailed from south of the border. Also, reggae, ska, and other island music found its way into many songs recorded on contemporary Christian music albums, following secular trends. In 1984 one of the most notable reggae-influenced recordings was "Love's Not a Feeling," a hit song for Steve Camp and Michele Pillar.

Trumpeteer and vocalist Phil Driscoll showed a distinct jazz flavor in much of his music. He had the remarkable ability to sound like the best of himself, Joe Cocker, Chuck Mangione, Bob Seger, and Ray Charles, all at once. No surprise, then, that white audiences, black audiences, younger audiences, older audiences, rock audiences, jazz audiences, and praise audiences all went for some facet of his music.

The bridging of racial divisions, such as was done in a minor way by Driscoll, had by 1984 not gone as far as some artists would have preferred. Andrae Crouch expressed his concern for the industry's separation of black and white gospel. Suffering from the lack of ample black gospel radio stations and the strong tendency of white gospel stations to avoid much of the black gospel music, many of the black gospel artists did not get adequate exposure.

However, many contemporary Christian artists who were black preferred to be contemporary Christian artists first, with no allegiance to one type of audience over another. Myrrh Records was successful in establishing strong markets on both sides of the racial fence for black artists such as Leon Patillo, Morris Chapman, Philip Bailey, Al Green, and others. Andrae Crouch and the Disciples had broken the ground with their albums on Light Records years before. But Andrae was right in his assessment overall, as music by some excellent performers found the bridging of racial barriers a considerable task. Perhaps Myrrh Records had taken the best move, by including all artists on the one label rather than creating labels specifically for black or white gospel music.

Toward the mideighties, Christian music finally began to wend its way in substantial amounts into the next frontier: the burgeoning video market. Working with considerably lower budgets than their secular counterparts, Christian labels and artists stepped up efforts at producing creative videos which would stand up against the secular ones.

Silverwind's colorful "Song in the Night" video, released in 1982, was one of the first creative clips (i.e., nonconcert videos) for contemporary Christian music. It had been preceded by Word's *More Than Music* video show and Sparrow's videotaped Barry McGuire concert, which resulted in his album *Inside Out* and a few other experiments in Christian video music.

Soon Swedish rock group Jerusalem had a video out, which was shown on MTV a few times. Also taping on video were the Archers in a Colorado concert performance. Within a few months, other artists joined the stream into video. As Christian television networks began requesting video clips for their programming, the labels and artists stepped up their efforts further.

By 1984 the artists on video representations of their music included, among several others, Jerusalem, Sheila Walsh, Steve Taylor, Mylon LeFevre, Amy Grant, DeGarmo & Key, Sandi Patti, Randy Stonehill, the 77s, Charlie Peacock, Russ Taff, Benny Hester, Leslie Phillips, and Michael W. Smith. Several secular crossover artists also produced an array of videos: Donna Summer, Bob Dylan, U2, Kansas, and others were included, although their overtly Christian songs were not necessarily the ones featured. Secular involvement was also noted increasingly in production, editing, and direction of many of the videos, as trained video creators in the Christian sector developed.

A few of the videos were successfully landed on programs and networks in the secular world, but it was tough going. MTV was pretty well a closed market, expressing virtually no interest in playing the Christian videos, regardless of how good they were. The large secular labels had virtually cornered the market for the largest music television network. In 1984 lawsuits began to test the exclusivity arrangements many of the big secular labels made with the dominant music video medium. In the meantime, Christian rock was for all practical purposes off-limits on MTV.

However, more interest and accessibility was attained on national and local video-clip shows, which were coming into vogue by 1984. The smaller music networks also showed more interest than the giant MTV. It was on those services that artists such as Steve Taylor, whose video of his song "Meltdown" was the first Christian rock video "hit," had a sporting chance to infiltrate the secular.

The main use of videos in the early eighties was in promotion of recorded product by the record labels and artists. Through displaying the various videos in record and book stores, record buyers were able to "get a little closer" to the recording artists.

In 1984 all of the major labels, and some smaller ones, were beginning to view the sales potential of videos at the consumer level. Because of the increasing demand for purchaseable or rentable videos, the labels obliged with their debut of sale-or-rent videos. And in the same year the first Christian "video-oriented" music store opened in Columbus, Ohio. Heartsong Records, Tapes, and Videos displayed a wall of fifteen video monitors in the store, allowing customers to see and hear their music.

28/ *International Ripples*

For at least a few years the summer of 1984 in the United States will be best remembered as the year of the Olympics in Los Angeles. The Games etched their way into the memories of millions of people around the world, especially Americans.

While the press gave vast coverage to the contests on the various playing fields and at the pools, there was extensive evangelistic activity going on behind the scenes. Close to one hundred different Christian organizations participated under the coordination of the 1984 Olympic Outreach Committee. More than eleven thousand young people and adults from seventy-seven countries were commissioned to participate in evangelistic activity during the Games.

Music and drama played a major part in those enthusiastic endeavors. At several locations around the greater Los Angeles area, Christian musicians and singers performed gospel music for residents and foreign visitors. Debby Boone, Andrae Crouch, Bob Bennet, Kelly Willard, and more than one hundred and fifty other artists and groups performed seven hundred hours of gospel music.

Christian music of all types and tempos had by 1984 become increasingly international in its scope and its outreach. The number of artists crisscrossing the globe on concert tours had grown to the point that overseas trips were considered almost commonplace. Communist countries, once virtually off-limits to most Christian musicians, especially Americans, began opening their doors at an unprecedented rate. Living Sound played in Poland. Scott Wesley Brown performed there and in other countries behind the Iron Curtain. In Brown's "I Care Letter" in 1984, he said, "While I love America and the spirit of her Constitution, my allegiance is to Christ and his kingdom. As I walked side by side with Christians of the USSR, Czechoslovakia, East Germany, and Poland, I realized that all men are potentially my brothers in Christ.

"It is tough for them," he added, "but Jesus never promised a life full of roses without thorns. It breaks my heart to see musicians without instruments, churches without organs, people without Bibles. This why I CARE exists. You and I can do something about it. We have the resources to provide so much to those who are in need. We can help in the revival these Christians long for."

As a result of Brown's concern for the church behind the Curtain, he compiled and produced an album of music from American and European Christian artists, entitled *All the Church Is Singing*. Brown's I CARE organization then placed the album cassettes in the hands of Christians in Communist countries. Through the "Adopt a Musician" program, Christian music groups from the West were invited to support Christian music groups from behind the Iron Curtain. Programs were being set up for Poland, Czechoslovakia, East Germany, and the USSR.

For American musicians, travel overseas became an eye-opening experience in which the dire need for the gospel was sorely evident. More than once an American musician, used to performing freely in the United States churches, coffeehouses, and auditoriums, left on overseas jaunts assuming that the rest of the world would be much like America, with its relatively open tolerance of Christianity.

But those same artists returned to the United States with a new appreciation of the concepts of freedom and grace as the result of visits to some countries. They were happy to be home, but loaded with a new burden for a dying world, and anxious to respond more fervently than ever before to Christ's Great Commission.

Travel to non-Communist countries was, of course, much more widespread and frequent, and requests from host countries came for more. There were even a few American performers who relocated in other countries, feeling the burden to do all their work there. Karen Lafferty moved to Holland for work with Youth with a Mission, and Barry McGuire moved to New Zealand, partly because of his zeal for reaching Asians for Christ.

Another type of global concern which intensified in the eighties was that of world hunger. Certain artists became very vocal on the matter and put their weighty support behind organizations whose goals were to fight hunger. Gene Cotton was one of the first of the contemporary Christian singers to carry the banner, as early as the midseventies, just before he crossed over into secular music and left Jesus music behind. Carrying on the cause in the next decade would be Randy Stonehill, Phil Keaggy, Sheila Walsh, Petra, and the Bill Gaither Trio, as well as others who supported the hunger-relieving work of Compassion International. They spoke up for Compassion's ministry by appearing in magazine ads, speaking about it in concerts, and singing about the plight of the undernourished in their music. "Who Will Save the Children?" was one of the most notable songs on the subject, released in 1984 on Randy Stonehill's album *Celebrate This Heartbeat*. Joining Randy on the song was Phil Keaggy.

Another effort to combat hunger was an album put together to benefit World Vision. Artists contributing a cut to the album included Barbara Mandrell, B. J. Thomas, Andrae Crouch, Evie Karlsson, Amy Grant, Dion, Keith Green, Walter Hawkins, the Imperials, and the Sweet Comfort Band. Keith Green's song "A Billion Starving People," released posthumously on a 1984 collection of Green songs, also was a poignant reminder of the plight facing many of the world's population. Some of the revenues from John Michael Talbot's albums were sent to a relief organization, Mercy Corps International.

The widening of the Christian world view among musicians and singers was aided in part by the efforts of Cam Floria and his Christian Artists Seminars. The annual gathering in Estes Park, Colorado, had proven to be a successful conclave of aspiring and established music makers and people in the associated industries. Over the years the workshops and seminars at the Estes Park location continued to widen in scope, presenting different views on the hows, whys, and wherefores of Christian music. The nightly concerts, over a week's period, featured more than fifty popular and up-and-coming musicians. It was at those concerts that several artists from foreign countries were introduced to American audiences.

In 1981 Floria and his counterparts in Europe coordinated the first Christian Artists Europe at DeBron Conference Center in Holland. Musicians were invited from all over Europe to join Americans for the conference. That first seminar had more American presence than some Europeans approved of. However, by the next year's seminar a more acceptable balance of clinicians and artists representing the European countries was reached. Participants even included Christian music people from behind the Iron Curtain.

Holland was a natural for such a gathering, according to one of the main coordinators, Leen La Riviere, who since 1969 had worked with the Continentals organization to see music ministry grow in Europe. A concert network—Continental Sound—had been developed over the years to aid musicians in touring and playing in various European cities and towns. The Continentals alone had six groups touring in Holland in 1983.

Continental Sound also published their own Dutch-language magazine, *Sjofar*, which was later incorporated into another Dutch publication, *Gospel Music Magazine*. Through Continental Sound and Youth for Christ (the latter of which had first ventured into music ministry soon after World War II), Holland, with a population of only fourteen million, had been the breeding ground for a surprisingly active Christian movement through music ministries.

"In 1969," said La Riviere, looking back fourteen years later, "Holland and neighboring Belgium counted three gospel groups and maybe ten youth choirs. As a result of the work of the Continental Singers and Continental Sound, in 1983 we count in the two countries about one thousand gospel groups, soloists, and youth choirs, with some of them joined in their own union. That means an average of fifteen thousand young people involved in gospel music in the two countries."

Music festivals, much like the Jesus festivals in America, drew crowds. Youth for Christ and Continental Sound each sponsored one annually through 1979. More than four thousand people attended them. In nearby Belgium, of which the northern half is Dutch-speaking, an autumn One Way Day was held, and a spring Pentecost evangelistic gathering drew nearly ten thousand visitors. The two yearly events were sponsored by a group known as Opwekking.

Flevofestival (originally called Kameperland) was an evangelistic festival aimed at the secular Dutch-speaking people. Its attendance annually since the midseventies averaged four thousand, and it was sponsored by Youth for Christ.

La Riviere spoke highly of the way in which the various organizations throughout the small European nation worked together cooperatively, including Continental Sound, Opwekking, GMI, Youth for Christ, *Gospel Music Magazine,* Euroconcerts, Christian Artists, and others. "The revival in music," he added, "has opened doors into radio and TV as well. NCRV and EO, two broadcasting services, started regular radio programs with gospel music, and television as well, featuring gospel musicians."

The longest-lived gospel-music group in Holland, according to La Riviere, was Burning Candles. Some of the Continental Sound artists included a rock band, Messengers; folk-country singer Wim Pols; the traditional/classical ensemble, Hymne; a jazz ensemble led by Carel Heinsius; Discipel; and scores of others. Also quite popular in Holland is the folk duo known as Elly & Rikkert, well-known performers who became Christians after their career was already going strong, and fellow-entertainers Gert & Hermien Timmermans.

As one travels south from Holland, through the French-speaking part of Belgium, and into France itself, the influence in the churches becomes heavily Catholic. In fact, 85 percent of the fifty-four million inhabitants of France are Catholic, 3 percent are Muslim, 1.5 percent are Protestant, and only .5 percent are reported to be born-again Christians, according to recent surveys. The French have a strong classical music background, similar to several other European countries. For a long time music had little to do with the church, according to Marc Brunet, whose Sephora Music organization was formed to help develop Christian music in French-speaking countries.

"The slow development of music in the church here," he explained in 1984, "is partly due to French reformer Calvin's disdain for music or instruments in church. Because of this limitation and persecution in past centuries, many of the great artists and intellectuals had to emigrate to such countries as Switzerland, Germany, and Holland. This left France with a cultural void in both the society and the church."

About twenty years ago, however, modern music styles started to show up in evangelistic churches (the few there were). Charles Road and Gerard Peilhon were the first to use guitar and compose their own chants (possibly similar to praise choruses of the American Jesus movement). The modern music was immediately controversial.

A lot of small musical groups were formed in France in the seventies, all part-time ministries rather than full-time professions. Two companies, SEMA and TRINITE, contributed greatly to the development of French music and served as pioneers in the work. They produced and recorded dozens of groups, the most well-known including "Les Temoins" (The Witnesses), "Les Reflets" (The Reflections), Jean Paul Andre, Jean Paul Ayme, "Naissance" (Birth), "Les Commandos du Seigneur" (The Commandoes of the Lord), and "Vent d'Espoir" (Wind of Spirit).

Others included the Cascades, Transit, Alain Faure, Les Benjamins, the Apostrophes, and Pasturages. Also making music during that all-important formative decade were Danie and Moise Hurtel, Intersection, the Roffidal Trio, Pierre and Jean Help, and the Emmanuel Trio. At that time, the only full-time performer was Gil Bernard, a former music hall singer who had been converted in the early sixties. He directed TRINITE.

The first event of national importance in gospel music for France came during Pentecost in 1972, according to Brunet. For three days, sixteen French groups performed a wide range of modern styles before an audience numbering about nine hundred, a sizable one for the time. Several organizations co-sponsored the event. A similar festival was held simultaneously in Belgium to the north.

As in Holland, Youth for Christ organized several music tours, using foreign bands and French groups. Festivals began to become more common in France, with one also in Switzerland nearby. An annual festival, the JEF Festival, was started in 1972.

As the development of gospel music continued, controversy again grew as to the validity, even the sanctity, of Christian music played with electric guitars. That argument dragged on in many countries just as it had in the U.S.

In spite of the disagreements and deliberation over the use of contemporary Christian music, it continued to develop. Sephora Music was formed by Marc Brunet in 1978. The next year, he began to publish *Sephora Music Magazine,* and introduced the first catalog of American and English records available to the French.

Certain American artists began making appearances in France, including Tom Howard, 2nd Chapter of Acts, Karen Lafferty, Larry Norman, and Living Sound. A few French bands got substantial exposure, including Philippe and Christian Chanson, Christian Gonzalez, and Jude 25. Still, none were traveling or performing full-time.

In 1980 a new record label appeared, called Editions CDE, working mainly within the circle of the Assemblies of God in France. In 1981 the new French government authorized the establishment of local radio stations. (European countries often had had only a few government-operated radio stations serving the respective nations, but that began changing.) These new stations opened the airwaves for gospel music as well as secular.

New studios and labels continued to develop in the eighties. In 1983, again during Pentecost, the most important musical event for gospel music in France took place, according to Marc Brunet. Two thousand people attended the Sephora Festival at Dijon, the first of its kind. With both French and foreign bands participating, the festival offered a centralized concept toward gospel music, with booths, expositions, and artistic productions such as mime, choreography, and films.

The summer of 1983 saw the rise of an antirock movement in France, with opponents using cassettes, videocassettes, and Christian reviews and conferences. Even though it remained as an original medium and was always appreciated by the youth, modern Christian music and secular music was put into question by many critics, much as in the States.

Brunet added that by 1984 there were about forty evangelical libraries in France, which sold mostly cassettes, though not all were contemporary. He also reported that there was more Catholic music

than Protestant Christian music, but it leaned more toward traditional sounds.

"Presently," he added, "there aren't more than about a dozen
full-time Christian musicians found in France. They don't count on
music as a living, and others only tour on their free time and during
the holidays."

For Spain and the Spanish-speaking nations, much of the work
in contemporary Christian music has been accomplished by Producciones de la Raiz. The organization was founded in the late seventies.

"It began in response to the need among Spanish Christians for
more adequate musical materials," Luis Alfredo Dias reported in
1984. "We organized the first festival of gospel music in 1977, and
later an encounter for Christian artists in 1980. We began to visit
religious and secular bookshops with the goal of greater distribution
of contemporary gospel music, with promotion through articles in
various magazines. We organized a trip to the Greenbelt Festival in
England and attended the Christian Artists Seminar in Holland.
Like the labor of ants . . . long, difficult, and often without apparent
results. But we remain clear in our purpose and firm in our goal,
assured that 'He who began the good work in us, will also accomplish it.' "

With four hundred million people living in Spanish-speaking
countries, Producciones de la Raiz had a formidable task ahead. But
with enthusiasm such as often seen in the pioneers of contemporary
Christian music in the United States, they kept plodding on. There
were tremendously encouraging developments.

"Together with IBRA-RADIO, an interdenominational organization dedicated to gospel broadcasting," Dias said, "we began in
early 1983 a weekly program of thirty minutes duration, with news
of international gospel music. The response to the program has been
very favorable."

A number of Spanish editions of recordings from around the
world were being published and distributed by the eighties, including imports from Maranatha! Music in the U.S. and GMI in Holland. Other releases included: *Nada Es Neutral* (Nothing is Neutral),
a new-wave album by a group known as 2000 DC; *Oye PaPa* (Listen,
Daddy), a musical based on the Lord's Prayer; and *Rockangular,* by a
group that composed themes within symphonic rock. "These productions," added Dias, "have been self-financed mostly by their
composers, together with the support of their churches, friends, and
families."

In addition to 2000 DC and Rockangular, there were several

other musicians making a notable impact on the gospel music scene in Spain and Spanish-speaking countries. Adolfo Rivero, an accomplished guitarist, had recorded three albums by 1984. Luis Alfredo Dias was born in Uruguay, where he started his music career. He then lived in the United States and Finland, where he recorded albums in both Finnish and Spanish. Also a painter, Dias had six albums to his credit. Resso (Echo) began making music ten years ago with a pop Christian sound. Paz (Peace) had done three recordings, all recorded live in concert. Alex Blanco, one of the founders of the group Resso, was also a teacher of the classical guitar and performed pop music as well. He was creator of the work, *Oye PaPa;* he then formed a group known as Tragaluz (Cellar Window), and had a recording with them called *Every Day.*

Jose de Segovia, a journalist living in Madrid, provided information on yet other Spanish musicians: Jose and Vicente Rodriguer, two brothers living in Germany as emigrants; Metamorfosis, a jazz band whose album *Butterflies and Elephants* received accolades as one of the best jazz records in Spain; and Vincente Forner, who started "Units" (United), one of the first gospel rock bands in Spain, and later made two recordings with his own group, Manantial.

Tours of artists and groups from other nations were coordinated by Prodduciones de la Raiz also. Adrien Snell from England, Karen Lafferty from Holland, Discipel from Holland, and a group known as Bob Hope from Sweden all sang the Good News in Spain in 1983 or 1984. *The Bible in Songs,* the first cassette for the evangelical market dedicated to children, came in Dutch form from Holland, and was in part translated into Spanish for the master tape, and released in Spain. Also in the works were Spanish editions of records by England's John Pantry and a Swedish group, Salt.

Spanish-speaking people were also introduced to their own gospel music magazine, *Entrelineas* (Between the Lines), published for the first time in the early eighties.

"Since our work began six years ago," Luis Alfredo Dias explained, "we have been confronted with the problem of distribution. There was no complete directory of religious bookshops in order to plan for serious marketing; thus, we began obtaining a complete list of places selling our music. After dozens of trips, covering most of the country by public transportation, we obtained what we wanted. Besides the ten evangelical bookshops, one hundred and ninety Catholic stores, plus some secular ones that also sell religious music, we visited nearly two hundred persons in charge of small church bookshops of all evangelical denominations. We have arranged with some of them for exclusive distribution. For the first time, the same music can be heard, learned, and sung by the complete body of Christ in Spain. We marvel at this miracle."

The interaction of Holland, France, and Spain provided a glimpse at the activity in contemporary Christian music throughout much of Europe. To go into each country in detail would require a full book in itself; it is unfortunate that they cannot all be covered here. In many of the European nations, the history would read much as the American history does, only in microcosm.

Portugal and Italy are predominantly Catholic countries where the evangelical movement of contemporary Christian music was just beginning to make ripples in 1984. In Switzerland, there was a small but growing contingent of gospel-music performers and creators.

Scandinavia's development of Christian music had been progressive and encouraging. A pioneer in the Scandinavian countries was Levi Petrus, a pastor of the old Pentecostal Church of Stockholm, Sweden. "He believed in the power of the music," explains Leen La Riviere, "so new music has a long tradition in Norway, Sweden, and Denmark."

Perhaps most familiar to Americans were Evie Tornquist Karlsson and her husband, Pele Karlsson. Evie was an early starter in her music career, singing as a young teenager. She was American, but her family's heritage was Swedish, and she hit the hearts of Scandinavians early on. In 1974 Kurt Kaiser introduced her to American audiences for the first time via a Word album, and she was immediately a favorite in the United States too. At first considered traditional by those wanting more rock-type Christian music, she managed to find acceptance in contemporary and traditional music circles. In the early eighties, she married Pele Karlsson, and they moved to California and recorded albums together, redeveloping traditional trends in their music, such as on their album *Restoration*.

Other Swedish artists with whom American Christian music fans had been acquainted in recent years included the excellent contemporary choral group Choralerna, who recorded an album with Danniebelle Hall for Sparrow Records, and hard-rock bands Edin-Adahl and Jerusalem, whose albums have been released through the Benson Company. A name to begin appearing in the eighties on records in the United States was Jan Groth, a former secular pop singer from Denmark who turned to contemporary Christian music. Other popular Scandinavian singers to be heard on the American side of the ocean were Solvei Larsen and Ingemar Olsson.

In West Germany, the battle with and within the church concerning the use of rock in gospel music continued. In the seventies, singer and writer Inge Bruck experienced a spiritual renewal which reportedly nixed her secular career, but she then successfully performed gospel music, including making appearances on radio and television. Andreas Malessa, the rock band Semaja, and Klaus and Hella Heizmann were other artists keeping the contemporary Christian music scene going in Germany. Concerts were on the increase in the eighties, with some fans begging for more. There were efforts at building a Christian music study center.

The development of contemporary Christian music in Britain closely paralleled that in the United States, but on a smaller scale. The cultural exchange between the United States and Great Britain saw musicals by Jimmy and Carol Owens hitting popularity in England (including *Come Together, If My People,* and *The Witness*), Liberation Suite from San Marcos, Texas making a mark in Ireland and England, and Larry Norman colluding with various friend musicians in Great Britain and performing in concerts and on record. In 1979 one British festival promoter, Tony Tew, said, "The pioneering music of Larry Norman has crossed the water, and we've learnt that it really is possible to be a Christian and a rock 'n' roll singer."

In the other direction, from east to west, came Malcolm & Alwyn, Garth Hewitt, Dave Pope, Judy MacKenzie, and Graham Kendrick, among the pioneers of overseas contemporary Christian music. Unfortunately, the tours of foreign artists in the United States met with little notice until the eighties.

Buzz and *New Christian Music* magazines were instrumental in communicating what was happening in Christian music in Britain. In the eighties they were joined by *Strait,* an earthy street paper which covered especially the more avant-garde aspects of the gospel-music scene.

And there was plenty which was avant-garde in Great Britain's Christian music. Two of the progenitors of the new-wave Christian music which would begin to flex its muscles in the eighties were Giantkiller and Ishmael United. The latter group, originally billed as Rev. Counta and the Speedoze, was led by a far-out vicar whose music was equally so, bold for its time.

Many of the more radical rockers were welcomed at England's annual Greenbelt festival, where a wide variety of musicians played before crowds in excess of sixteen thousand. Garth Hewitt, writing in the Greenbelt program for 1979, explained, "Greenbelt has only one criterion (apart from musical standards—which are applied honestly!), and that is that the band or artists must be Christian—then it is up to them how they glorify God." This brought charges from some observers who complained that the musicians and bands never did anything "spiritual," but the promoters were quick to remind the critics that Greenbelt was not to be compared with the other Christian festivals around the world; it was unique.

Cliff Richard, who appeared at Greenbelt, released a few gospel-oriented albums in England, but only a couple of them made it to the U.S. His *Small Corners* LP was a complete collection of popular contemporary Christian songs, but was available in the United States only by special order. His *Help It Along* album helped to generate monies for the TEAR Fund, a organization for fighting world hunger, a cause of which Cliff was a well-known supporter. Cliff also continued putting one or two token Christian-lyric songs on his pop albums in America.

Myrrh Records imported much of the music being recorded on the Myrrh label's British editions, doing short runs in the States, but providing a bit of an opportunity for record collectors to pick up on the British music without having to go the expensive route. Andrew Culverwell, a British singer, was first brought over via record by Manna Records, and then picked up by Word's DaySpring label.

In the eighties, there was a stepped-up emphasis on importing the music being created and performed in countries other than the United States. Sheila Walsh, already recorded and well-known in her native Scotland and the rest of Great Britain, arrived on U.S. shores with fanfare celebrating her first American release, *Future Eyes,* on Sparrow Records. Her music varied from Helen Reddy-styled ballads to new-wave music and modern rock in the Sheena Easton vein. Her first American concert tour, complete with special effects on stage, was well received, and by 1984 she had released her second U.S. album, and her video of the song "Mystery" was placed on sale, backed with American Steve Taylor's "Meltdown" video. The two rock performers embarked on an Australian concert tour in the late part of the year.

In the same year Refuge and Pilgrim America Records, both distributed by The Benson Company, brought in more imported contemporary Christian music. Artists featured on the labels included Adrien Snell (who broke relatively new ground when some of his works were presented on national television in Britain and Holland), John Pantry, Barry Crompton, Andy McCarroll & Moral Support, Paradise, the Barratt Band, Bryn Haworth, and Fresh Air. Other names cropped up almost monthly, as a "British explosion" was heralded by the various labels.

South Africa, Australia, and New Zealand also developed contemporary Christian music, though it was not as quick to reach the United States. To the advantage of the Americans, the British, the Australians, the New Zealanders, and the South Africans, English was a common language. And furthermore English was a fairly universal language. Many of the citizens of Europe and other continents had at least a rudimentary knowledge of English as a second language, allowing some degree of freedom for English-speaking artists on recordings or in concert.

Conversely, the musicians who knew only their non-English language found little success in performing before American audiences, who had by tradition been disinterested in learning or understanding music in other languages. Even Spanish-language songs, which communicated to the high percentage of Mexican and Spanish-speaking people in the United States, only came through on albums in a trickle.

Part of the reason for the indifference among American Christians was the extraordinary abundance of contemporary Christian music generated in English. There was no purpose, they reasoned, in listening to languages they couldn't understand. That response was typical for Americans, but they unfortunately missed out on some quality music.

There was much more tolerance for other languages in the European countries, where the people were much more used to international exchange and interlingual communication.

In the meantime, American Christian music makers extended their reach to include parts of the world long neglected as far as gospel music was concerned. Cam Floria addressed the gospel music industry in 1983 with an observation and challenge. Citing the progress made in Europe already, he turned the industry's attention elsewhere:

"Asia and the Third World are a bigger challenge," he said, "but with more potential than all the rest of the world combined, because of the phenomenal growth of Christianity in those countries and because most of the people in the world live there. But they are way behind—you have to look *hard* to see how far back they are.

"Yet, I believe the really important future for the gospel-music industry could be out there. Just think where *we* were only thirty years ago!"

Floria then referred to various musicians who had begun the work there already, including Otis Skillings, Chris Beatty, and Jimmy Owens. He referred to Barry McGuire's move to New Zealand, and the new Christian Artists Asia Music Seminar, first held in 1982. Also he noted that four Asian seminars would be held back to back in 1984, in Singapore, Hong Kong, the Philippines, and Korea.

"Music influences people," he continued, "especially young people. I was told recently by the leader of one of the world's outstanding youth organizations that by 1990 50 percent of the world's teenagers will be Asians.

"You say, 'But it's the Christians who will use our music and buy our cassettes. Are they there?'

"Yes. Two hundred and fifty evangelical churches in the little country of Singapore, over seven hundred in Hong Kong, innumerable hosts of Christians in the Philippines, and I was told by a knowledgeable Chinese distributor that 30 percent of the whole population of South Korea is Christian. But they have very little Christian music to play on their Sony Walkmans!

"Why?" he questioned. "Because we have all but forgotten the world that exists past Europe! But, believe me, it *is* the future. The gospel continues to change our world, and the music of the gospel will follow. . . .

"The opportunity is here, now. If we don't fill the void with our music, someone else will fill it with theirs. We must embrace Asia and the Third World. They are the future."

29/ Muscle Shoals

About one hundred and twenty-five miles to the southwest of Nashville is a neighborhood of four fairly small Alabama towns straddling the wide Tennessee River. They are Florence, Sheffield, Tuscumbia, and Muscle Shoals—towns with names foreign to all but residents, travelers, musicians, and music fans.

In Florence is the birthplace of W. C. Handy, "The Father of the Blues." But more musicians probably know of the Muscle Shoals area for another musical reputation, built in the sixties and seventies. While nearby Nashville laid claim to the title of Music City, USA, Muscle Shoals started developing its own clientele of musicians in rock, soul, and country music. The city-limits sign still proudly proclaims: "Welcome to Muscle Shoals, Hit Recording Capital of the World."

Indeed, for a period of several years there was always something in the national Top Ten charts that was recorded there. The list of artists who recorded in that remote corner of Alabama included, among others, Clarence Carter, Aretha Franklin, Candi Staton, Paul Simon, Rod Stewart, Willie Nelson, Cat Stevens, and Art Garfunkel.

The communities became a haven in those years for recording artists and studio musicians. Tucked away from the hustle and bustle of the Nashville scene and Los Angeles or New York studios, it was an attractive retreat for musicians to come and do their thing. In many cases, their "thing" included the extensive use and abuse of drugs, from marijuana to cocaine.

Quickly Muscle Shoals residents began to stereotype the entire music community there as no more than some sort of front for orgiastic debauchery. Even the churches took a hands-off stance.

In 1980, after a slowdown in the music business, the Muscle Shoals area once again hit the trade news when Bob Dylan went there shortly after his widely reported conversion to record his *Slow Train Coming* album at Muscle Shoals Sound.

One of the musicians who played on the Dylan sessions was Ronnie Eades, a saxophonist member of the famed Muscle Shoals Horns. Eades had been in the area since 1968, and had worked his way virtually to the top, including a three and a half month tour with Elton John in 1974. But even after that, and even as he blew the sax for Dylan, his life was skidding toward the bottom. His major problem was alcohol—a case of beer a day—plus more than his share of drugs. He had the reputation in music circles as the "town drunk."

"I was the life of the party," he said, looking back in 1984 with cleared vision, "always cuttin' up and everything. I never let anybody know whether I had problems or not. Deep down inside, when I got by myself, I knew that there was a problem. I'd try to drink those problems away, but it didn't work. I'd be miserable, then I'd go outside with some people. We'd start drinkin', cuttin' up, carryin' on. It was okay for awhile. Then after I got back to myself again, there it was. It wouldn't go away."

For recording engineer Jerry Masters, the tremendous success the Muscle Shoals music business had had with hit records and plentiful times helped to cover up a serious state of affairs in his own life. "I was always the first one to roll a joint, always the first one to mix up the mushrooms. I did an entire Rod Stewart album one time on mushrooms. I would do anything that would desensitize me. I got so good at engineering that I'd get blasted away and still cut hit records. It didn't matter anymore."

Meanwhile, Eades was lovingly but continually witnesssed to by his daughter, a new Christian. "She tried to get me to go to church," he recounted later. "I thought it was a joke."

Eades was playing in clubs around the Muscle Shoals area for a living. He recalls the line of reasoning he took in order to turn down his daughter's invitation. He thought, "The way I've met most of those Christians that I know was in these clubs. I don't want to have anything to do with this. I'm just as good as they are. What do I need with this? What do I need with God?"

For nearly six years several people had been praying for Eades. Finally his wife to be and his daughter got him to the church. "I'm gonna go once to get you off my back," he told them. "Then I don't wanta hear anything else about it."

"So I went to this full-gospel church and there was something different about it," Eades recalls. "It wasn't so bad. Something snapped inside of me. I acted like I didn't want to go back, but I went for about eight Sundays following. I still stayed in the clubs. As I went to church, conviction, truth, everything started comin' on. I *knew* that's what I needed! But a lot of pride and everything else was still in the way.

"After about eight weeks I couldn't stand it any longer. I still played the club that Saturday night, but I went down to the altar the next morning. I believe I got saved in that club. My eyes started to open. From drinking a case of beer a day, I had one beer that Saturday night, and I couldn't keep *that* down!

"I was very confused. I said, 'What is this?' Even when I was sick, I could drink beer! But I know it was the Spirit of the Lord coming inside me, and that mess just couldn't stay, couldn't live.

"That Sunday night, that was it. I said, 'Here's my life, Lord; as big a mess as it's in, you got it.' "

The memorable date for Eades was in 1981. He was thirty-nine years old when he made the decision. Eades and forty-one-year-old engineer Jerry Masters didn't know each other at the time, but they were later to become best of Christian friends.

Masters had attempted to run from his own problems by going to Florida, on his way to the Keys to get a job on a fishing boat. But he stopped over in Miami with some friends, who got him a job working at the famous Criteria Studios, where top hits like those by the Bee Gees were to be recorded.

"Everything I did was a hit," he recalls. But he also recalls spending three-quarters of his money on cocaine, "trying to fill the void in me."

"While in Miami I started reaching out to God," he continues. "I'd go out on the sunroof of the studio every day and pray. But I didn't know what I was praying to. To me, God was some giant guy in the sky with a big stick and a white beard. I prayed and asked him to send me a wife. He did, and she was saved. So I started getting the Word, whether I wanted it or not."

Masters ultimately moved back to Birmingham, about three hours drive south of Muscle Shoals. The binges continued. "I was drinkin' real heavy, and it was *killing* me, and I knew it. I'd go on cocaine binges for three or four days at a time and do nothing but take cocaine and drink Scotch. I would get so strung out, I'd take about ten Valium to try and come down. A couple of times I think I came close to dyin'—just layin' there in my bed, by myself, in my apartment."

Jerry's wife filled a void in his life, but he says not *the* void that was killing him. Following his move to Birmingham, he spent a year on retainer for a studio where he did virtually no work. "They paid me, but rarely worked me," he recalls. "I sat around, rolled joints, played video games. That ran out, so I came back to Muscle Shoals, checking unemployment. My life had been so good; now it was nose-diving."

Masters went out to a ranch owned by one of the successful studio owners. "There was a Bible sitting on the table there," he remembers, "left there by the studio owner's wife. I'd been drinking vodka straight.

"I just opened the Bible. I looked down at this Scripture, Deuteronomy 28:5. It says, 'You will take a new wife, and for a period of one year you will not go to work, you will not go to war, you will do nothing but stay home and take care of your wife.'

"That's exactly what had just happened to me! I'd been given a year with my new wife, who I'd prayed for, to enjoy her and all that. I looked back and I started thinkin' about all the times I'd used to get drunk and take speed and smoke grass and ride motorcycles fearlessly, and I realized God had his hand on me all those years. I started cryin', and I cried for about two days. And I couldn't figure out why I was cryin'!

"I called my wife, Edie, and I said, 'What in the world's goin' on?' She said her church down there in Birmingham had been prayin' for me."

Next a pastor told Jerry to phone Ronnie Eades. "He didn't know Ronnie; he just knew of him from another musician who was a Christian, Randy Cutlip. I called Ronnie and said, 'Can you pray for me? I'm havin' a real rough time.'

"He said, 'Sure. I'll be glad to.' I hung up the phone and went to the studio, and he was sittin' there waitin' for me.

"Ronnie started sharing what God had done in his life. He'd been saved a year and two days. Boy, the tears started coming, and inside I was screaming, 'I wanna be saved! I wanna be saved! I wanna be saved!' But I didn't say anything. Ronnie left, and I went and had a meeting with the studio owner. I got back in my car and headed back to Birmingham. Somewhere between here and there I got saved! By the time I got home I was a different person.

"I noticed I only drank about one glass of wine that night. I didin't think anything about it. I usually got up and started drinkin' as I got out of bed, and drank all day. But the next day I got up and I felt *so good!* I didn't want anything to bring that down. So I waited until that night, and I drank one beer. Then I drank another glass of wine, and said, 'Man, this stuff doesn't feel right.'

"For six years I had never gone to bed without taking a Valium. I couldn't! I had to stagger to bed to go to sleep. Also, I had smoked grass for thirty years. In the last ten years, I had smoked at least three joints a day. So I had to be under those three influences to even think of layin' down and tryin' to go to sleep.

"The Spirit of God spoke to me that day, though, and said, 'I want you to go back there and lay down and close your eyes.' I went back and laid down and closed my eyes, and that's the last thing I remember. I woke up the next morning totally delivered from alcohol, Valium, marijuana, and cocaine. None of it can enter my body now. God delivered me supernaturally overnight of all that junk. If I'd have gone to the hospital, it would've taken me six months to a year to dry out. That was May 2, 1982."

The conversions of Eades and Masters were just two instances of what would become an almost steady stream of changed lives in those mid-sized Alabama towns. The roll was being added to down yonder in a revival which would sweep through the music industry in an area with no less than seven recording studios.

Lenny LeBlanc, who was successful with a pop hit, "Falling," by LeBlanc and Carr, became a Christian in 1981. When contemporary Christian singer Michele Pillar came to the area to record her first solo album, she met Lenny "by providential 'chance.'" The result was a duet on her first album. Lenny later signed with Heartland Records in Florida to do his own Christian albums.

Cindy Richardson, who toured extensively with Crystal Gayle as backup singer, became a Christian after attending Ronnie Eades' Bible study. When Ava Aldridge, a songwriter and publisher who had co-written the pop hit song, "Spendin' the Night Together," was invited to sing at church with Lenny LeBlanc, she was born again.

Added to the list were Joey Holder and Steve Herbert. Jerry Wallace, a producer and songwriter ("Even the Nights Are Better," by Air Supply) was also won to the Lord.

Guitarist Will McFarlane, one of the first of the Muscle Shoals musicians to become a Christian, also became one of the most vocal and engaging spokesmen of the revival going on there.

But ask any of these Muscle Shoals musicians and they'll readily tell you of the hopes and aspirations they have for their studio cities to become a center for *Christian* recording activity. And the way things were going by late 1984, they were right on target. The number of contemporary Christian albums coming out of Muscle Shoals had greatly increased, including two by Michele Pillar, two by Will McFarlane, two by Lenny LeBlanc, and one each by Robyn Pope, Cindy Richardson, and others.

"Muscle Shoals is just another town as far as location goes," said Jon Phelps, president of Heartland Records, who recorded several projects there in mid-1984. "But there is a pouring out of the

Holy Spirit and an anointing from God on the people of this town. It has spread from one person to the next. It's so obvious. I've seen it mostly in the music community.

"This town doesn't look like it's going to lose its vision. If it did, it would repeat what people have done over and over again. I just believe their hearts are square on the nose."

"Muscle Shoals is pregnant," says Eades. "Something is fixin' to be birthed here that's big. He told us we're going to be a part of it, and the Lord's gonna put us doin' exactly what He wants us to be doin'."

"I think by the time your book's out, it'll be exactly what it was here fifteen years ago," adds Jerry Masters, "except it'll be for the Lord. I think it'll be a center for cutting records for Jesus."

Watching the Muscle Shoals musicians build each other up is very reminiscent of the Jesus movement of some fifteen years ago. Masters was referring to the rock and country industry which thrived there in the sixties and seventies, but it was during that same time that musicians were first creating contemporary Christian music some two thousand miles away on the West Coast, such as in the Calvary Chapel community. Talking to Eades, McFarlane, Masters, and the others is like witnessing an enthusiasm and unity of purpose unequaled in much of Jesus music since those early days. Just as there was always guidance and support offered by the Calvary Chapels for their musical missionaries, there is a group spirit and support for the Muscle Shoals musicians in several churches.

"There are three or four churches that are really going out of their way to open their doors to us, to support us in ministry when we do go out of town, or just out on the streets of our own community," says Will McFarlane. "It was the Lord who impressed upon us that we didn't have the right or the unction to go into somebody else's town and tell them how we think they ought to live their lives if we weren't being recognized, raised up, or submitted to eldership in our own local fellowships. If nobody recognized or laid hands on me, to send me out from my own local body or from a fellowship— be it a home fellowship or a church building—or at least some accountability as we submit ourselves one to another, then I shouldn't be going out.

"The gospel is a corporate Word. It is *together* with *all* the saints that you grasp the width and height and depth of the love of Christ. None of us feel that it's an individualistic thing."

There is another interesting thing to note about the musicians in Muscle Shoals. They're older, more mature, rock-generation musicians whom the Lord blessed at a much later age than most of the

Jesus musicians of the Jesus movement. While countless Christian musicians still eye the climb to success and stardom in order, they say, to use their stardom as a witness, Masters and the others have come directly from there. And while some of the more derisive of their fellow-musicians may view them as has-beens, Masters replies, "We've been at the top, and we know what it's like. We *chose* to be where we are now."

Choosing to be more selective in the music they record now means that their work is usually not as lucrative as it used to be. Some of the musicians have humbled themselves to the point of digging ditches to make the money they could be making playing on stoned-out sessions and hanging around with certain famous musicians. "I don't mind doing construction work and all that," says saxophonist Eades. "The Lord's just teachin' us patience, to persevere and depend on him for our needs."

Eades, for one, has chosen to stay away from the secular sessions. "The one thing I play on now is contemporary Christian music, which down here in this area at this particular time is not enough to make a living by. The budgets for Christian music are cut short. You might make one hundred or two hundred dollars on an album, whereas we used to make one thousand, sometimes two thousand dollars a week.

"It's gone from a whole lot to nothing. But the meaning of life has changed for me now. I want to help other people. I want to help other musicians who are in the same place that we've been, and these kids that think, 'Hey, man, if I was like that, I'd be okay.'

"The Lord's leading us into schools and prisons to say, 'Hey, you wouldn't. We've been there, man, and there ain't nothing there. The bottom line is: You've gotta have Jesus to survive. That's the only way.'"

Coming to surface in Muscle Shoals were the Paul/Timothy relationships referred to much earlier in this history. The musicians of the area are anxious to make it a center for Christian recording projects, working with Christian songwriters and performers whether they be trained or novice. Recording there, they say, is more than just an in-studio experience.

"It's such a small place that our lives are an open book to one another," adds Will McFarlane. "Fellowship keeps us close and pressing on. If I step out of line in this town, every youth group will find out within a few hours. We're accountable for our actions here.

"People can come in and know that churches are going to be praying for their record while we're making it here. They know that people are going to be able to come into the studio and break bread with them and pray before each song is cut. In many other places, you'd get lost in the studios and never get that. Here, it's a family matter.

"You record in Muscle Shoals, and all of a sudden people are showin' up in the studio with food for you, because they know you're hungry. They see the Kingdom actually expressed here. And that expresses life to the folks who aren't Christians who are actually playing on the dates. Many times all the musicians on the dates are not believers, and they're seeing something different too."

"I think the Lord," adds Jerry Masters, "had decided there's so much talent in this town, and he's tired of it being used for the enemy, and he's takin' over this town!"

The scene was an urban university campus in a large southeastern city. On this particular 1984 night a brisk fall wind cut through the open-air hallways of the school's arts complex, catching people in short sleeves off-guard.

A table with a coffee urn, soft drinks, chips, and crackers sat across from the auditorium entrance. About forty people had come tonight to the Christian "coffeehouse."

Represented in the forty people was a cross section of college-aged personality types: the studious, the nervous, the retiring, the brash. While one man madly raced through the pages of his Bible searching for an elusive passage, another left through the back door to light up a cigarette, then lingered to hear the music performed on the stage.

The music represented a cross section too, a potpourri of music styles. The featured singer performed using recorded tracks. Later other people were invited to sing a song or two. One sang country and Dylan-styled music, complete with a harmonica holder resting on his neck. Another sang praise choruses, which a few people present knew and others picked up gradually. A third person offered a singalong ditty. Another did folk music. Finally the coffeehouse director sat at the piano and sang two more songs.

Most of the numbers were simple; a few were surprisingly good. In fact, one or two were good enough that they shouldn't have been heard only by the few people there that night. These original Christian songs communicated on a one-to-one level with the people scattered in the audience. No fancy shows; the atmosphere was laid back. The scene was remarkably reminiscent of the coffeehouse ministries of the early Jesus movement, where much of the early Jesus music was born.

The city in which the coffee house ministry was located had several contemporary Christian concerts scheduled in the coming weeks. There were several radio stations programming Christian music for anyone who wanted to tune in. There were hundreds of churches in the metropolitan area. But sitting there, one sensed that all of that Christian activity was passing these particular students by.

There was surely a reason they came—perhaps for fellowship, perhaps to kill boredom, or perhaps to seek answers to big questions. The few people who worked the coffeehouse ministry were providing a badly needed way station, a place of spiritual nurture, often for people who would never go to the concerts, listen to the radio, or attend the churches. This particular coffeehouse was just as important as the ones which ministered a decade and a half earlier to the same type of people.

That same fall night, some two thousand miles away near Dallas, Texas, there were even more indications that coffeehouse ministries were needed as much as, if not more than, ever before. More than five hundred persons (nearly nine hundred in the final session) attended the 1st National Street Ministries Conference, which carried the theme, "Training *you* to take Jesus to the streets of America." Seven street-level outreach ministries sponsored the conference, which featured twenty-seven teaching and training workshops.

Chuck Girard provided the music and talks on "using praise and worship as a weapon." Among the guest speakers were David Wilkerson, Judy McPheeters, Jonathan Gainsbrugh (director of Worldshakers for Christ and publisher of a street-ministries directory), John Dawson (director of Youth with a Mission in California and National Olympic Outreach Director for the Games just past), Gary Greenwald (pastor of Eagle's Nest Church in California and director of his own national rock music seminars), and Scott Hinkle (of his own outreach ministry).

The high attendance for the first annual conference indicated a definite interest in maintaining street-level ministries throughout the United States and elsewhere. The directory published by Gainsbrugh listed more than three hundred such ministries, estimated to be less than half the actual number of coffeehouse and street-level para-church outreaches in the U.S. Many Christians, in fact *most* Christians, were not even aware of the work going on in the streets of cities and towns. The work was not heavily publicized, nor was it glamourous.

"God is bringing together an army of what Jonathan Gainsbrugh calls 'attack sheep,'" one report on the conference read. "A result of the conference was the formation of the International Street

Ministry Association (IMSA) to serve as a clearinghouse and liaison between street ministries.

"Certainly," the report continued, "any hunger for souls is good news, as is encouragement to those in front-line ministries. At the same time, however, there was one prominent speaker who blasted Christian rock and received a good hand from many in the audience. Indeed, the musical direction of the conference toward praise and worship was somewhat surprising, at least in its relationship to evangelism."

Though the conference showed a possible mellowing of musical attitudes and tastes, there were many who saw the continued validity of using rock as an evangelistic medium. No place was its effectiveness more evident than in prisons, jails, and detention centers. Christian rockers such as DeGarmo & Key, the Rob Cassells Band, and Resurrection Band often played in everything from juvenile halls to penitentiaries, and with excellent results. Other artists, such as Canada's Gene Maclellan, composer of the sixties hit, "Put Your Hand in the Hand," opted for more moderate music in their concerts behind prison bars. In many cases the Christian music presented by these singers was the first encounter with the gospel the prisoners had ever had.

In spite of this evangelistic work and the street-level ministries, there still lingered a question in 1984 as to whether contemporary Christian music had been used effectively or efficiently to evangelize, or whether such hopes and efforts had been lost in the hubbub of its success as a commercial industry.

"We've done a great job of converting the church to accept rock and roll," one Christian recording engineer pondered, "but I don't know how well we've done in converting people to Jesus with the music."

Rather than being a negative assessment of the contemporary Christian music scene, the comment was an astute and healthy consideration worth note. If no one would question the effectiveness of the music, it would ultimately have no value, through neglect.

Much like Christian radio, Christian music ministered mostly to Christians, or at least the churched.

Stan Moser, the executive vice-president of Word Records, gave a glimpse at his company's target market in a special *Billboard* magazine article written by Bob Darden. An informal survey, evidently taken by Word at a gathering of "thousands of church-oriented young girls," yielded that about 40 percent had never heard of Amy Grant, two-thirds had never heard of Sandi Patti, and only 20 percent had heard of Leslie Phillips, a newer artist on Word's Myrrh label.

"Even with our increased dent, we've still got a long way to go," he (Moser) says. "Our statistics show that about 50% of the U.S. population is active in some way in church. Roughly about 100 million people. Only 10% of that figure ever frequents Christian bookstores or shops, which is where the bulk of our albums are sold. So our market universe to this point has only been 10 million people.

"That means when someone like Amy Grant nears a million units sold, she's penetrating the universe that encompasses the other 90 million Christians who are 'secular' in terms of their buying habits. Even surveys of longtime Petra fans show that those same fans are buying five or six secular albums by people like Def Leppard, Journey, or Led Zeppelin for every Petra LP they buy.

"That means we still have a huge untapped market in that 90 million. It is for all intents and purposes a secular market that's not going to be offended by our message. That's where our next thrust is going to be."

Five years ago, that same marketplace would not have allowed Leslie Phillips to even mention something like extramarital sex. Today, as the scope of the artist broadens, so has the willingness of the market grown to include more than just one topic in gospel music.

"The Bible most definitely addresses salvation," Moser says, "but it also addresses issues like honesty, integrity, homosexuality, and whatever. For example, we've had a series of powerful anti-abortion songs in the past few years, something our audience would never allow to be mentioned before. The relevant message is still salvation, but specific songs can now deal with specific topics and that's opened up a whole lot more freedom of expression lyrically and musically for our artists. And that's given them the opportunity to reach a wider audience—that 90 million we're talking about."[1]

Those ten million people which Moser referred to earlier are also the ones which show the most likelihood of listening to Christian radio. By 1984 the number of Christian music stations had increased to an impressive number, many of them programming a mix of light contemporary and bright M.O.R. Christian music. That format was the most common among stations which were considered contemporary. A fewer number programmed straight contemporary music, more up-tempo than the mixed format. But even by the mideighties, only a handful of stations, if that many, programmed Christian rock as their main music format.

KLYT in Albuquerque was one of the few ultracontemporary stations. Since it was noncommercial, there was more freedom in format; there was not a commercial quota which had to be met each month. Christian rock radio, when done commercially, had very little chance because of the reticence of sponsors to go onto such a station. In most cases the sponsors advertising on Christian radio paid heed to the complaints of the older, established businessmen with which they wished to do business. With that cadre, rock just didn't hit it. However, as always, there were a few exceptions. Historic KYMS in Santa Ana, one of the pioneer contemporary Christian stations, leaned toward the rock side with a good measure of success and positive response. The Orange County area and the West Coast were excellent testing grounds for rock radio, since so many of the Christian new music groups hailed from that region. Far away, in Chattanooga, Tennessee, long-time southern-gospel outlet WMOC was reported to have switched to a "progressive" Christian rock format in late 1984.

Most of the rock music being heard on Christian stations was via locally produced or nationally syndicated radio shows which sometimes aired on both Christian and secular radio stations. Shows such as "Joy Song" in Oklahoma City, "American Christian Rock Countdown" from Kokomo, Indiana, Laurie de Young on WKLQ in Grand Rapids, Michigan, and "The Brian Mason Show" out of Nashville kept contemporary music of varying degrees of rockiness on the air. Another favorable outlet for Christian rock proved to be the college radio stations.

One of the main changes in Christian radio over the preceding decade had been a noticeable increase in the number of stations serving individual markets. There were several metropolitan areas that were served by as many as four or five Christian *music* stations, and more if one counted the stations carrying taped teaching programs. In addition, there were a few markets where more than one Christian station appeared in the coveted ratings books, right in the company of the secular stations, albeit fairly low on the totem pole.

Radio broadcasters were encouraged to pay more attention to improving their sound, cleaning up their signal, gearing up their sales, and polishing up their image so as to compete head-to-head with the secular big guys, rather than compare themselves and compete with other Christian stations in their or other markets. Brad Burkhart's monthly column in *MusicLine* magazine preached it, and the speakers at the National Gospel Radio Seminar each year reiterated it.

In the early eighties, several powerhouse radio stations came on with contemporary Christian formats: XERF, the station on which Wolfman Jack had wailed years before, became Love 16. Fifty-thousand-watt WAPE in Jacksonville and WCFL in Chicago both became Christian-music stations, with WCFL advertising "America's most powerful Christian radio signal." Other stations under the same ownership as WAPE and WCFL were expected to go gospel in late 1984. Fifty-thousand-watt stations covered large geographic areas, especially at night, and the dream of contemporary Christian music for the whole nation, even the small, outlying towns, looked to be reality.

Several stations, though not covering the geographical areas of the AM powerhouses, managed to pull impressive ratings in their areas when compared with other religious broadcasters. Stations such as WXLN in Louisville, Kentucky, KCFO in Tulsa, Oklahoma, KBIQ in Seattle, Washington, WLIX in Long Island, New York, and WDJC in Birmingham, Alabama, were a few.

Typical of radio, though, sudden changes came to some of them, even though the ratings looked good. Tulsa's KCFO, with some of the top ratings for a Christian station in the country, suddenly let its staff go in the middle of 1984 and switched to a syndicated contemporary format. In a similar move, the staff of WDJC in Birmingham, which enjoyed good ratings for its coverage of north-central Alabama, suddenly changed its format to southern gospel without a moment's warning to the listening audience. WDJC had been a contemporary station a year or so earlier, but gradually modified its format until the sudden move in October 1984.

However, Birmingham proper was not left without Christian radio, or even contemporary Christian music radio. WCRT kept the contemporary flag waving in the market, and with increasing ratings. The Alabama city was typical of a multiplying number of areas with a variety of religious stations to choose from. Birmingham had an extraordinary number; listeners could choose from ten available signals, running the gamut from all preachers to contemporary music.

As stated before, Christian radio was probably reaching mostly Christians. Christian music and record sales were aimed at mostly Christians. What about evangelism to the lost? Was there any?

And furthermore, should music even be used for evangelism? Some antagonists thought not. More than once, an anticontemporary-music preacher or evangelist or writer would cite that the Scriptures basically referred to music as being a vertical conduit, for use in praising the Lord. Nowhere, the opponents added, was the use of music for evangelism justified.

Yet the majority of people in contemporary music or gospel music in general felt that nothing in the Scriptures ever preached *against* it, and over the years music had proven to be an increasingly important part of everyone's life. So why not hit them where they live?

But the burden of evangelism, or even renewal, through music seemed to always fall on the musicians, the singers, the concert promoters, the agents, the radio stations, or the record labels. At least that's where the public let it fall.

Much of the burden should have rested with the audiences, the Christians who partook of the music for their own edification. Christian music fans and followers were frequently reminded by the singers and musicians, often to no avail, to bring friends and neighbors with them when they came to concerts, especially unsaved friends. Much too often, though, Christians neglected to do so, opting for the entertainment aspect, or assuming that their friends would say "No," and figuring that it would just be too much trouble.

One artist, when asked what the difference was between American audiences and those in other countries, replied, "The Americans are fat. They've gotten so much Christianity, they take it for granted. It's always there when they need it, but if they feel that they don't need it, they fall asleep. In other countries, the people are starving for the Word, spoken and sung. They want every chewy morsel they can get."

In reality, there were many starving people in the United States as well. They were next door, in the offices, in traffic, in the next booth at quick-food restaurants, even in one's own families. They were the very ones who could greatly benefit from the music many Christians took for granted or even used as a pacifier. Yet, those hungry people hadn't been invited in for the feast.

The "Give the Gift of Music" slogan used by record labels to sell more product was well chosen. Not only would the gift keep on giving as a friend or associate or relative listened to a record over and over; it may have kept on giving in life-changing ways virtually immeasurable. The thoughtfulness of a believer in inviting a friend to a Christian concert (at the risk of being told "No" a dozen times) might ultimately be a permanent gift. Furthermore, the example a believer set by what music he or she listened to might very well witness to the unbeliever as well.

But really more important than the gift of music may be the love behind it, the attitude in which it was given. Consider the scene at a 1979 New Year's Eve concert held in an ice-skating rink in Denver. The Christian concert had been advertised on secular and Christian radio stations, with the secular ads only giving a slight hint that the music would be anything other than what the listeners of the station were used to hearing.

It was an evening of top Christian rock bands and solo performers; no one could complain about the quality. But the advertising had brought in a most interesting variety of people, a hybrid mixture of straight Christians, hip Christians, straight non-Christians, and not-so-straight non-Christians.

During intermission many of the Christians (who made up the majority that night) greeted each other in the foyer of the rink, hugging and smiling. In the center of the area stood a young girl, perhaps thirteen, dressed fit to kill, with overdone makeup to match.

At first glance there was nothing unusual. But as Christians continued greeting and hugging each other, it became fairly obvious what the difference was. She stood alone. As Christians stood in groups of a dozen or so, carrying on animated conversations, the lone girl stared, first at one group, then another.

But she wasn't smiling. Christian love was being exchanged virtually under her nose, but none of it was being given to her.

The Christians were too busy hugging each other.

> So go paint your face, little one,
> And try and keep the pace,
> And though you have someone who loves you,
> You still feel homely. . . .
> But, little one, you're not alone;
> We all have felt the same way that you do.
> And when you see that God has made us like we
>   are to better do His will,
> Then there's no need to hide or change your face
> Or try and keep the pace,
> For I have seen you through the eyes of Jesus,
> And you're beautiful,
> You're so beautiful.[2]

They're all around us, everywhere I see
All those lonely faces all staring back at me
So tell me what's the answer
How are we to go?
By the power of the Spirit, we've got to let them know

That we're A Colony of Heaven, strangers in this land
    To show the world around us
    That the Kingdom is at hand
    A Colony of Heaven, for everyone to see
    All the life of Jesus Christ in you and me

'Cause they've all seen our churches, they've heard
    our list of rules
And they've felt our judgment and watched us play
    the fools
We've got to make some changes to show our love is
    true
And just stop the imitation and do what we must do

We're A Colony of Heaven, strangers in this land
    To show the world around us
    That the Kingdom is at hand
    A Colony of Heaven, for everyone to see
    All the life of Jesus Christ in you and me

As the Lord said to the Father, I'm in you as
    you're in Me
May they also be made one in us, that the whole
    world might believe

We're A Colony of Heaven, strangers in this land
    To show the world around us
    That the Kingdom is at hand
    A Colony of Heaven, for everyone to see
    All the life of Jesus Christ in you and me.*

---

* Words and music by Will McFarlane. Published by Wilmac Publishing and
Snellsong.

Appendix A
"Religious" Songs Which Reached the Billboard Top 100 Pop Charts 1955–1984

Following is a list of songs of a "religious" nature, generally in keeping with Judeo-Christian concepts. Each of the songs appeared on the *Billboard* Top 100 singles charts between 1955 through 1984. The recording artists listed are not all Christians. Obviously, songs such as "Stairway to Heaven," "Kiss an Angel Good Morning," or "You'll Never Get to Heaven If You Break My Heart" are omitted. Likewise, songs expressing other faiths, such as Seals' and Crofts' "Hummingbird" and George Harrison's "My Sweet Lord," are not included. "Superstar," from *Jesus Christ Superstar,* was included due to its historical significance.

1955
Angels in the Sky—*Crew Cuts*—#13—Mercury 70741
Bible Tells Me So—*Don Cornell*—#7—Coral 61467
Bible Tells Me So—*Nick Noble*—#22—Wing 90003
He—*Al Hibbler*—#7—Decca 29660
He—*McGuire Sisters*—#12—Coral 61494

1956
Every Time (I Feel His Spirit)—*Patti Page*—#87—Mercury 70971
Give Us This Day—*Joni James*—#30—MCM 12288
Mary's Boy Child—*Harry Belafonte*—#15—RCA Victor 47-6735
The Good Book—*Kay Starr*—#89—RCA Victor 47-6617
Sinner Man—*Les Baxter*—#82—Capitol 3404

1957
(There'll Be) Peace in the Valley—*Elvis Presley*—#39—RCA Victor EPA 4054
There's a Gold Mine in the Sky—*Pat Boone*—#28—Dot 15602

Chart information taken from Joel Whitburn's Record Research, compiled from *Billboard's* "Pop" charts.

1958
He's Got the Whole World (In His Hands)—*Lauri London*—#2—Capitol 3891
He's Got the Whole World in His Hands—*Mahalia Jackson*—#69—Columbia 41150
Wonderful Time Up There—*Pat Boone*—#10—Dot 15690

1959
Battle Hymn of the Republic—*Mormon Tabernacle Choir*—#13—Columbia 41459
Deck of Cards—*Wink Martindale*—#7—Dot 15968
When the Saints Go Marching In—*Fats Domino*—#50 Imperial 5569

1960
Wings of a Dove—*Ferlin Husky*—#12—Capitol 4406

1961
Child of God—*Bobby Darin*—#95—Atco 6183
Michael—*Highwaymen*—#1—United Artists 258

1962
None

1963
Dominique—*The Singing Nun*—#1—Philips 40152
Michael—*Steve Alaimo*—#100—Checker 1054

1964
All My Trials—*Dick & Deedee*—#89—Warner Bros. 5411
Amen—*Impressions*—#7—ABC-Paramount 10602
I Believe—*Bachelors*—#33—London 9672
Michael—*Trini Lopez*—#42—Reprise 0300
Oh, Rock My Soul—*Peter, Paul & Mary*—#93—Warner Bros. 5442
Tell It on the Mountain—*Peter, Paul & Mary*—#33—Warner Bros. 5418
You'll Never Walk Alone—*Patti LaBelle & Blue Belles*—#34—Nicetown 5020 & Parkway 896

1965
Crying in the Chapel—*Elvis Presley*—#3—RCA Victor 47-0643
Crying in the Chapel—*Adam Wade*—#88—Epic 9752
Let's Get Together—*We Five*—#31—A & M 784
Michael—*C.O.D.'s*—#41—Kellmac 1003
People Get Ready—*Impressions*—#14—ABC-Paramount 10622
Sinner Man—*Trini Lopez*—#54—Reprise 0405
Turn! Turn! Turn!—*Byrds*—#1—Columbia 43424
You'll Never Walk Alone—*Gerry & The Pacemakers*—#48—Laurie 3302

1966
He—*Righteous Brothers*—#18—Verve 10406

Chart information taken from Joel Whitburn's Record Research, compiled from *Billboard's* "Pop" charts.

1967

Get Together—*Youngbloods*—#62—RCA 47-9264

1968

Amen—*Otis Redding*—#36—Atco 6592
Battle Hymn of the Republic—*Andy Williams*—#33—Columbia 44650
Daddy Sang Bass—*Johnny Cash*—#42—Columbia 44689
You'll Never Walk Alone—*Elvis Presley*—#90—RCA Victor 47-9600

1969

Crystal Blue Persuasion—*Tommy James & the Shondells*—#2—Roulette 7050
Dammit Isn't God's Last Name—*Frankie Lane*—#86—ABC 11224
Get Together—*Youngbloods*—#5—RCA 47-9264
Jesus Is a Soul Man—*Lawrence Reynolds*—#28—Warner Bros. 7322
Kum Ba Ya—*Tommy Leonetti*—#54—Decca 32421
Oh Happy Day—*Edwin Hawkins Singers*—#4—Pavilion 20001
Sweet Cherry Wine—*Tommy James & the Shondells*—#7—Roulette 7039
That's the Way God Planned It—*Billy Preston*—#62—Apple 1808
Turn! Turn! Turn!—*Judy Collins*—#69—Elektra 45680
You'll Never Walk Alone—*Brooklyn Bridge*—#51—Buddah 139

1970

Amazing Grace—*Judy Collins*—#15—Elektra 45709
Are You Ready—*Pacific Gas & Electric*—#14—Columbia 45158
Church Street Soul Revival—*Tommy James*—#62—Roulette 7093
Everything Is Beautiful—*Ray Stevens*—#1—Barnaby 2011
Fire and Rain—*James Taylor*—#3—Warner Bros. 7423
Fire and Rain—*R. B. Greaves*—#82—Atco 6745
Fire and Rain—*Johnny Rivers*—#94—Imperial 66453
Holy Man—*Diane Kolby*—#67—Columbia 45169
I Heard the Voice of Jesus—*Turley Richards*—#99—Warner Bros. 7397
Jesus Is Just Alright—*Byrds*—#97—Columbia 45071
Oh Happy Day—*Glen Campbell*—#40—Capitol 2787
Spirit in the Sky—*Norman Greenbaum*—#3—Reprise 0885
Spirit in the Sky—*Dorothy Morrison*—#99—Buddah 196
Stealing in the Name of the Lord—*Paul Kelly*—#49—Happy Tiger 541
Stoned Love—*Supremes*—#7—Motown 1172
Superstar—*Murray Head*—#74—Decca 32603

1971

All My Trials—*Ray Stevens*—#70—Barnaby 2039
Come Back Home—*Bobby Goldsboro*—#69—United Artists 50807
Deep Enough For Me—*Ocean*—#73—Kama Sutra 525
Grandma's Hands—*Bill Withers*—#42—Sussex 227
Life—*Elvis Presley*—#53—RCA 47-9985
Mighty Clouds of Joy—*B. J. Thomas*—#34—Scepter 12320
My Sweet Lord—*Billy Preston*—#90—Apple 1826
Put Your Hand in the Hand—*Ocean*—#2—Kama Sutra 519
Superstar—*Murray Head*—#14—Decca 32603

Chart information taken from Joel Whitburn's Record Research, compiled from *Billboard's* "Pop" charts.

Take My Hand—*Kenny Rogers & First Edition*—#91—Reprise 1018
Think His Name—*Johnny Rivers*—#65—United Artists 50822
Top 40 of the Lord—*Sha Na Na*—#84—Kama Sutra 528
Turn Your Radio On—*Ray Stevens*—#63—Barnaby 2048
Wedding Song (There Is Love)—*Paul Stookey*—#24—Warner Bros. 7511

1972

Amazing Grace—*Royal Scots Dragoon Guards*—#11—RCA 74-0709
Day By Day—*Godspell*—#13—Bell 45, 210
I'll Take You There—*Staple Singers*—#1—Stax 0125
Jesus Is Just Alright—*Doobie Bros.*—#35—Warner Bros. 7619
Joy—*Apollo 100*—#6—Mega 615-0050
Jubilation—*Paul Anka*—#65—Buddah 294
Me and Jesus—*Tom T. Hall*—#98—Mercury 73278
Morning Has Broken—*Cat Stevens*—#6—A & M 1335
Speak to the Sky—*Rick Springfield*—#14—Capitol 3340
That's The Way God Planned It—*Billy Preston*—#65—Apple 1808
Wedding Song (There Is Love)—*Petula Clark*—#61—MGM 14431
Wholly Holy—*Aretha Franklin*—#81—Atlantic 2901

1973

He—*Today's People*—#90—20th Cent. 2032
I Knew Jesus (Before He Was a Star)—*Glen Campbell*—#45—Capitol 3548
Jesus Is Just Alright—*Doobie Bros.*—#35—Warner Bros. 7661
Put Your Hands Together—*O'Jays*—#10—Philadelphia International 3535
Why Me—*Kris Kristofferson*—#16—Monument 8571

1974

City in the Sky—*Staple Singers*—#79—Stax 0215
Lord's Prayer—*Sister Janet Mead*—#4—A & M 1491
There Will Never Be Any Peace (Until God Is Seated at the Conference Table)—
    Chi-Lites—#63—Brunswick 55512

1975

L-O-V-E (Love)—*Al Green*—#13—Hi 2282
Operator—Manhattan Transfer—#22—Atlantic 3292

1976

None

1977

You Light Up My Life—*Debby Boone*—#1—Warner/Curb 8455

1978

Belle—*Al Green*—#83—Hi 77505
Rivers of Babylon—*Boney M.*—#30—Sire Hansa 1027

1979

All Things Are Possible—*Dan Peek*—#78—Lamb & Lion 817
Gotta Serve Somebody—*Bob Dylan*—#24—Columbia 1-11072

Chart information taken from Joel Whitburn's Record Research, compiled from *Billboard's* "Pop" charts.

1980

Do Right—*Paul Davis*—#23—Bang 4808
Hold On—*Kansas*—#40—Kirshner 4291
The Good Lord Loves You—*Neil Diamond*—#67—Columbia 11232
Wondering Where The Lions Are—*Bruce Cockburn*—#21—Millennium 11786

1981

None

1982

None

1983

Yah Mo B There—*James Ingram & Michael McDonald*—Q-West QWT 7-29394
Your Unconditional Love—*Donna Summer*—Mercury 814088-7

1984

(Pride) In the Name of Love—*U2*—Island 7-99704

Chart information taken from Joel Whitburn's Record Research, compiled from *Billboard's* "Pop" charts.

Appendix B
The Contemporary Christian
Music Family Tree—1963–1978

The early contemporary Christian music recording artists

On the following pages is a comprehensive list of the singers and musicians who first recorded what is now known as contemporary Christian music. These artists developed music in various styles: folk, Jesus music, rock, jazz, and others.

The list was included in the 1979 and 1980 editions of this book, when it was titled *Why Should the Devil Have All the Good Music?* An attempt was made at that time to list beside each name the styles each artist or group employed, according to categories which seemed fairly descriptive at the time. Since then, even the descriptive terms have changed to some degree, but they still convey the general idea.

Since 1978, musicians and artists have come from all fields of pop and gospel music to become part of the contemporary Christian music family. To add the names of each and every such artist would almost require a book in itself. However, including this initial list of artists who first recorded contemporary Christian music presents a family tree of sorts—a record showing the early roots of what we now call contemporary Christian music.

Types of music performed by each artist or group are indicated by the first series of letters in each entry. The two major categories are contemporary gospel (stemming from the traditional church and gospel music) and Jesus music (stemming from secular pop-music styles). In this list, "rock music" is used to designate recorded music from secular sources which crossed over to some degree into the contemporary Christian music field of interest. "SR" indicates that some or all albums by that artist or group were released on secular record labels only. Whether or not those artists were actually Christians is not indicated. In many cases, combinations of code letters are used to identify the artists' styles more specifically.

225

In cases where an artist's recordings originated from a country other than the United States, the country is indicated by an abbreviation in italics. The artists of some countries, such as France, Spain, Holland, Germany, and those of Scandinavia, were unfortunately not incorporated into this original listing. However, many of them are recognized in Chapter 28.

Catholic contemporary music and Jesus music such as that covered in this book have historically appealed to different audiences. Catholic contemporary music had not permeated the non-Catholic scene to any great degree when the listing was done, nor has it to the present time. Therefore, Catholic contemporary music, of which the majority was of a folk nature, is indicated by its own classification, the letters "CM."

Recordings of religious cults, or those recordings and artists deemed by the author more anti-Christian than Christian (such as *Jesus Christ Superstar*) are excluded from this list, although they are included in some of the other appendices for different reasons.

Inclusion of any recording or artist on this list does not represent endorsement of the particular recording or artist, nor does it indicate the quality of the recordings. Many of the albums referred to are no longer available or carried by the actual labels. Many of the artists who continue to record have moved to other labels since 1978; only their labels prior to that year are included here.

For the collector of contemporary Christian music, however, this listing should provide an excellent checklist as he or she pores through garage sales and second-hand record bins.

This list would hardly have been possible without the untiring help of Dan Hickling. Dan applied endless hours of research for its compilation.

DESCRIPTION OF CATEGORIES:

Music Types:
CG—Contemporary gospel
CL—Classical
CM—Catholic music
CO—Comedy
FM—Folk music
JM—Jesus music
JZ—Jazz
PS—Praise/Scripture
RM—Rock music from secular source
SG—Soul gospel
SR—Secular release

Countries of Origin:
AU—Australia
CN—Canada
IT—Italy
SW—Sweden
UK—United Kingdom

Special Codes:
Ca—Cassette only on some releases
8T—8-track tape only on some releases
( )—When there are two groups with same name, the state or country of origin is given in parentheses.

CG	*Action Scene '71* (sampler)—Impact
CG/CO	Act One Company—Greentree
CG	Acts—custom
CG	Adams, J. T. & the Fireside Singers—Word
JM	Adams, Randy—Star Song
JM/UK	Advocates—Dovetail
JM	Agape—Mark
CM/JM	Agape/St. Paul's School Choir—Mace
PS	Agape Force—Candle Co., Word
CM/FM	*A Hundred Fold* (sampler)—World Library
8T/JM	Airborne—Solid Rock Sound
CM/JM	A Joyful Noise—Ignatius House
JM	Albrecht & Roley—Airborn
JM	Albrecht, Roley & Moore—White Horse
JM/UK	Alethians—Myrrh
JM	Alexandersen, Stephen—White Horse
SR/SG	Allen Group, Rance—Gospel Truth, Truth, Capitol
SR/JZ	All-Occasion Brass Band—MCA
JM	All-Saved Freak Band—Rock the World
CG	Alpenglow—JoySong, House Top
JM	Altman, Terry Ross—Paraklete
CG	Amason Twins—Herald
CG	Amigos—Heart to Heart
CG/JM	Amplified Version—New Pax, Chrism

CG	Andrus, Sherman—Impact, Shalom
CG	Andrus, Blackwood & Company—Greentree
SR/JM/CN	Apocalypse—Generation
JM/CG	Archers—Charisma, Impact, Light
CG	Arhelger, Jerry—Herald
PS	*Arise and Shine* (various)—Scripture in Song
JM	Ark—Spirit
CG/JM	Armegeddon Experience—M/M
JM/SG	Artistic Sounds—Savoy
JM	Aslan—Airborn
JM/CG	*A Time and A Place* (sampler)—Creative Sound
JM/UK	Atwood, Bill—Dovetail
CG/JM	Autry, Tom—Star Song
JM	Ayala, Bob—Pure Joy, Myrrh
CM/FM	Backwood—Pretzel
CG	Bailey, Stan—Klesis
JM	*Because I Am* (soundtrack)—Clear Light
JM/CG	*Beginnings* (sampler)—Sonrise Mercantile
CG/FM	Believers—Doxa
CM/JZ	Bellson Trio, Howard—World Library
CM/FM	Berakah—custom
CM/JM/IT	Berets—Blue Bell, Avant Garde
SR/RM	Berkery, Pat w/ Spur—Glascow
JM/CG	*Best of Christian Grit* (sampler)—NewPax
JM	Bethlehem—Maranatha

CG	Common Ground—Tempo	SR/JZ	Davis, Rev. Gary—Folklore, Prestige
PS	*Communion* (various)—Birdwing	JM	*Dawntreader One* (sampler)—Star Song
JM	Concrete Rubber Band—American Artists custom	JM	Daybreak—Holy Kiss
CM/FM	Condon, Tom—World Library	CG	Daylight—Edify
CG	Continentals—Light, Word	CG	Dayspring—Word
CG	Cook, Cheri—Solid Rock Sound	SR/JM	Deasy, Mike—Capitol
JM/UK	Cook, David—EMI	JM	Deasy, Mike & Kathie—Sparrow
CF/CN	Cooney, Sr. Lorna—Unicom, Praise	JM	DeGarmo & Key—Lamb & Lion
JM	Copalello, Pat—Kerygma	JM/CG/SG	DeGrate, Don & the Delegation—Sword, Shalom
CG/UK	Cordner, Rodney—Dorian, Pilgrim	CG/JM	Deliverance—Image VII, NewPax
CG	Coryell, Randy—Image VII	JM	Denzien, Rick—Superior
JM	Cotton, Gene—Monya, Impact, Myrrh	CG	Devers, Marcy—Olde Towne
CG	Crain, Jim—Star Song	SG	Dickerson, Ron & the Tranquillity—New Day
CM/FM	Creed, Dan—NALR	CM/FM	Diesel, Paula—Avant Garde
JM	Crimson Bridge—Myrrh	SG	Dixon, Jessy—Light
CG	*Cross & The Switchblade* (soundtrack)—Light	JM	Dogwood—Lamb & Lion, Myrrh
CG	Cross Current Community—Avant Garde	JM	Dove—Myrrh, Shalom
JM/CG/SG	Crouch, Andrae & the Disciples—Light	JM	Drake, Ed—Holy Kiss
		CM/JM	Dumin, Frank—Avant Garde
SR/JM	Crusaders—Capitol	CG	Duncan, D. J. W/Tim Goble—Destiny
CG	Cruse Family—Canaan	JM	Dust—Myrrh
JM	*Cry 3* (soundtrack)—Clear Light	JM/FM	Dust & Ashes—Avant Garde
CG/JM	Cull, Bob—Armchair, Maranatha	JM	East of the Altar—custom
		JM	*Easy Said . . .* (musical)—CMP
CM/FM	Cullen, Pat II—Joral		
CG/UK	Culverwell, Andrew—Polydor, DaySpring	CG	*Edify Volume 1* (sampler)—Edify
CG	Curry, Marie—Herald	CM/FM	Edwards, Deanna—TeleKetics, NALR
CM/FM	Curzio, Elaine—Avant Garde	CM/JM	Edwin, Robert—Avant Garde, Fortress
CG	Dalton, Larry—Light	JM	Eldridge, Rick—Herald, Klesis
JM	Dalton, Michael—Sounds of Joy	SR/RM	Electric Prunes—Reprise
JM	Damascus—Eden	CM/JZ	Elia, Tim—NALR
JM	Damascus Road—JesuSongs	SR/JZ	Ellington, Duke—Prestige, RCA
CM/FM	Dameans—FEL, TeleKetics, NALR	JM/FM	Ellis & Lynch—Raven, Ra-O
SR/JZ/CN	Dandy, Trevor—Zaza	JM	Emmanuel—Chalice
JM	Daniel Amos—Maranatha	CG	Epstein, Kathie—Petra
CG	Danny, Wayne, Paul—Image VII	JM	Eternal Savings and Trust Company—Amphion
CG	Daubenton, Georgene—Edify	JM	Eternity Express—Skylight Sing
JM/UK	Davies, Graham—Sharing		

JM/FM	Greenway, Blake—Century One		'74 (sampler)—custom
CM/FM	Griffen, Ron &	SG	Hill, Tessie—Peacock
	the Leaven—FEL	CM/FM	His People—World Library
CG/JM	Grine, Janny—Sparrow	CG	Holm, Dallas (& Praise)—
CM/FM	Group—World Library		New Sounds, Impact, Greentree
CG/JM/SG	Grover, Teddy & Joy—	JM	Honeytree, Nancy—
	custom, Greentree		Superior, Myrrh
CM/FM/JM	Gutfruend, Ed—	JM	Hoopes, Dick—Celebration
	Epoch VII, NALR	SR/JM	Hope—A & M
		JM	Hope of Glory—Shalom,
CM/FM	Habjan, Sr. Germaine—FEL		Tempo, Chrism
CG/CN	Hakumu—Christopher	JM	Hopkins, Dave—custom
SG	Haley, Josh—Songbird	JM/FM	Horn & Alexander—Bridge
JM/SG	Hall, Danniebelle—	CG/UK	*Hosanna* (musical)—
	Light, Sparrow		Reflection
CG	Hall, Duann—custom	JM	Howard, Tom—Solid Rock
JM	Hall, Pam Mark—	JM	Howell, Doug—Trinity, Eden
	Aslan, Spirit	CG	Hubbell, Larry—Myrrh
CG/JM	Hall, Sammy—Faith, Impact,	CM/FM	Hurd, Bob &
	NewPax, Pax		Whitebird—FEL
JM	Hallelujah Joy Band—	JM	Hurlburt, Steve—Last Adam
	Creative Sound	CG	Hutton, Ramona—Impact
CM/RM	Haney, Lynn—Tribute	JM	Hybl, Scott—Ark
JM	Haney, Marc—Bride		
CG	Harlan, John, Todd—Disciple	CG	Icthus Team—Destiny
CG	Harris, Larnelle—Word	CG/PS	*If My People*
JM/FM(NM)	Harvest—Gospel Towne (FM)		(musical)—Light
JM(CA)	Harvest—Pure Joy	JM	Imago Dei—Caelix
JM	Harvest Flight—Destiny	CG	*I'm Here, God's Here, Now*
JM/FM	Haun, Mike & Jerry		*We Can Start* (musical)—Light
	Blacklaw—custom	CG	Imperials—Impact, DaySpring
SR/SG	Hawkins, Edwin—Pavillion,	CG	*In the Spirit*
	Buddha, Birthright		(sampler)—Bridge
SG	Hawkins, Tramaine—Light	CO	Isaac Air Freight—Maranatha
SG	Hawkins, Walter—Light	JM/UK	Ishmael—Dovetail
SR/UK	Haworth, Bryn—Island, A & M	CG	*It's Getting Late*
JM/UK	Hayles, Lou—Myrrh		(musical)—Light
JM	Heard, Mark—AB, Airborn		
JM	Henderson, Ken—Straight	CM/FM	Jabusch, Willard F.—
JM/UK	Henderson, Stewart—Dovetail		One O One
CG	Henley, Bob & Jane—Singcord	JM/FM	Jackson Brothers—custom
CG	*Here Comes the Son*	SG	Jackson Company, Henry—
	(musical)—Light		Myrrh, Gospel Truth, Birthright
CG	Heritage—Medallion	SG	Jackson, Madeline Manning—
JM	Annie Herring—Sparrow		NewPax
FM	Hershberg, Sarah—FEL	SR/RM	James, Tommy—Roulette
SR/JM	Hester, Benny—VMI, Spirit	JM	J.C. & Co.—custom
JM/UK	Hewitt, Garth—Myrrh	JM	J.C. Power Outlet—Myrrh
CG/JM	Hibbard, Bruce—Seed, Myrrh	CG/CO	Jeremiah People—
CG/JM	Hildebrand, Ray—Word,		Continental, Light
	Myrrh, Tempo	JM	*Jesus Festival of Music*
JM	*Hill Country Faith Festival*		(sampler) Creative Sound

CG	*Love* (musical)—Tempo	SR/CL/RM	*Mass* (opera)—Columbia
JM/PS	Love Inn Company—New Song	JM	Matthews, Randy—Word, Myrrh
JM	*Love, Peace, Joy* (sampler)—Myrrh	JM	Matthews, Taylor & Johnson—NewPax
JM	Love Song—Good News	JM	Mattson, Dave—Myrrh
CG	Love Song Strings—Creative Sound, Mighty Wind	JM	McCrary—Light
CG	Lovette, Carol Jean—Celebration	SR/FM	McCurdy, Ed—Folkways
		JM	McGee, Barry—Sword
CG	Lowe, Candi—custom	JM	McGuire—Greentree
CG/JM	Lucas, Sharalee—Word, Petra, Greentree	JM	McGuire, Barry—Myrrh, Sparrow
		JM	McHugh, Phill—Triad, Jesus Folk, Lamb & Lion
JM/UK	MacKenzie, Judy—Impact, EMI	CG/UK	McKee, Mary—Pilgrim
CG/UK	Maggee, Len—Impact, Dovetail, Grapevine	JM	McPheeters, Charles—Landmark
JM/UK	Malcolm & Alwyn—Myrrh, Pye, Key	JM	McVay, Lewis—Maranatha
		CG	Medema, Ken—Word
JM	Malool, Greg—Herald	CM/FM	Medical Mission Sisters—Avant Garde
CG/JM	Manley, Jim—New Wine		
CG	Mann Singers, Johnny—Light	JM	Meece, David—Myrrh
JM(PA)	Manna—Manna	CG	*Meet God, Man* (opera)—Concordia
JM(FL)	Manna—Herald		
JM	*Maranatha! 1—The Everlasting Living Jesus Music Concert* (various)—Maranatha	JM/UK	*Meet Jesus Music*—Profile, Dovetail
		JM	Melton, Carol—Agape
JM	*Maranatha! 2* (various)—Maranatha	JM	Messenger—Light
		CG	Messengers of Love—custom
JM	*Maranatha! 3—Rejoice in the Lord* (various)—Maranatha	CG	Michael & Tamara—Birthright, New Life
JM	*Maranatha! 4* (various)—Maranatha	CM/FM	Miffleton, Jack—World Library
JM	*Maranatha! 5* (various)—Maranatha	SR/SG	Mighty Clouds of Joy—ABC Dunhill
JM	*Maranatha! 6—A Family Portrait* (various)—Maranatha	JM/UK	Mighty Flyers—Myrrh, Trust
		JM	Millenium—custom
PS/CG	Maranatha Singers—Maranatha	CG	Miller, Jimmy—Pure Joy, DaySpring
PS/CG	Maranatha Strings—Maranatha	CG	Mills, Walt—Impact, Myrrh, DaySpring
JM	Mark, Pam—Aslan	SR/RM	Mind Garage—RCA
JM/CN	Marnoch, Ray—custom (FM)	SR/CM/RM	Mission—Tribute, Avant Garde, Paramount
CG	Marsh, Don (Brass Orchestra)—Impact	CM/RM	Mitchell, Ian & Caroline—FEL
JM	Martin, Rich—Sonburst	JM	*Moment of Truth* (various)—custom, Sonrise Mercantile
CG/CN	Martin, Sara Dale—Profile	SR/CG/JM	Monda, Dick—Verve

CM/JZ	Montague Trio, George—FEL
CM/FM	Montfort Mission—Warner Brothers, GIA
SR/RM	Moonrakers—Shamley
CM/CG	Moore, Alan—World Library
JM/FM	Moore, Mickey & Becki—Maiden
JM/FM	Moore, Ron—Airborn, Creative Sound
CM/FM	Mudd, C.P.—Jonah
JM/CN	Murphy, Ray & Dana Gillespi—Christopher
CG/UK	Murray, Gwen—Dovetail
JM	Mustard Seed Faith—Maranatha
JM	*Mystery Revealed* (sampler) —Creative Sound
JM/UK	Narnia—Myrrh
CG	*Natural High* (musical)—Light
CG	Nelson, Dan—Listen
JM	Nelson, Erick—Maranatha
CM/FM	Nester, Leo—World Library
JM	New Beginning—custom
CG/JM	Newbury Park—Creative Sound
CG	New Californians—Tempo
CM/FM	New Canticle—Word of God
CG	*New Covenant* (musical)—Light
JM	New Covenant/Grace—Dayspring House
CG	New Creation—custom
CG	New Creation—Heritage
CG/PS	New Creation Singers—Family Crusades, Birdwing
CG	New Dawn—Greentree
CG	New Directions—Herald
CG	New Folk—Impact
CG	New Folk—custom
CG	New Hope (Singers)—Light, Tempo
CG/UK	New Horizon—Pilgrim
CG/JM	New Jerusalem—Trinity
JM	New Life—Trinity
CG	New Neighborhood—Creative Sound

CG	New Sky Singers—Volume III
PS	New Song—New Song Ministries
CG	*New Vibrations* (musical)—Light
CG	New Village Singers—Edify
JM	New Wine—Deep
CG/FM	*New Wine Sound* (various)—New Wine
CG/FM	*New Wine 2* — New Wine
CG	New World—FourMost
JM	Norman, Larry—Capitol, Impact, One Way, Verve, MGM, Solid Rock, AB, Street Level
FM/JM/CN	North Wind—Master's Collection
JM/UK	Nutshell—Myrrh
CG	Oak Ridge Boys—Columbia
CG/JM	Oaks Band—Rockland Road
JM	O'Connell, James—Sonburst
JM	Omartian, Michael (& Stormie) —ABC Dunhill, Myrrh
JM	One Song—Paula
JM	One Truth—Sonrise Mercantile, Greentree
PS	ORU Vespers—Celebration
SR/JM	Overland Stage—Epic
JM	Owens (-Collins), Jamie—Light
CG	Owens, Jimmy—Word, Light, Impact
JM	Owens, Jon—Gospel Now Sound, Psalms & Proverbs, Windy
CM/FM	Page, Paul F.—Pretzel
JM/FM	Pampayan, Ted—Silent Seed
JM	Pantano/Salsbury—Solid Rock
JM/UK	Pantry, John—Maranatha
JM	Parable—Maranatha
JM/UK	Parchment—Pye, Myrrh, Grapevine

CM/FM	Parker, Tom—World Library
CM/FM	Patenaude, Andre—Shrine
JM	Pattons—Candle Co.
CG/JM	Paxton, Gary S.—NewPax, Pax
JM(CA)	Peculiar People—custom
JM	Peek, Dan—Lamb & Lion
CG/FM	*People Got to Be Free* (various)—FourMost
PS	People of Praise—custom
CG/CN	Pepper, Pat—Master's Collection
JZ	Person, Houston—Savoy
CG	Petersen, Dave—Freedom
JM	Petra—Myrrh
JM	Phoenix Sonshine—Destiny, Maranatha
JM	Pilgrim 20—CHM
FM	Pires, Barbara—custom
CG/CN	Pollard, Elaine—Praise
CG/UK	Pope, Dave—Myrrh
JM/UK	Potter, Phil—Genesis
CG/CN	Potter's Clay—Today
JM	Powell, Steve—Wineskin
CG/CN	Power & Light Co.—Today
JM	*Power Music* (sampler)—Myrrh
JM	Praise—Creative Sound, custom
CF/JZ/JM	*Praise the Lord in Many Voices, Volumes I-III*—Avant Garde
SG	Preston, Billy—Myrrh
FM	Pritcher, Joan—custom
JM	Psalm 150—Manna
JM/FM	Quinlan, Paul—FEL, NALR
JM/CN	Quintessance—Christopher
JM	Rainbow Promise—Wine Press
CG	Rambo, Reba—Impact
CG	Random Sample—Tempo
CG	Raney, Sue—Light
CG	*Real Thing, The* (various)—Word
FM/JM/UK	Reality Folk—Profile

JM/FM	Rebirth—Avant Garde, custom
JM/CN	Reborn—custom
JM(NJ)	Redemption—Triumphonic
JM(TX)	Redemption—Evan Comm
CG	Reflection—Word
CG	*Relevant* (sampler)—Bridge
JM	Remnant—custom
CG	Renewal—Rockland Road
CM/FM	Repp, Ray—FEL, Myrrh, Agape, Joral
CG	*Requiem for a Nobody* (various)—Light
JM/CN	Restoration—Praise
JM/CA	Resurrection Band—custom, Star Song
JM/CG	Rettino, Ernie—Maranatha, Windchime
SG/CN	Revelation Company—Master's Collection
JM/UK	Reynard—Grapevine
FM	Rich, Linda—Inter-Varisty
CG/JM/UK	Richard, Cliff—Columbia, Word, Light, EMI
JM/FM	Ridings, Rick—Selah
JM	Rising Hope—custom
CM/FM	Roamin' Brothers—FEL
CM/FM	Roamin' Collars—World Library
CG	Robbins, Terri—custom
JM	Roberts, Austin & Advent—NewPax
JM/SG	Robinson, Eddie—Myrrh
JM	Rockwood—Dharma
CG	Romero, Judy—Lamb & Lion
JM	Ron & Shirley w/ Universe—custom
JM	Ross, Nedra—New Song
CM/FM	Rousseau, Robert—FEL
JM	Ryder, Dennis—Hosanna
CM/FM	St. Louis Jesuits—NALR
JM	Salmondt & Mulder—custom
FM/JM/CN	Salte, Arlen—Eagle Creek
JM	Salvation Air Force—Myrrh
CM/FM	Sanders, Skipp—World Library
PS/CA	Sandquist, Ted—New Song

JM	Spring of Joy—Lamb & Lion
CG/JM	Springwater—Springwater
CG	Spurrlows—Word, Light, Tempo
JM	Stanley, Carl—Light
SR/SG	Staple Singers—Stax
JM	Stearman, Dave—Celebration
SR/CG	Stevens, Ray—Barnaby
JM	Stewart & Kyle—Grapevine, Chrism
JM	Stonehill, Randy—Solid Rock, One Way
JM	Stookey, Noel Paul—Warner Brothers, Neworld
JM	Strathdee, Jim—New Wine
SR/JM	Street Christians—PIP
JM	Sugar Chuck—Jasper
CM/JZ	Summerlin, Ed—Avant Garde
SR/JM	Summers, Bob—MGM
JM	Suncast—Daybreak, Myrrh
JM	Sundquist, James—Lamb & Lion
JM	*Superjubilation!* (sampler)—Myrrh
JM	Suriano, Gregg—Behold
CG	Sutter, Lynn—DaySpring
JM	Sweet Comfort (Band)—Maranatha, Light
SR/RM	Sweet Revival—SSS
JM/CN	Sweet Spirit—Christopher
SG/JM(NY)	Sweet Spirit—Shalom
JM	Sycomore—Celebration
CM/FM	Sylvester, Erich—Epoch VII
CG	Take Three—Bridge
JM	Talbot Brothers—Warner Brothers, Sparrow
JM	Talbot, John Michael—Sparrow
JM	Talbot, Terry—Sparrow
JM	*Tales from the Tube* (Soundtrack)—Creative Sound
PS	Tamarah—custom
CG/JM	Tami Cheri—Light, Superior
SR/CL	Tashi—RCA Red Seal
JM	Taylor, Danny—Jubal, Tempo, NewPax

JM	Taylor, Emmett—Kerygma
JM	Taylor, Joe—Ark
CG	*Teen Challenge Praise* (various)
JM/CG	*Teen Scene* (various)—Charisma
CG	*Tell It Like It Is* (musical)—Light
CG	*Tell the World in '73* (musical)—Light
CM/FM	Temple, Sebastian—St. Francis
CM/FM	Temple/Hershberg St. Francis
CM/FM	10.15—custom
JM	Terry Group, The Pat—Myrrh, custom
JM/SG	Thedford, Bili—Good News
CG/UK	The Genesis—Pilgrim
CG	Theisen, Maribeth—Celebration
JM	Third Day—custom
JM	Thomas, B.J.—Myrrh
CG	Thomas, Harry—Destiny
CG	Thomas, Tina—Superior
JM/FM	Tim & Dale—Ark
JM	*Time to Run* (soundtrack)—World Wide, Creative Sound
JM	Tom & Dan—FEL
CG/SW	Tornquist, Evie—Majestic, Signatur, Word
CG/JM	*To the Children of the King* (various)—Sheep Shed
SR/SG	Townsley, Jr., Nat—ABC Peacock
JM	Tranquility—Chrism
JM	Trinity—Living Waters
CG	Truth & His Associates—Truth
CG/JM	Truth—Impact, Paragon
JM	*Truth of Truths* (musical)—Oak
CM/FM	Tucciarone, Angel—World Library
JM	Ugartechea, Becky—Maranatha
JM	*Ultima Thule* (sampler)—Creative Sound
CG	Union, The—Elkanah
CG	Unknown Quality—

Appendix C
Music Comparison Chart

A listing of contemporary Christian musicians, their music, and what their music sounds like.

The first edition of the following chart, which compares the music of contemporary Christian artists to that of secular performers, appeared in the September 1982 issue of *Group* Magazine. An updated version appeared in the June-August 1984 issue, and another appeared in J. Brent Bill's book, *Rock*, published by Revell in 1984.

At first such an idea for comparing secular and Christian music didn't set well with some industry people, who preferred to think that Christian music was unique in its style, and comparison to the world's music would only sully its reputation. Those with a more realistic view knew that much of the contemporary Christian music had inescapable secular parallels, since many of the singers and musicians grew up under the same musical influences as their secular counterparts. The lyric content, not the music style, was what made contemporary Christian music different. When it came to style, only a few Christian artists had what could be considered a truly "unique" sound.

Many record-buying Christians, it turned out, wanted and needed such a chart. Anyone who had recently become a Christian or a Christian music fan could be easily overwhelmed by strange names on albums they had never heard of. Only through friends and (in some areas) the radio could they have any idea of which Christian artist performed what style of music. Sure it was *Christian* music, but was it rock? country? jazz?

Shortly after the first somewhat rudimentary chart was published in 1982, letters for reprint permission began arriving weekly. They came especially from music ministers and youth leaders who saw the value in using the chart as an avenue to alternative music for their young people or adults, many of whom had never before taken interest in Christian music.

For much the same reason, we are including the chart here. Contemporary Christian music has grown so much that no matter what the style of music, there is probably a Christian artist somewhere performing it. With quantity and quality constantly increasing, contemporary Christian music has become an excellent alternative.

Keep in mind that the comparisons listed here are for music style only, obviously not for lifestyle. A comparison mentioning AC/DC does not imply that the Christian counterpart uses questionable lyrics or stage attitudes. Likewise, a reference to Culture Club does not infer that the Christian counterpart dresses in women's clothes or wears lipstick and eye shadow.

This Music Comparison Chart is, unavoidably, somewhat arbitrary, partly because so many Christian musicians and singers continue to record a potpourri of styles, rather than settling in on one. Partly to blame is the tendency of the artists and record companies to attempt to get the greatest mileage out of the record by seeking a common denominator in their music: a type of identity crisis. On the other hand, many artists are constantly changing and progressing into new musical genres. One reader, for instance, might disagree that Daniel Amos sounds like ELO, because that reader has not heard the earlier Daniel Amos albums, on which they *did*. The comparisons deal with an overview of the artists' album catalog, not just the most recent record. The main thing to remember in using the chart is what it suggests: If you like (or liked) artist "A" in secular music, then there's a good chance you'll like some of the music of "B" in Christian music. It's a start, not a Bible.

An asterisk (*) indicates that an artist has developed his or her own recognizable sound, often with no direct parallel among the better known secular artists. A double asterisk (**) indicates an artist whose recordings are on a secular label, which may be purchased through secular record stores as well as some Christian bookstores. A blank space indicates that no specific comparison has been determined.

My sincerest thanks go out to the disc jockeys, writers, music fans, friends, and National Christian Youth Congress delegates who have all contributed to making the chart as comprehensive as it is. Also, thanks to *Group* magazine for their willingness to print the chart in the first (and second) place.

Permission must be obtained from the publisher of this book

for reproduction of this chart in any fashion. Suggestions, corrections, and additions are welcome at all times and may be sent to the author in care of the publisher for later consideration and possible incorporation.

THE MUSIC COMPARISON CHART

A listing of contemporary Christian musicians, their music, and what their music sounds like

CHRISTIAN ARTIST	SOUNDS LIKE . . .	TECHNO-POP	PUNK	NEW WAVE	HEAVY METAL	HARD ROCK	POP ROCK	ROCKABILLY/NOSTALGIC ROCK	SOUTHERN ROCK	CLASSICAL ROCK	RENAISSANCE ROCK	JAZZ	REGGAE	DISCO	FUNK	BLUES	SOUL	SOUL GOSPEL	SOUTHERN GOSPEL	COUNTRY ROCK	COUNTRY	FOLK/ROCK	ACOUSTIC	BALLAD	CLASSICAL	COMEDY/HUMOR	POP
After the Fire (ATF)** (Epic)	Psychedelic Furs, Human League, Falco, The Fixx	●		●			●																				
Dennis Agajanian (Light/Sparrow)	Eddie Rabbit, Gordon Lightfoot, Johnny Cash, Johnny Lee							●												●	●	●	●				
Andrus, Blackwood & Co. (Greentree/Nissi)	★						●												●								
Archers (Light/Songbird)	★					●	●							●					●								
Steve Archer (Myrrh)	★						●																	●			

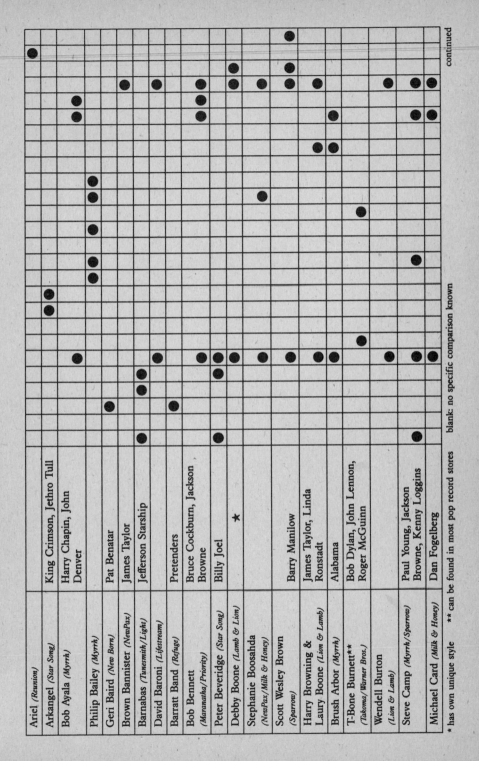

continued

* has own unique style   ** can be found in most pop record stores   blank: no specific comparison known

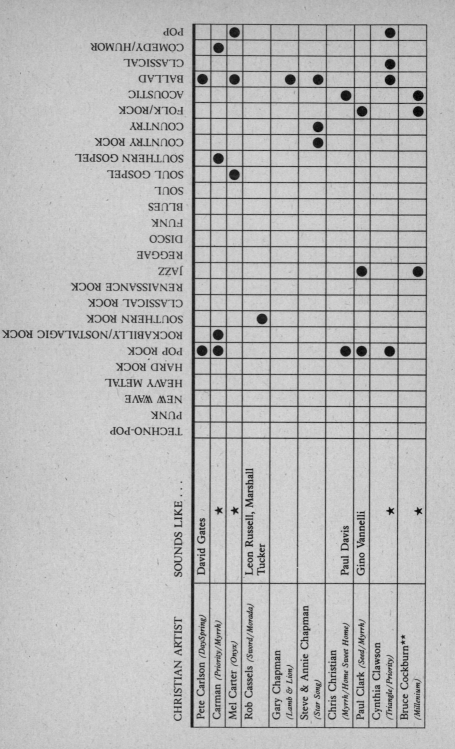

CHRISTIAN ARTIST	SOUNDS LIKE . . .	POP	COMEDY/HUMOR	CLASSICAL	BALLAD	ACOUSTIC	FOLK/ROCK	COUNTRY	COUNTRY ROCK	SOUTHERN GOSPEL	SOUL GOSPEL	SOUL	BLUES	FUNK	DISCO	REGGAE	JAZZ	RENAISSANCE ROCK	CLASSICAL ROCK	SOUTHERN ROCK	ROCKABILLY/NOSTALGIC ROCK	POP ROCK	HARD ROCK	HEAVY METAL	NEW WAVE	PUNK	TECHNO-POP
Pete Carlson *(DaySpring)*	David Gates				●																	●					
Carman *(Priority/Myrrh)*	★	●	●		●					●											●	●					
Mel Carter *(Onyx)*	★										●																
Rob Cassels *(Sword/Morada)*	Leon Russell, Marshall Tucker																			●							
Gary Chapman *(Lamb & Lion)*					●																						
Steve & Annie Chapman *(Star Song)*					●			●	●																		
Chris Christian *(Myrrh/Home Sweet Home)*	Paul Davis					●																●					
Paul Clark *(Seed/Myrrh)*	Gino Vannelli						●										●					●					
Cynthia Clawson *(Triangle/Priority)*	★	●		●	●																	●					
Bruce Cockburn** *(Millenium)*	★					●	●										●										

Artist (Label)	Unique style	Comparison
Daniel Consiglio (*Epoch/NALR*)	★	
Continentals (*Christian Artists*)	★	
Denny Correll (*Myrrh*)		David Clayton-Thomas, Ray Charles
Kemper Crabb (*Star Song*)	★	
Billy Crockett (*DaySpring*)		Culture Club, Michael Jackson
Andrae Crouch (*Light/Warner Bros.*)	★	
Cruse (*Priority/Nissi*)	★	
Cindy Cruse (*Nissi*)		Cindy Lauper
The Cruse Family (*DaySpring/Impact/Priority*)		
Morgan Cryar (*Star Song*)	★	
Rick Cua (*Refuge*)		The Outlaws, Robbie Dupree
Andrew Culverwell (*DaySpring*)		
Daniel Amos (*Solid Rock/NewPax/Alarma/Refuge*)		The Tubes, Talking Heads, Devo, ELO, The Cars, INXS
Daniel Band (*Lamb & Lion/Refuge*)		Rush, Triumph, Quiet Riot, Ratt, Crocus
David & The Giants (*Priority/Myrrh*)		Cheap Trick, Bruce Springsteen
DeGarmo & Key (*Lamb & Lion/Power*)		Doobie Bros., Allman Bros., Michael McDonald, Yes, The Cars, Hall & Oates

* has own unique style   ** can be found in most pop record stores   blank: no specific comparison known

continued

CHRISTIAN ARTIST	SOUNDS LIKE...	POP	COMEDY/HUMOR	CLASSICAL	BALLAD	ACOUSTIC	FOLK/ROCK	COUNTRY	COUNTRY ROCK	SOUTHERN GOSPEL	SOUL GOSPEL	SOUL	BLUES	FUNK	DISCO	REGGAE	JAZZ	RENAISSANCE ROCK	CLASSICAL ROCK	SOUTHERN ROCK	ROCKABILLY/NOSTALGIC ROCK	POP ROCK	HARD ROCK	HEAVY METAL	NEW WAVE	PUNK	TECHNO-POP
Teri DeSario (DaySpring)	Sheena Easton, Quarterflash, Barbra Streisand, Christine McVie				●																	●			●		
Dion (DaySpring)	★						●						●									●					
Dixie Melody Boys (Lifeline)					●			●	●	●																	
Jessy Dixon (Light/Power)											●	●															
Phil Driscoll (Mighty Horn/Sparrow)	Joe Cocker, Ray Charles, Chuck Mangione				●												●		●			●					
Roby Duke (MCA Songbird/Good News)	Boz Scaggs, Christopher Cross, Kenny Loggins																					●					
Bob Dylan** (Columbia)	★					●	●				●		●								●						
Edin-Adahl (Refuge)	Asia															●							●		●		
David Edwards (Myrrh)	Cars, Human League, Bruce Springsteen, Rick Springfield																					●	●		●		
Joe English (Refuge/Myrrh)	Gino Vannelli																					●	●				

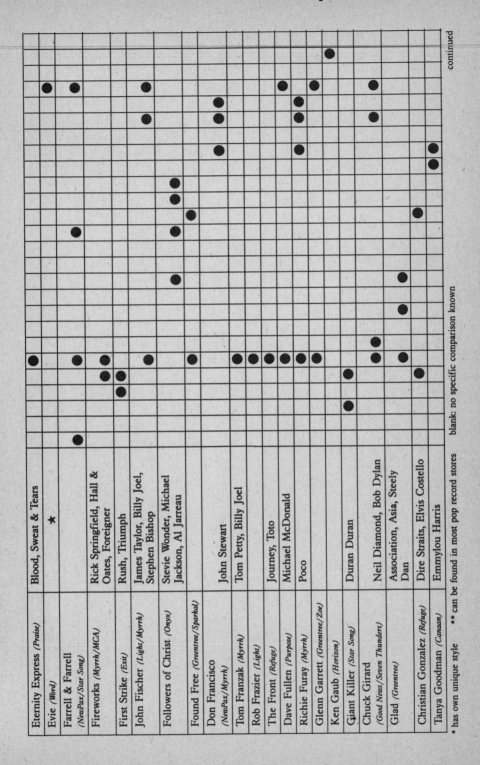

Eternity Express (Praise) — Blood, Sweat & Tears

Evie (Word) — ★

Farrell & Farrell (NewPax/Star Song)

Fireworks (Myrrh/MCA) — Rick Springfield, Hall & Oates, Foreigner

First Strike (Exit) — Rush, Triumph

John Fischer (Light/Myrrh) — James Taylor, Billy Joel, Stephen Bishop

Followers of Christ (Onyx) — Stevie Wonder, Michael Jackson, Al Jarreau

Found Free (Greentree/Sparkal)

Don Francisco (NewPax/Myrrh) — John Stewart

Tom Franzak (Myrrh) — Tom Petty, Billy Joel

Rob Frazier (Light)

The Front (Refuge) — Journey, Toto

Dave Fullen (Purpose) — Michael McDonald

Richie Furay (Myrrh) — Poco

Glenn Garrett (Greentree/Zoe)

Ken Gaub (Horizon)

Giant Killer (Star Song) — Duran Duran

Chuck Girard (Good News/Seven Thunders) — Neil Diamond, Bob Dylan

Glad (Greentree) — Association, Asia, Steely Dan

Christian Gonzalez (Refuge) — Dire Straits, Elvis Costello

Tanya Goodman (Canaan) — Emmylou Harris

* has own unique style   ** can be found in most pop record stores   blank: no specific comparison known

continued

CHRISTIAN ARTIST	SOUNDS LIKE...	POP	COMEDY/HUMOR	CLASSICAL	BALLAD	ACOUSTIC	FOLK/ROCK	COUNTRY	COUNTRY ROCK	SOUTHERN GOSPEL	SOUL GOSPEL	SOUL	BLUES	FUNK	DISCO	REGGAE	JAZZ	RENAISSANCE ROCK	CLASSICAL ROCK	SOUTHERN ROCK	ROCKABILLY/NOSTALGIC ROCK	POP ROCK	HARD ROCK	HEAVY METAL	NEW WAVE	PUNK	TECHNO-POP
Thomas Goodlunas & Panacea (Exit)	Kansas, Moody Blues																		•				•				
Nancy Grandquist (NewPax)					•						•								•			•					
Amy Grant (Myrrh/A & M)	★				•						•											•					
Al Green (Myrrh)	★																										
Keith Green (Sparrow/Pretty Good)	Elton John																					•					
Steve Green (Sparrow)	★				•																						
Janny Grein (Sparrow)	Terri Gibbs, Juice Newton		•	•	•	•	•																				
Jan Groth (Refuge)	Bruce Springsteen, Bob Seger				•																		•				
Tami Gunden (Light)																							•				
Pam Mark Hall (Aslan/Star Song/Reunion)	Joni Mitchell, Nicolette Larson, Pat Benatar				•		•															•					
Larnelle Harris (Word/Impact)	★				•							•															
Harvest (Milk & Honey)	Alabama			•	•		•	•		•																	

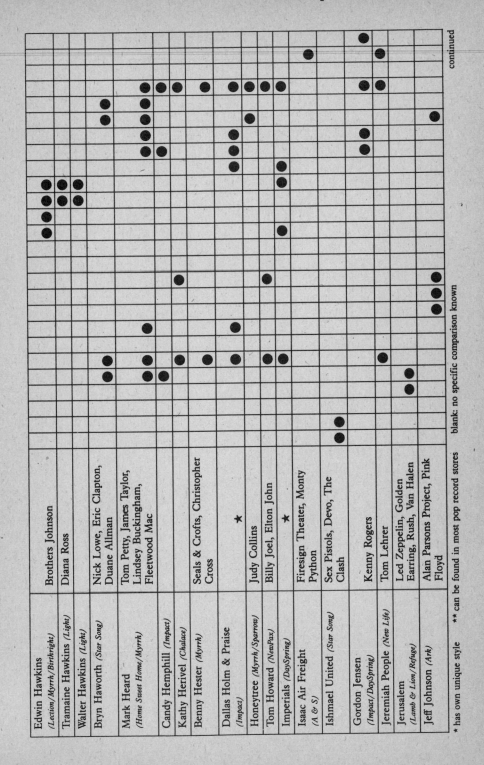

Edwin Hawkins
(Lection/Myrrh/Birthright)

Tramaine Hawkins *(Light)*

Walter Hawkins *(Light)*

Brothers Johnson

Diana Ross

Bryn Haworth *(Star Song)*

Nick Lowe, Eric Clapton, Duane Allman

Mark Heard
(Home Sweet Home/Myrrh)

Tom Petty, James Taylor, Lindsey Buckingham, Fleetwood Mac

Candy Hemphill *(Impact)*

Kathy Herivel *(Chalace)*

Benny Hester *(Myrrh)*

Seals & Crofts, Christopher Cross

Dallas Holm & Praise
(Impact)

★

Honeytree *(Myrrh/Sparrow)*

Judy Collins

Tom Howard *(NewPax)*

Billy Joel, Elton John

Imperials *(DaySpring)*

★

Isaac Air Freight
(A & S)

Firesign Theater, Monty Python

Ishmael United *(Star Song)*

Sex Pistols, Devo, The Clash

Gordon Jensen
(Impact/DaySpring)

Kenny Rogers

Jeremiah People *(New Life)*

Tom Lehrer

Jerusalem
(Lamb & Lion/Refuge)

Led Zeppelin, Golden Earring, Rush, Van Halen

Jeff Johnson *(Ark)*

Alan Parsons Project, Pink Floyd

* has own unique style   ** can be found in most pop record stores   blank: no specific comparison known

continued

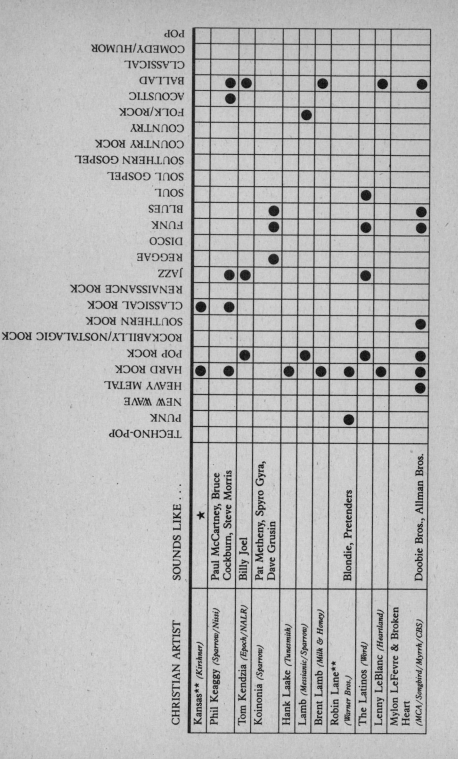

CHRISTIAN ARTIST	SOUNDS LIKE . . .	POP	COMEDY/HUMOR	CLASSICAL	BALLAD	ACOUSTIC	FOLK/ROCK	COUNTRY	COUNTRY ROCK	SOUTHERN GOSPEL	SOUL GOSPEL	SOUL	BLUES	FUNK	DISCO	REGGAE	JAZZ	RENAISSANCE ROCK	CLASSICAL ROCK	SOUTHERN ROCK	ROCKABILLY/NOSTALGIC ROCK	POP ROCK	HARD ROCK	HEAVY METAL	NEW WAVE	PUNK	TECHNO-POP
Kansas** *(Kirshner)*	★																		●				●				
Phil Keaggy *(Sparrow/Nissi)*	Paul McCartney, Bruce Cockburn, Steve Morris				●	●											●						●				
Tom Kendzia *(Epoch/NALR)*	Billy Joel				●												●		●			●					
Koinonia *(Sparrow)*	Pat Metheny, Spyro Gyra, Dave Grusin												●	●		●	●										
Hank Laake *(Tunesmith)*																							●				
Lamb *(Messianic/Sparrow)*							●															●					
Brent Lamb *(Milk & Honey)*					●																		●				
Robin Lane** *(Warner Bros.)*	Blondie, Pretenders																					●	●			●	
The Latinos *(Word)*												●		●			●					●					
Lenny LeBlanc *(Heartland)*					●																		●				
Mylon LeFevre & Broken Heart *(MCA/Songbird/Myrrh/CBS)*	Doobie Bros., Allman Bros.				●								●	●						●		●	●	●			

Artist (label)	Comparison
Liberation Suite *(Star Song/Myrrh)*	Chicago, Saga
Liberty *(Sound Chaser)*	
Lifesavors *(A & S/Refuge)*	
Kerry Livgren** *(Kirshner/CBS)*	Kansas, Journey, E, L&P
Will McFarlane *(Refuge)*	
Malcolm and the Mirrors *(A & S)*	Rick Springfield, The Tubes
Darrell Mansfield Band *(Polydor/A & S)*	
Kenny Marks *(Myrrh)*	
Randy Matthews *(Spirit)*	Joe Cocker, Leon Russell
Barry McGuire *(Sparrow)*	★
Ken Medema *(Word/Glory Sound)*	Harry Chapin, Tom Sullivan
David Meece *(Myrrh)*	Barry Manilow, Andy Gibb, Jack Wagner
John Mehler *(A & S)*	Kinks, The Babys, The Cars
Mercy River Boys *(Canaan)*	Oak Ridge Boys
Mighty Clouds of Joy *(Myrrh)*	James Brown
Mickey & Becki Moore *(Maiden)*	Peter, Paul & Mary
Tim Miner *(Nissi)*	Hall & Oates, Michael McDonald
Ron Moore *(Airborn/Refuge)*	Neil Young, John Mellancamp

* has own unique style   ** can be found in most pop record stores   blank: no specific comparison known

continued

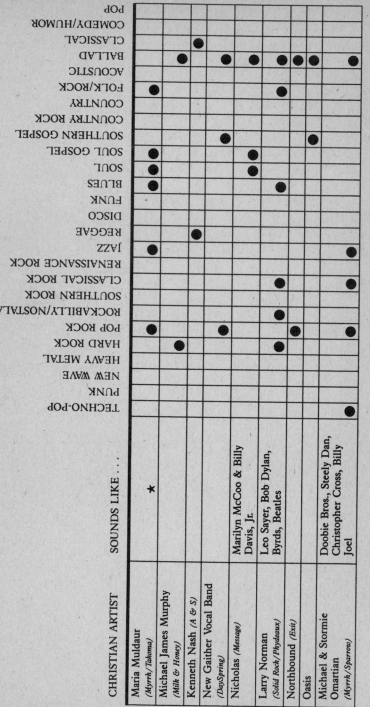

CHRISTIAN ARTIST	SOUNDS LIKE	POP	COMEDY/HUMOR	CLASSICAL	BALLAD	ACOUSTIC	FOLK/ROCK	COUNTRY	COUNTRY ROCK	SOUTHERN GOSPEL	SOUL GOSPEL	SOUL	BLUES	FUNK	DISCO	REGGAE	JAZZ	RENAISSANCE ROCK	CLASSICAL ROCK	SOUTHERN ROCK	ROCKABILLY/NOSTALGIC ROCK	POP ROCK	HARD ROCK	HEAVY METAL	NEW WAVE	PUNK	TECHNO-POP
Maria Muldaur *(Myrrh/Takoma)*	★						•				•	•	•				•					•					
Michael James Murphy *(Milk & Honey)*					•																		•				
Kenneth Nash *(A & S)*				•												•											
New Gaither Vocal Band *(DaySpring)*					•																	•					
Nicholas *(Message)*	Marilyn McCoo & Billy Davis, Jr.				•					•	•	•															
Larry Norman *(Solid Rock/Phydeaux)*	Leo Sayer, Bob Dylan, Byrds, Beatles				•		•						•						•		•	•	•				
Northbound *(Exit)*					•	•																•					
Oasis					•					•																	
Michael & Stormie Omartian *(Myrrh/Sparrow)*	Doobie Bros., Steely Dan, Christopher Cross, Billy Joel				•												•		•								•

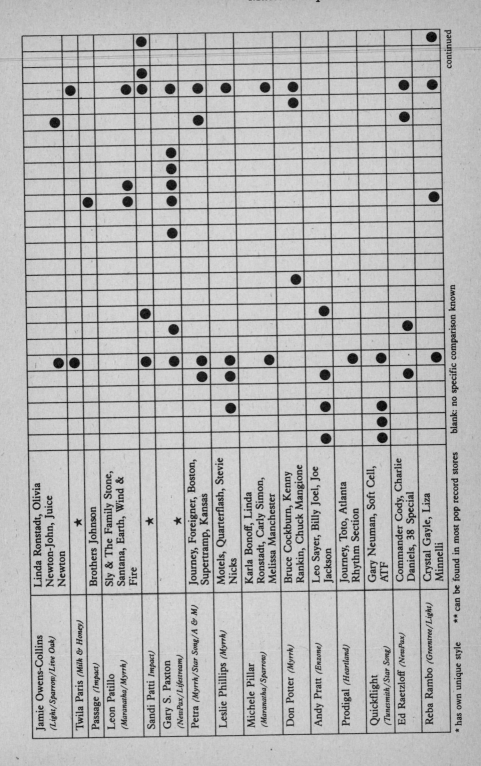

* has own unique style   ** can be found in most pop record stores   blank: no specific comparison known

continued

CHRISTIAN ARTIST	SOUNDS LIKE . . .	POP	COMEDY/HUMOR	CLASSICAL	BALLAD	ACOUSTIC	FOLK/ROCK	COUNTRY	COUNTRY ROCK	SOUTHERN GOSPEL	SOUL GOSPEL	SOUL	BLUES	FUNK	DISCO	REGGAE	JAZZ	RENAISSANCE ROCK	CLASSICAL ROCK	SOUTHERN ROCK	ROCKABILLY/NOSTALGIC ROCK	POP ROCK	HARD ROCK	HEAVY METAL	NEW WAVE	PUNK	TECHNO-POP
Resurrection Band (Rez Band) (Star Song/Light/Sparrow)	Rainbow, Rush, Jefferson Airplane, AC/DC, Triumph, Iron Maiden, Twisted Sister																						●	●			●
Cliff Richard** (EMI)	★				●																	●					
Cindy Richardson (Heartland)					●																						
Phillip Sandifer (Urgent)					●																						
Connie Scott (Sparrow)	Laura Branigan, Donna Summer																					●					
Seawind** (A & M/Horizon)	★				●									●			●					●					
2nd Chapter of Acts (Myrrh/Sparrow/Live Oak)					●																	●					
Semaja (Refuge)	Santana ★																●		●			●					
September (Sugar)	Sheena Easton																					●	●				
Servant (Tunesmith/Rooftop/Myrrh)	Joan Jett and the Blackhearts, Go-Gos																					●	●				●

Artist	Comparison
Seventy-Sevens (Exit)	ATF, Talking Heads
Tim Sheppard (Greentree)	
Silverwind (Sparrow)	Abba, Olivia Newton-John
Michael W. Smith (Reunion)	Jack Wagner
Stephen Soles (Good News)	
Billy Sprague (Reunion)	
Spurr & MacNeill (A & S)	
Stalnecker	*
Candi Staton (Beracah)	*
Randy Stonehill (Solid Rock/Myrrh)	Elvis Costello, Rick Springfield, Jackson Browne, Bruce Springsteen
Noel Paul Stookey (Neworld/NewPax)	Peter, Paul & Mary
Streetlight (Sparrow)	Stevie Nicks, Little River Band
Stryper (Enigma)	Motley Crue
Sweet Comfort Band (Light)	Styx, Raydio, Toto
Russ Taff (Myrrh)	Michael McDonald, Doobie Bros., Hall & Oates
John Michael Talbot (Birdwing/Sparrow)	*
Terry Talbot (Birdwing/Sparrow)	Eagles, Harry Chapin, Poco
Tamarack (MRC)	Seawind
Steve Taylor (Sparrow)	Devo, Pretenders, Police, Elvis Costello
Terry Taylor (Refuge)	David Bowie

* has own unique style   ** can be found in most pop record stores   blank: no specific comparison known

continued

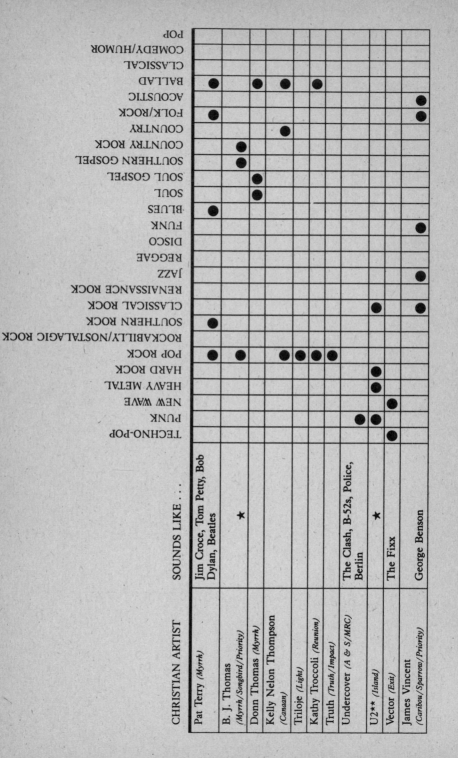

CHRISTIAN ARTIST	SOUNDS LIKE . . .	POP	COMEDY/HUMOR	CLASSICAL	BALLAD	ACOUSTIC	FOLK/ROCK	COUNTRY	COUNTRY ROCK	SOUTHERN GOSPEL	SOUL GOSPEL	SOUL	BLUES	FUNK	DISCO	REGGAE	JAZZ	RENAISSANCE ROCK	CLASSICAL ROCK	SOUTHERN ROCK	ROCKABILLY/NOSTALAGIC ROCK	POP ROCK	HARD ROCK	HEAVY METAL	NEW WAVE	PUNK	TECHNO-POP
Pat Terry *(Myrrh)*	Jim Croce, Tom Petty, Bob Dylan, Beatles				●		●						●							●		●					
B. J. Thomas *(Myrrh/Songbird/Priority)*	★																					●					
Donn Thomas *(Myrrh)*									●	●	●	●															
Kelly Nelon Thompson *(Canaan)*					●			●																			
Triloje *(Light)*					●																	●					
Kathy Troccoli *(Reunion)*					●																	●					
Truth *(Truth/Impact)*																						●					
Undercover *(A & S/MRC)*	The Clash, B-52s, Police, Berlin																									●	
U2** *(Island)*	★																		●				●	●		●	
Vector *(Exit)*	The Fixx																								●		●
James Vincent *(Caribou/Sparrow/Priority)*	George Benson					●	●							●			●		●								

Artist (Label)	Comparison
Karen Voegtlin (Greentree/Light)	
Alwyn Wall (Star Song)	John Lennon, Beatles
Randall Waller (Tunesmith)	Rick Springfield
Sheila Walsh (Sparrow)	Sheena Easton, Helen Reddy, Eurhythmics
James Ward (Lamb & Lion)	Stephen Bishop, Boz Scaggs
Matthew Ward (Sparrow)	Stevie Wonder
Mike & Rose Warnke (Myrrh)	Rodney Dangerfield
The Watchmen (Lifestream)	
Ira Watson (Sozo)	Peaches & Herb, Earth, Wind & Fire
Wayne Watson (Milk & Honey)	Dan Fogelberg
Lisa Welchel (Nissi)	Madonna, Cindi Lauper
Wendy & Mary (Birdwing)	*
White Heart (Myrrh)	Toto
Malcolm Wild (A & S)	John Lennon, Beatles, Tom Petty
Fletch Wiley (Star Song)	Chuck Mangione
Kelly Willard (Maranatha)	Crystal Gayle
Mark Williamson Band (Myrrh)	
Marlow Scott Wilson (Refuge)	Cindi Lauper
Winans (Light)	
John & Vicki Jo Witty (Word)	*

* has own unique style   ** can be found in most pop record stores   blank: no specific comparison known

Notes

Chapter 1: Eve of Destruction

1. Edward E. Plowman, *The Underground Church* (Elgin, Ill.: David C. Cook, 1971), p. 25.
2. Billy Graham, *The Jesus Generation* (Grand Rapids, Mich.: Zondervan, 1971), p. 24.
3. *Ibid.*, p. 20.
4. *Ibid.*, p. 45.
5. Dennis C. Benson, *The Now Generation* (Richmond, Va.: John Knox Press, 1969), p. 118.
6. *Ibid.*, p. 17.
7. Norman Vincent Peale, "The Surging Spirit," *Guideposts*, November 1971, p. 4.
8. Plowman, *Underground Church*, p. 10.
9. John 15:12, KJV.
10. Matt. 5:9, KJV.
11. Matt. 5:22, KJV.
12. Peale, "Surging Spirit," p. 4.
13. "The New Rebel Cry: Jesus Is Coming," *Time*, June 21, 1971, p. 56.
14. Patrick Corman, "Freaking Out on Jesus," *Rolling Stone*, 1971, p. 24.
15. "The New Rebel Cry," p. 5.

Chapter 2: He's Everything to Me

1. Darryl E. Hicks, "Thurlow Spurr—PTL's Music Man," *The Singing News*, September 1, 1978, p. 17A.
2. "He's Everything to Me" by Ralph Carmichael. Copyright © 1964 Lexicon Music, Inc. ASCAP. All rights reserved. International copyright secured. Used by special permission.
3. "Jimmy Owens Discusses Pop Music in the Church: Part 2," *Rock in Jesus*, September/October 1972, pp. 13, 14.
4. "The Salvation Army: The Band Marches On—With a Rock Beat," *Right On!*, February 1973, p. 14.

Chapter 3: Jesus Is Just Alright

1. © 1968 Paul Simon. Used by permission.
2. *Hit Parader*, January 1971, p. 27.

Chapter 4: Jesus Christ S.R.O. (Standing Room Only)
1. W. Bender, "Rock Passion," *Time*, November 9, 1970, p. 47.
2. "Religious Rock," *New Yorker*, November 7, 1970, p. 39.
3. *Ibid.*
4. Bender, "Rock Passion," p. 47.
5. "Pop Testament," *Newsweek*, November 16, 1970, p. 96.
6. *Ibid.*
7. Cheryl A. Forbes, "Superstar: Haunting Questions," *Christianity Today*, December 4, 1970, pp. 38, 39.
8. *Ibid.*
9. Clifford Edwards, "Jesus Christ Superstar: Electric Age Messiah," *Catholic World*, August 1971, p. 220.
10. "Jesus Christ Superstar review," *Business Week*, September 11, 1971, pp. 46, 47.
11. *Jesus Christ Superstar* review, *Time*, October 25, 1971, p. 64.
12. "Pop Testament," *Newsweek*, p. 96.
13. Cheryl A. Forbes, "From Bach to O'Horgan," *Christianity Today*, December 3, 1971, pp. 42, 43.
14. *Jesus Christ Superstar* review, *Time*, p. 66.
15. Billy Graham, *The Jesus Generation* (Grand Rapids, Mich.: Zondervan, 1971), p. 131.
16. "Controversy Rages Over 'Superstar,' " *Planet*, March 1972, p. 26.
17. D. P. Scaer, "Jesus Christ Superstar," *Springfielder*, March 1971, p. 298.
18. Forbes, "Superstar: Haunting Questions," p. 39.

Chapter 5: Little Country Church
1. "Why Should the Devil Have All the Good Music?," copyright © 1973 by Glenwood Music Corporation/Straw Bed Music. Used by permission. All rights reserved.
2. "One Way," copyright © 1973 by Glenwood Music/Straw Bed Music. Used by permission. All rights reserved.
3. "Why Should the Devil Have All the Good Music?"
4. "I Wish We'd All Been Ready," copyright © 1969 and arrangement © 1972 by Beechwood Music Corporation/J. C. Love Publishing Company. Used by permission. All rights reserved.
5. *Ibid.*
6. "I Can't Wait," copyright © 1972, 1976 by Word Music, Inc. All rights reserved. Used by permission.

Chapter 6: Turn Your Radio On
1. Norris McWhirter, *Guinness Book of World Records* (New York: Sterling Publishing Company, Inc., 1962), revised American edition, 1977, p. 237.
2. Michael J. Conner, "The Electric Church," *The Wall Street Journal*, September 4, 1974, p. 32.
3. Dennis C. Benson, *The Now Generation* (Richmond, Va.: John Knox Press, 1969), p. 17.
4. Pat Robertson with Jamie Buckingham, *Shout It from the Housetops* (Plainfield, N.J., Logos International, 1972), p. 202.
5. *Ibid.*, p. 204.

Chapter 7: Day by Day
1. Charles M. Austin, "Honest Exuberance," *Christian Century*, August 4, 1971, p. 938.

2. Tom Prideaux, "On This Rock, a Little Miracle," *Life*, August 4, 1972, p. 20.
3. H. Elliott Wright, "Jesus on Stage: A Reappraisal," *Christian Century*, July 19, 1972, p. 786.
4. Joseph Barton, "The Godspell Story," *America*, December 11, 1971, p. 517.
5. H. Elliott Wright, "Jesus on Stage," p. 786.
6. David Brudnoy, "Hosanna!," *National Review*, August 17, 1973, p. 898.

Chapter 8: Pass It On
1. Cathy Steere, *Impact*, July 1972, p. 3.
2. Randy Matthews, © New Bay Psalter Music Press, Inc./Paragon Music Corp., 1975.

Chapter 10: It's Only Right
1. "Easter Song," by Anne Herring. Copyright © 1974 Latter Rain Music (AS-CAP). Used by permission.

Chapter 11: The Rock That Doesn't Roll
1. Bob Larson, *Rock & the Church* (Carol Stream, Ill.: Creation House, 1971), p. 54.
2. *Ibid.*, p. 78.
3. *Ibid.*, p. 69.
4. Letter to the Editor, *Cornerstone*, Vol. 6, Issue 37, June/July 1977, p. 4.

Chapter 12: All Day Dinner
1. Liz Neuman. "Expectation," *Jesus '76—Mercer Program Book*, p. 5.

Chapter 13: Let Us Be One
1. Letter to the Editor, "Thankful," *Lincoln Star*, April 18, 1975.

Chapter 14: Superstar
1. John Anderson, *Rolling Stone*, January 29, 1976.
2. David Winter, *New Singer, New Song* (Waco, Tex.: Word, 1967), p. 130.
3. Jerry Hopkins, "Cliff Richard: An Elvis for Christ," *Rolling Stone*, April 13, 1972, p. 18.
4. *Ibid.*
5. "Just Plain Noel Stookey," *Right On!*, March 1973, p. 5.
6. *Ibid.*

Chapter 16: Gospel Light
1. 1 Cor. 1:18, NASV.
2. Psalm 75:6, 7, paraphrased.

Chapter 17: Time We Returned
1. Richard Quebedeaux, *The Worldly Evangelicals* (New York: Harper & Row, 1978), p. 168.
2. 1 Timothy 4:12.
3. 1 Peter 5:5-7.
4. "It's Time We Returned," words and music by Michael C. Johnson. Copyright © 1977 Paragon Music Corp. Used by permission.

Chapter 21: Crossing Over from the Other Side
1. For further information on several of these artists, consult the Bibliography. Thirteen artists' testimonies are included in *I've Got a New Song*, written by Paul Baker (Scandinavia Publishers, 1983).
2. Kenneth Boa and Kerry Livgren, *Seeds of Change* (Westchester, Ill.: Crossway Books, 1983).

Chapter 24: Coping with Burnout
1. Words and music by Candi Staton. Copyright Beracah Publishing Company, ASCAP. Reprinted by permission.

Chapter 30: Gospel Music: Christian Witness
1. Bob Darden, "Major Labels: Poised on the Brink of Breakthrough with Pop Music's Fastest Growing Genre," *Billboard*, September 29, 1984, p. G-5.
2. From "Try and Keep the Pace," by Bob Ayala. Copyright Word Music, Inc. and Pure Joy Music.

Bibliography

(Several of the books listed in this bibliography are now out of print. Copies may still be found in some Christian bookstores or church libraries. *Indicates a book especially recommended.)

The Jesus Movement

Beck, Hubert. *Why Can't the Church Be Like This?* St. Louis, Missouri: Concordia, 1973.

*Benson, Dennis C. *The Now Generation.* Richmond, Vir.: John Knox Press, 1969.

Blessitt, Arthur. *Life's Greatest Trip.* Waco, Tex.: Word Books, 1970.

——; with Walter Wagner. *Turned on to Jesus.* New York: Hawthorne Books, 1971.

——. *Tell the World: A Manual for Jesus People.* Old Tappan, N.J.: Fleming H. Revell, 1972.

Briscoe, Stuart. *Where Was the Church When the Youth Exploded?* Grand Rapids: Zondervan, 1972.

*Graham, Billy. *The Jesus Generation.* Grand Rapids: Zondervan, 1971.

Lindsey, "Holy" Hubert. *Bless Your Dirty Heart.* Plainfield, N.J.: Logos International, 1972.

Moody, Jess. *The Jesus Freaks.* Waco, Tex.: Word Books, 1971.

Ortega, Reuben, compiler. *The Jesus People Speak Out!* Elgin, Ill.: David C. Cook, 1972.

Pederson, Duane; with Bob Owen. *Jesus People.* Glendale, Calif.: Regal Books, 1971.

*Plowman, Edward E. *The Underground Church.* Elgin, Ill.: David C. Cook, 1971.

*Quebedeaux, Richard. *The Young Evangelicals.* New York: Harper & Row, 1974.

262

———. *The Worldly Evangelicals.* New York: Harper & Row, 1978.

Struchen, Jeanette. *Zapped by JESUS.* New York: A. J. Holman, 1972.

Two Brothers from Berkeley. *Letters to Street Christians.* Grand Rapids: Zondervan, 1971.

Music and Media

Anderson, David L. C., compiler. *The New Jesus Style Song Book.* Minneapolis: Augsburg Publishing House, 1972.

Aranza, Jacob. *Backward Masking Unmasked.* Shreveport, La.: Huntington House, 1983.

Baker, Paul. *I've Got a New Song.* El Cajon, Calif.: Scandinavia Publishing House, 1983.

Benson, Dennis C. *Electric Evangelism.* Nashville, Tenn.: Abingdon Press, 1973.

——— *The Rock Generation.* Nashville, Tenn.: Abingdon Press, 1976.

Bill, J. Brent. *Rock and Roll.* Old Tappan, N.J.: Fleming H. Revell, 1984.

Blanchard, John. *Pop Goes the Gospel.* Evangelical Press, 1985.

Doney, Malcolm. *Summer in the City.* Berkhamsted, Hertfordshire, England: Lion Publishing, 1978.

Edmondson, Frank M., compiler. *Jubilation Songbook.* Waco, Tex.: Myrrh Music, 1976.

Hart, Lowell. *Satan's Music Exposed.* Huntingdon Valley, Penn.: Salem Kirban, Inc., 1980.

Haynes, Michael K. *The god of Rock: A Christian Perspective of Rock Music.* Lindale, Tex.: Priority Publications, 1984.

Hicks, Darryl E. and Dr. David A. Lewis. *The Todd Phenomenon.* Harrison, Ark.: New Leaf Press, 1979.

Knuteson, Roy E. *Rock Music and the Christian.* Wheaton, Ill.: Chapel of the Air, 1972.

La Riviere, Leen. *Kaf and Koren (Chaff and Grain).* Rotterdam, Holland: Continental Sound, 1975, 1980. Published in Dutch.

Larson, Bob. *Rock.* Wheaton, Ill.: Tyndale House Publishers, 1980.

——— *Rock and Roll: The Devil's Diversion.* Carol Stream, Ill.: Creation House, 1967.

——— *Rock and the Church.* Carol Stream, Ill.: Creation House, 1971.

——— *The Day Music Died.* Carol Stream, Ill.: Creation House, 1972.

——— *Hippies, Hindus and Rock and Roll.* Carol Stream, Ill.: Creation House, 1972.

Lawhead, Steve. *Rock Reconsidered.* Downers Grove, Ill.: InterVarsity Press, 1981.

——— *Turn Back the Night.* Westchester, Ill.: Crossway Books, 1985.

Mars, Peter. *Violent Orders for the Subliminal.* Troy, Mich.: Board-well, 1982.

Noebel, David. *Christian Rock: A Strategem of Mephistopheles.* Manitou Springs, Col.: Summit Youth Ministries, date unknown.

—— *The Legacy of John Lennon.* Nashville, Tenn.: Thomas Nelson Publishers, 1982.

—— *The Marxist Minstrels: A Handbook on Communist Subversion of Music.* Tulsa, Okla.: American Christian College Press, 1974.

—— *Rock 'n' Roll: A Prerevolutionary Form of Cultural Subversion.* Manitou Springs, Col.: Summit Ministries, date unknown.

Peters, Dan and Steve. *Why Knock Rock?* Minneapolis: Bethany House Publishers, 1984.

Peters, Dan, Jim and Steve. *Documentation Part I: What the Devil's Wrong with Rock Music?* St. Paul: Zion Christian Life Center, 1980.

—— *Documentation Part II: Rock Music Research.* St. Paul: Zion Christian Life Center, 1981.

Peters, Jim and Gentle Touch. *Documentation III: What the Devil's Wrong with Rock Music?* St. Paul: Gentle Touch Ministries, Inc., 1983.

Robertson, Pat, with Jamie Buckingham. *Shout It from the Housetops.* Plainfield, N.J.: Logos International, 1972.

Scarborough, William R., editor. *National Christian Booking and Program Directory.* Laguna Hills, Calif.: Christian Booking and Program Directory, 1983.

Schaeffer, Franky. *Addicted to Mediocrity.* Westchester, Ill.: Crossway Books, 1981.

Whitburn, Joel C., compiler. *Joel Whitburn's Top Pop Records 1955-1972* and yearly supplements and updates. Menominee Falls, Wisc. 53051 (P.O. Box 82).

Autobiographies and Biographies

Boa, Kenneth and Kerry Livgren. *Seeds of Change.* Westchester, Ill.: Crossway Books, 1983.

Boone, Pat. *A New Song.* Carol Stream, Ill.: Creation House, 1970.

Boone, Pat. *Together.* Nashville: Thomas Nelson, 1979.

Cash, Johnny. *Man in Black.* Grand Rapids, Mich.: Zondervan Publishing House, 1975.

Crouch, Andrae, with Nina Ball. *Through It All.* Waco, Tex.: Word Books, 1974.

Holm, Dallas. *This Is My Story.* Nashville: Impact Books, 1980.

Medema, Ken, with Joyce Norman. *Come and See.* Waco, Tex.: Word Books, 1976.

O'Neill, Dan. *Troubador for the Lord: The Story of John Michael Talbot*. New York: Crossroad, 1983.

Richard, Cliff. *Which One's Cliff?* London, England: Hodder & Stoughton, 1977.

Ross, Scott, with John and Elizabeth Sherrill. *Scott Free*. Old Tappan, N.J.: Chosen Books, 1976.

Thomas, B. J., with Jerry B. Jenkins. *Home Where I Belong*. Waco, Tex.: Word, 1978.

Thomas, B. J. and Gloria. *In Tune*. Old Tappan, N.J.: Fleming H. Revell, 1983.

Williams, Paul. *Dylan—What Happened?* South Bend, Ind.: And Books/Entwhistle Books, 1980.

Winter, David. *New Singer, New Song: The Cliff Richard Story*. Waco, Tex.: Word Books, 1967.

Index

My very special thanks go out to Claude Crain for his initial index and the early formative work which went into this index.